THE
ARGENTO
SYNDROME

Published in the USA by:
BearManor Media
PO Box 1129
Duncan, Oklahoma 73534-1129
www.bearmanormedia.com

ISBN 978-1-59393-567-2

Printed in the United States of America.
Cover design by Silver Ferox Design. Cover Illustration by Micah Maté.
Book design by Brian Pearce | Red Jacket Press.

THE
ARGENTO
SYNDROME

DEREK BOTELHO
ILLUSTRATED BY MICAH MATÉ

BEARMANOR MEDIA

TABLE OF CONTENTS

"GREAT WORKS OF ART HAVE GREAT POWER."

THE STENDHAL SYNDROME

ACKNOWLEDGMENTS

This book would be nothing without the help of many people, and I would like to give them my heartfelt gratitude for their time and energy. Micah Maté, my partner in crime and friend for 20 plus years; I am eternally grateful. Jeff Burr, thank you for feedback and well, for listening when it mattered, and even when it didn't. Erik Guczwa, what can I say? Without you, I'm nothing! David Del Valle, for pushing me in the right direction. Eriq Chang, it's all lemon sponge cake and bear claws. Very special thanks to Maitland McDonagh, just following a path…I am honored to walk it. Luigi Cozzi, for the barrage of e-mails I apologize. Thank you very much for answering every single one! Simone Arrighi, thank you for the photos and everything else you've done over the years. To everyone I interviewed for the project, thank you very much for your cooperation, it is greatly appreciated. Lastly, to Dario and Asia Argento, knowing you both means more than you will know. Grazie mille e tanti abbracci!

A very sad, but special thank you to Diana Romero, who leant me that copy of *Unsane/Tenebrae* all those years ago. Who would have known what watching that single film would start? I hope you're somewhere safe, and watching a lot of great movies!

INTRODUCTION

François Truffaut, in the audio recordings of his legendary interview with Alfred Hitchcock, said:

One senses the importance of dreams in all your work…we go back to the fairy tale. It's starting from the premise of the man alone. By terrifying things, that unconsciously you seem to fall into in the field of the dream, which is often based on peril and isolation…Your type of logic often irritates the critics. This is to some degree the logic of dreams. It's obvious in pictures like Strangers on a Train, *which is a succession of strange forms, one on top of the other overlapping almost like a nightmare.*

Hitchcock replies simply, "I think it occurs because I'm never satisfied with the ordinary. I can't do well with the ordinary."

This (above) could have very easily been spoken about Argento, as many critics over the years have decried his "lack of logic," or the artificiality of his films, even the more "realistic" ones. Perhaps *Tenebrae* would illustrate the best example of this suspect reading of his films. On the surface, Argento has presented a fairly by-the-numbers murder mystery compared to many of his other films. However, the version of reality presented by Argento of Rome is that of a not-so-distant future, with a wealthy population that has dwindled, as society has for some reason weeded out the lower class almost entirely. Everyone seems to be upper-middle class or a street urchin. Even the beautiful female thief, who steals paperback novels, lives in a nicely appointed apartment. Does she steal out of maniacal need, or is it merely out of boredom, bred of entitlement? This question is never answered, nor should it be. It isn't necessary to understand the "logic"

of the world Argento is creating. It is merely his version of reality, as Hitchcock created his own version through his many films, reaching an epoch with *Vertigo*.

Granted, Hitchcock never made anything as delirious or psychedelic as *Suspiria* or *Inferno*, but *Vertigo* does have a touch of the supernatural and surreal, even if it is part of a ruse to further Scotty's involvement in Madeline's plight. By the time Scotty figures out what is going on, he has been consumed by Madeline in every conceivable way a human can be with another, and does not resemble any kind of reality in the outside world. The mise-en-scène is entirely built out of artificial parts from the depths of Scotty's obsessions.

I'm not attempting to prove the critical trope that Argento is the "Italian Hitchcock" or a "garlic flavored Hitchcock," as several critics have suggested over the years. Merely, like Brian De Palma and numerous directors throughout modern cinema, that Hitchcock has had an indelible impression on the development of film as an art form. I have no evidence that Argento and Hitchcock crossed paths in life, yet they have obviously done so artistically: to what degree is debatable, yet the fact stands.

François Truffaut, like Argento, began his career as a film critic and then moved into creating films himself. Truffaut had a reputation of being quite vitriolic toward movies he saw little merit in, and upon beginning to write and direct his own films, walked back many of his harsher criticisms and began to see the aspersions he cast upon others in his own work. Argento's work will most likely never attain the critical or academic praise Truffaut or Hitchcock enjoyed throughout their careers, nor many of his fellow Italian filmmakers like Fellini or Antonioni, yet that does not make his vision less valid or important — merely different.

It is simply Argento's daring to slash and burn his own path through the jungles of other "horror" film directors, past and present, and to stand out as truly unique, which at the least commands a modicum of respect whether you like his work or not. His influence on the horror film specifically cannot be denied. I would make the argument that Argento isn't so much a horror film director any more than Hitchcock made "B" thrillers, which is how many of the "A"-list stars in Hollywood saw his work.

Like Brian De Palma, many critics have accused Argento of misogyny over the years. I don't agree with labeling either director as such, as they both murder men and women, yet both have said they would rather photograph women as opposed to men. And Hitchcock was certainly famous for his love of a certain blond type.

From the first time I saw *Tenebrae* at age thirteen, I was immediately struck by Argento's use of cinematic technique in ways I had never seen. From the camera crawl on the roof in *Tenebrae* to the violent primary color palette of *Suspiria*, Argento has always experimented with the thriller and supernatural in his own unique way, tying the two genres together and creating a singular style. With every film, his experiments with ideas, themes, and technique continued to grow over the course of a now four-decade — and growing — career.

Armed with the blessing of Asia Argento on the title of my book — she said it was "smart" — the journey to writing it has been long and unforgettable. What was originally conceived as a collection of interviews, turned into my college thesis project: a documentary about Argento's films, which, due to money, was never completed. Yet the more I worked on the project as a documentary, something kept tapping me on the shoulder, suggesting I go back into it as a book. As part personal memoir, collection of interviews, and essays on the films, the structure of this work has evolved over time. Some of the films begged a more detailed look, while others, I felt, didn't need so much digging into.

The last time I saw Dario was in Los Angeles in 2010, and at dinner he introduced me to a few people. "This is Botelho; he is writing a book *for* me." Dario's charming misuse of the word "for" in the place of "about" made me smile, and his complete lack of deigning me worthy of a first name was equally amusing. Yet in a way, he was right; I am writing this book for him in hopes that my contribution to the study of his work helps others in understanding his place in film history.

Derek Botelho and Dario Argento at the Cinequest Film Festival in San Jose, CA. FROM THE AUTHOR'S COLLECTION.

MEETING A MASTER

In March of 2000, Dario Argento was being honored at the Cinequest Film Festival in San Jose, California. Seeing as I lived only an hour away and might never have the opportunity to see Argento in person, I had to go see him. He was slated to attend several days of the festival, and the organization would screen a selection of his films with him introducing most.

The first night Dario was to attend the festival, they were screening *Suspiria*, where he would be given their "Maverick Spirit Award" and do a Q & A after the showing. Needless to say, I was excited to see the man and hear his thoughts on his career. As the screening time neared, I gathered the courage to approach a festival volunteer to ask if it would be possible to meet Dario beforehand. Luckily, she was able to get me a meeting with Dario, as brief as it was. I can't even remember what I was thinking as I approached him, because it was just too bizarre to really be happening. Would he be what I expected of a guy who spent years murdering hapless men and women onscreen with a gusto I had never witnessed in American filmmakers? Would he be able to say much to me? I didn't have any gauge on his grasp of English either. I was just happy to be able to meet him. The festival worker took me into the lobby of the theater where Dario was standing alone, looking very small and frail. I was surprised then, and still am, how little he is.

Without a word, he walked over to me and said, "Hello, I am Dario!" all smiles and shining eyes. With an amused smile, I said, "Nice to meet you. I am Derek." I was a bit taken aback by his warmth as he gave me a hug.

I kept going: "I just wanted to tell you how much your work has changed the way I watch movies…and I really admire your vision…and how you stick to it

come hell or high water." It really was that awkward as I, again, didn't know how much of what I was saying he would understand. Of course, he responded very cordially to my freakishly stilted speech. You would think I was the one who spoke English as a second, or maybe third, language.

"Thank you," he said. "I just wanted to meet you and say hello, but I must go eat something while the movie is showing. After the movie, we will talk more."

"Ok, enjoy your dinner. I will see you later."

Now, even at this point in my life at twenty-three, I had seen *Suspiria* probably ten or so times, but never in a theater with a crowd. It was great! People laughed, screamed, laughed some more. This was my first time to see one of Argento's movies in a theater, and the crowd was electric, although there were a few walkouts from attendees who had obviously never seen the movie and didn't know what they were in for.

Once the film was over, Dario walked into the theater, waved to everyone, and smiled from ear to ear, and the crowd got up and went nuts cheering him on. He stood in front of the screen, beaming and soaking up the praise. Things soon calmed down as the moderator of the Q & A went up and announced they would take questions from the audience after a brief talk together. I believe it was after this short talk that a translator was brought up and just stood there as Argento chose to answer all the questions in English, which was very charming and resulted in some perhaps unintentional comedy. My favorite being when he proclaimed, with his arms raised almost as if he were cheering on his favorite football team, "I am bisexual! I love everyone! I love men, I love women!" I am paraphrasing from memory, but I am sure he was only referring to his adoration for the crowd and how happy the turnout made him feel. He also referred to Nicole Kidman and Tom Cruise in Stanley Kubrick's last film, *Eyes Wide Shut*, as "Muppets," and further explained that he disliked the movie very much and that he was saddened by how a once-great director had made something so bad.

Someone asked about the edits made to the print of *Suspiria* that had been shown, which I assume was the edited version distributed in the U.S. by Fox, and Argento said there were some sixty plus cuts made to the film to get that R rating. After explaining this, I recall he said, "These people, the censors, should be put in prison. Would you go to a museum and cut up a painting you don't like?"

Near the close of the evening, the moderator handed Argento the "Maverick Spirit Award," which resembles a glass unicorn horn; he proceeded to put it on his head and kind of shrug down as if in ridicule of his worthiness of such a trinket of a lifelong contribution to cinema. Oh, this burden, she's heavy!

After a Q & A that lasted more than an hour and a half, Argento walked into the lobby of the theater and proceeded to sign autographs and take pictures until it seemed everyone was satisfied and had a chance to lavish some form of praise upon him. As anyone who has spent any time around Dario can attest, he is quiet and introverted until he gets excited about something and then explodes! I can't help but think many people, when they meet him, are surprised just how meek and "normal" he is. He makes films that are loud and garish, but I suppose it is where he chooses to put that energy.

Before I left the theater that evening, I asked Dario, while he was signing a photograph for me and my friend Henry, if it would be possible to talk to him again. He asked if I was coming to the screening of *Tenebrae* the next day, and I told him that I planned on being there. He said, "Good, meet me a half hour before and we will talk." So with the promise of an exciting day to come, I drove home and didn't sleep much.

Early the next afternoon, I arrived at the theater where *Tenebrae* was being screened. Dario met me as promised, and we sat in the lobby and talked for a bit about the festival. After this talk, another volunteer of the festival came up to us and told Dario that he was needed to prep for the screening coming up. So he asked me if I would like to meet him that evening and talk more. Of course I would. So we planned to meet at the restaurant of his hotel later that night.

Argento rushed off to present the afternoon's screening of *Tenebrae*. Shortly after sitting down in the theater, a festival volunteer came in to introduce Dario and give us some bad news: the festival wasn't able to find a print of *Tenebrae*, so they would be projecting the DVD. The collective groan that went up in the crowd was a little scary. With that, Dario came into the room shortly after and apologized, then jumped right into his short speech.

Standing in front of the crowd, he very quietly said, "I said everything last night after *Suspiria*, so I don't have any more to give. The only way I can reveal more is to be naked." Someone in the audience yelled, "Take it off!" And surprisingly, he did! In his boxer shorts and shoes, Dario told a few stories of the making of *Tenebrae*, most notably that working with Anthony Franciosa was difficult due to the actor's constant drinking. "I don't care if you drink, just don't do it on my set!" On the heels of that comment, he told us how difficult it was to watch Franciosa make out with Daria Nicolodi — his longtime girlfriend — take after take. "The bastard ruined the shots just to make me watch more!" And on the censorship the film had around the world: "Here in the U.S., the film was cut by more than ten minutes; this is ridiculous. How is it even the same film? And they called it *Unsane!*"

After the screening of *The Bird with the Crystal Plumage* that evening, I went to the Fairmont Hotel to meet Dario. It's still surreal to think about sitting in the restaurant drinking Heineken and eating Goldfish crackers with this man. He was amused by the crackers and held them up and made them swim through the air. "They are like fish!" he proclaimed with innocent glee; it was amusing to say the least.

During our conversation, he asked me if I had lived in the bay area my entire life, which I had up to that point, and he told me that it was his first visit. With much joy, he told me about visiting some of the locations Hitchcock used to shoot *Vertigo*. A far more amusing story followed about being taken to *Le Video*, an enormous video store in San Francisco, where he was overjoyed to find an entire section of his films, after asking the clerk, "Do you have any of Dario Argento's films?" He said one of the clerks recognized him and asked him to sign some of the videos they had for rent, which he said he did.

For a few hours, we sat and drank (ate a lot of Goldfish crackers), talked about his films, and he told me some very random things about them. I learned that *The Bird with the Crystal Plumage* took a long time to get financed and he was horrified nobody would take him seriously since he was just a critic, but that his reputation as a critic gave him a name. The pan and scan videotape of *Deep Red* in the scene with Marcus and Carlo talking in the piazza in front of the fountain: "All you can see is the fountain! It's ridiculous. The statue doesn't talk!" This prompted me to ask him what aspect ratio he favored to shoot in. He was confused by my question in English, so I said in my awful Italian, "Schermo panoramico o piatto?/Widescreen or flat?" while drawing one rectangle bigger than the other on a napkin! I don't know when he figured out what I was trying to say, but his eyes got wide and he said a bit sadly, "Ah, I like the scope, it's bigger! You have more visual space to fill. I made all the early movies like this. But with video, a lot of distributors don't want this because it makes them harder to show on TV and videotape. A lot of people don't like widescreen on TV. I shot *Opera* in Super 35 so you can shoot for 1.33 and scope at the same time." And when I thought about it, this made sense, since RAI Italia largely funded the film.

We had watched *Tenebrae* earlier in the day, and he told me that the English and French posters had the image of the woman with the slashed throat covered up by the red ribbon. "It looks silly; it's not a children's movie, why cover it up? It is supposed to be a strong image!"

I took this opportunity to ask him why he decided to undress at the screening of the film earlier that day. He laughed and said, I am sure, emboldened by a few beers, "I didn't know how else to answer any more questions. I like to reveal myself to the audience. I didn't know what else to say!"

I had recently seen *Trauma* for the first time, and I asked him what it was like to work with Asia, as an actress, at that time.

> *It was wonderful; we have an even greater bond now that we have worked together as actor and director. She was very nervous and upset when we shot the scene in the bathroom. Her covering up her breasts, she was hiding from me! But when we shot the rough scenes for* The Stendhal Syndrome *and* Phantom of the Opera, *we both cried at times and then shot the scenes as actor and director, not father and daughter.*

As the evening was wrapping up and as I became more comfortable talking with the man about many things I had wondered about as a fan, I told him as

someone who was considering going to film school that I would like to have the chance to watch him work. Now, I assumed he would say something like, "Oh, yes that would be nice," or something equally as dismissive but polite. Instead, what I heard was, "I am starting to shoot in May; you come to Italy and visit." With that, Dario took my program from the festival and tore off part of one of the pages, wrote down his phone number, and told me to call his assistant to arrange the set visit. We said our goodbyes and he hugged me and told me he would see me soon. Indeed, he would.

FOREWORD

I do not know what price I shall pay for breaking what we film historians call "Silentium." Regardless, I feel compelled to comment on Derek Botelho's volume of Argento lore, *The Argento Syndrome,* a very personal investigation into the director many historians have come to refer to as "The Italian Hitchcock." Yet Argento is his own man, in nearly every sense of that well well-worn phrase, because, as a director, one only has to glance at the current crop of genre films we have come to know as "slasher" movies, to see the debt other filmmakers already owe this man and his overwhelming influence on the genre as a whole for the last three decades.

Horror films, good ones that is, tend to operate on a dream logic, whose atmosphere covers a multitude of sins, since the atmosphere of the piece is everything. The self self-contained scripts, the sometimes lack luster performances; the result must always be form over content, as dreams become nightmares over and over again in the psychotic landscapes of Argento's universe. These blood-drenched fantasies resonate to a large number of fans that revere this director for what he has brought into their lives. The artifice of the traditional giallo films of the '60's, combined with the atrocity of violence, is forever part of Argento's stylization as a director who discovered, and then was able to translate, great beauty to the screen within the trappings of the horror film itself.

For a film book to be successful, it must supply its readers with a special point of view, from which to appreciate the films at hand, and so it was with Derek's book, since I for one was not that much of a dyed-in-the-wool admirer of the films of Dario Argento, that made me reassess the man's work. When Derek first asked me to chat with him about Argento for this book.

I had, of course, seen most of the canon, but perhaps no more than one screening at a time of any given film except *Suspiria,* which I have admired ever since it came out. It was Derek's sense of astonishment that what began for him as a documentary in the making, had morphed into a book that got my attention, and, as we began to discuss each film in detail, I realized that I was neglecting a major talent in the genre, primarily because of my own misinterpretations of several of his films.

As we began our dialogue, I discovered that I really admired more of Argento's oeuvre than I first suspected, so that, coupled with Derek's historian's knowledge of Argento's individual films, opened the door for further investigation. After we did the first interview, I began to screen Argento's films all over again, during which time Derek started sending me selected chapters to read, as he began the editing process for the final read through before publication. I soon discovered that Derek Botelho is a tireless advocate when it comes to something he feels strongly about, and I began to realize that these films represented something essential to his involvement in cinema as well as his trajectory as a writer. He took up the gauntlet and made the pilgrimage to Rome (at Argento's request) to be an eyewitness to Argento filming *Sleepless* in 2000. I was also struck by his connection to the Argento family; he managed to do what most film buffs never dare to even try to accomplish and that is a direct dialogue with the object of your admiration. Derek found a more than sympathetic ear from both Argento himself and then his two daughters.

Through Derek's personal and rather unique vision of Argento's world, I then rediscovered my own fascination with this director's fever dreams of surrealism

interwoven with the psychotic role playing of his protagonists. As with masterworks like *Suspiria* and then
again his Disney inspired fantasy *Inferno*. If if you try
and allow yourself to abandon any preconceived notions
of traditional horror films as I did, being from a gen-
eration brought up on Universal nightmares, Hammer
Horrors, and then finally landing in the sunlight of
Italian gothic, which opened the doors into the realms
of darkness to be found in foreboding castles looming
over frightened townships. If you can accomplish this,
then Argento's films might have the same effect on you
they did me, as if I had just began to read the works
of Poe or Lovecraft for the first time, then moving on
to De Quincey and the Arabian Nights. It is a journey
devoutly to be wished.

Ti penso sempre,
David Del Valle

L'UCELLO DALLE PIUME DI CRISTALLO

THE BIRD WITH THE CRYSTAL PLUMAGE

Being Argento's first film as a director, *The Bird with the Crystal Plumage* was far from the first of his films that I saw. However, when I finally did watch it with a friend of mine, who had only seen *Suspiria* and *Phenomena* up to that point, we were both impressed by the clean Agatha-Christie-like plot and just how different it was from almost everything else Argento has made. It has none of the supernatural touch of the "Three Mothers Trilogy" or the nonsensical histrionics of many of his other "realistic" films. Yet it does have an amazingly assured hand guiding it, especially in light of the filmmaker's inexperience behind a camera.

From the opening moments of Argento's first film as a director, he is able to set a mood that is quite different from most films of this type, as the film's opening credit sequence is entirely focused on the villain and the pursuit of his next victim in a nice subversion of the norm. Typically, structure dictates that we first get to know the protagonist and then meet the antagonist through their experience. Argento wastes no time in getting the story going, as the opening credits let us in on a murder from inception to act. Yet we only hear the murder take place, subconsciously telling the audience that what you hear is just as important as what you see; and sometimes more so.

The girl's murder is announced the next day in the newspaper, as we meet Sam Dalmas (Tony Musante) and his friend Carlo (Raf Valenti) at a newsstand. They are on their way to the institute that commissioned Sam's latest work: a study on the preservation of rare birds. Carlo tells Sam, in possibly my favorite line of dialogue in the film — as it is completely

ridiculous — "I forgot to tell you that thing you wrote has been a great success with the experts, you know?" And Sam goes on to self-deprecate and tell us some back story about himself as an American writer living in Rome along with his model girlfriend. (Aren't they all artists and models or actresses in these films?)

Tony Musante had been a stage and film actor of some note in the 1960s up to this point, appearing in *The Detective*, playing a homosexual murder suspect opposite Frank Sinatra. His television work included an episode of *The Alfred Hitchcock Hour* and the *DuPont Show of the Week* episode "Ride With Terror," in which he would later reprise the same role of Joe Ferrone in the feature film version directed by Larry Peerce. This adaptation of the one-hour TV drama into film, titled *The Incident,* had a very impressive cast, including Martin Sheen, Ruby Dee, Ed McMahon, Beau Bridges, and Donna Mills. The film was Musante's as well as Sheen's first major work in a feature. Just previous to *Bird*, Musante had worked on *Metti, una Sera a Cena* (One Night at Dinner), strangely titled *The Love Circle* for English territories, which Argento cowrote, and it was this project that prompted Argento to ask Musante to play Sam Dalmas.

Inside the Wilkinson Institute, Sam and Carlo walk among cases of specimens of birds of all sizes, a tie-in to the title, which is just a non sequitur until the vital clue is revealed in the mystery. It's obvious the way that Sam reacts to not wanting a copy of his book that he has written it not out of pleasure or passion but of necessity. He has no interest in birds, only in making a living. The next scene is arguably the most famous set piece in the entire film. Sam is walking down a lonely, dark street later that evening. Exactly what has he been doing since he picked up that check? Sam comes upon a brightly lit art gallery with huge glass doors facing out onto the street. He stops across the street and looks inside to two figures: a redheaded woman dressed all in white, struggling on a staircase with what appears to be a man, dressed head to toe in black, and brandishing a knife. Is this the same person in the opening of the film? Or simply someone dressed in a similar fashion? Could the woman be someone else in a photograph we haven't been shown yet? Or was this completely spontaneous and done out of desperation? And why would the killer murder someone in such a brightly lit, conspicuous place?

The allusion to performance art and murder being art comes to mind, with the setting of such an act being a place of artistic expression. Almost two decades later, Argento would bring this to light further when he directed a fashion show for the house of Trussardi, where the models were stalked by a killer dressed much like the one we see here. Or perhaps Argento is winking at the Grand Guignol — that vaunted theatre of

the bizarre and horrific. The art gallery set, designed by Dario Micheli, is a fantastic space for such a scene. It is sparse, with ample room for the action to take place and yet, with the various point of view angles, it has a sense of claustrophobic dread that neither the audience nor the characters can escape from. Everything about the gallery is potentially dangerous, from the staircase with a dangerous-looking rake to the sharp bird claw sculpture that suggests violence is imminent.

Our first glimpse of Monica Ranieri (Eva Renzi) is odd. We don't see her from Sam's point of view, rather from behind her, looking out into the street in Sam's direction. Although we are with the hero and on his journey, the camera still shows us another side of things; are we complicit with the murderer as in the opening scene in the darkened room, and is this our first encounter with this girl in distress, the murderer's point of view? Or is it, as I theorize, Argento giving us a sly clue that, like Sam, we don't yet realize the importance of? Throughout this shot, with grim determination to win this struggle, Monica's face has a strange expression; there is almost a smile playing

Tony Musante is trapped in Argento's gallery of horrors. COURTESY OF THE DEL VALLE ARCHIVES/UMC PICTURES.

across her lips at one point, as her red hair keeps our focus on the right side of the frame, while a knife juts into the bottom left.

The knife soon finds its way into Monica's abdomen; the killer jumps off of the staircase and onto the floor of the art gallery and runs through a door in the back. As Monica stumbles down the stairs, she has noticed Sam and is pleading with him to help her. He approaches the gallery for a better look, and suddenly the pair of outer glass doors close behind him, trapping him like a lizard in a terrarium. With the hero now as trapped as the victim, the audience becomes the eyes and ears of both Sam Dalmas and Monica Ranieri, as neither has the means to call for help or escape their shared predicament.

Of course, when someone shows up on the street outside the gallery doors, he is deaf and can't hear what Sam is saying. After a few tries to get him to understand, the man just walks away. But in short order, the police and an ambulance arrive. This is the first great instance of Dario's black humor creeping into his characters and the situations he places them in.

In this scene, Argento's affection for all things voyeuristic really gets a workout. We have Sam watching Monica struggle for life, and in turn Monica watching Sam, as he is helpless to come to her aid. Of course, the audience is naturally in the position of voyeur, as that is the primary goal of cinema, to show and reveal through sight and sound. The sense of helplessness is palpable all the way around with this expertly constructed sequence that we will see again and again through Sam's fractured memory. In fact, every time he recalls the night in question, we are shown a slightly different version of events, as is the fault of memory. Argento has long been a student of psychology and is fascinated by the human mind and the foibles of the human condition. What follows is a story taken from *Witness For the Defense: The Accused, the Eyewitness, and the Expert Who Puts Memory On Trial* by Dr. Elizabeth Loftus and Katherine Ketcham, St. Martin's Press, 1991, which serves to illustrate the case for Sam's lack of a razor sharp memory of the evening's events:

Two men in their mid-twenties were hunting for bears in a rural area of Montana. They had been out all day and were exhausted, hungry, and ready to go home. Walking along a dirt trail in the middle of the woods, with the night falling fast, they were talking about bears and thinking about bears. They rounded a bend in the trail and approximately twenty-five yards ahead of them, just off the trail in the woods, was a large object that was moving and making noise. Both men thought it was a bear, and they lifted their rifles and fired. But the 'bear' turned out to be a yellow tent with a man and a woman making love inside. One of the bullets hit the woman and killed her. When the case was tried before a jury, the jurors had difficulty understanding the perceptual problems inherent in the event; they simply couldn't imagine how someone would look at a yellow tent and see a growling bear. The young man whose bullet killed the woman was convicted of negligent homicide. Two years later, he committed suicide.

This dramatic case demonstrates what psychologists call 'event factors'–those factors inherent within a specific event that can alter perception and distort memory. It was a dark night and in darkness, different colors can't be distinguished and details can't be resolved. The two hunters had strong expectations and motivations — they anticipated that they might see a bear, they wanted to see a bear, and they were nervous, excited, and exhausted from a long day in the woods. When they saw something large, moving, and making noise, they automatically assumed that it was a bear, raised their rifles, and shot to kill.

Per this example, Argento's deft inversion of the expected works quite well in this scene, as Sam assumes he sees a woman struggling to get away from a man who is trying to kill her, when in fact the opposite is true, as we will learn later. Lamberto Bava's film *Morirai a Mezzanotte (You'll Die at Midnight)* also uses the same conceit, with a woman struggling with a man who is assumed to be a killer.

Visually, there is a nod to the old Western idea that good guys wear white and the bad guys are in black. Monica is wearing a white jumpsuit and the assumed murderer is wearing all black. This could stem from Argento's exposure to the Italian westerns he worked on, such as *Five Man Army, Today We Kill, Tomorrow We Die!*, and, of course, *Once Upon a Time in the West*. But even these Westerns tend to subvert expectations people had built up from watching American Westerns over the years. These films have a very specific feel to them, which set them apart from their American counterparts.

Monica's husband Alberto Ranieri (Umberto Raho) — who is also the owner of the gallery — shows up soon after the police. He is wearing a black jacket, much like the one that Sam saw the killer wearing earlier. The rest of the scene really belongs to Enrico Maria Salerno as Inspector Morosini. He is all business, yet wearing a jaunty hat and looking for all intents and purposes like he is out for a night on the town. Our modern Sherlock Holmes gives Sam a tour of the gallery and asks him at various points what he saw, what he touched, and not to touch anything else! But of course, he breaks his own rules when picking up a black glove lying on the ground that very well may be evidence, and he touches it with his bare hands to test whether the material on it is or isn't blood.

In short time, our hero is embroiled in the mystery at hand, as Inspector Morosini has Sam sitting in on a lineup where the immortal line, "Ursula Andress

Italian poster for Lamberto Bava's You'll Die at Midnight. COURTESY THE DEL VALLE ARCHIVES/ MEDUSA.

belongs with the transvestites, not the perverts," is uttered, referring to a transvestite in the lineup of suspects. Morosini interrogates him in his office and takes his passport away in a great comic scene. "Do you have your passport?" Morosini inquires. "Yes, it's right here," says Sam. Sam hands Morosini his passport, assuming he is only going to look at it, and instead he quickly puts it in his desk drawer. "We can't have you moving around," he says dryly.

Sam isn't the only one caught up in this waking nightmare. His girlfriend, Julia, who is also working in Rome as a model, naturally becomes a target of the killer. She is played by Suzy Kendall, most known for being in *The Penthouse* and *To Sir, With Love*. She gives Julia a nice depth and sense of self, and she has no qualms about speaking her mind and defending herself and Sam from the police and their attacker in equal measure. Argento struck gold with Kendall, who was married to Dudley Moore at the time. She is, of course, beautiful, but also a skilled and certainly willing actress to be more than a pretty face, as is usually one of the only requirements for films of this type. Interestingly, the role of Julia was originally offered to Daria Nicolodi, but scheduling and her lack of film experience most likely kept the role out of grasp.

As the investigation kicks into high gear, we are introduced to a pimp named Garullo, nicknamed "So long" because he must say the phrase or else he will stutter. A proud member of the lower classes, Garullo boldly says to Sam, "It must have been a gentleman, some rich guy. They're the ones that have thoughts like this." I have always been intrigued by Argento's rather bold comments on the wealthy in his work. He largely deals with middle class people. Typically, the wealthy are the ones who are the most damaged and do the most damage in return. This can be seen in the corruption in the Terzi family from *Cat O' Nine Tails,* and *Phenomena,* where Jennifer is shipped off to a boarding school by her famous actor father, who is completely disconnected from his child and only speaks to her through his lawyer and agent, it seems. In *The Tram* episode of *Door into Darkness* — Argento's miniseries from 1973 — the main character gives this small speech at the end: "There are intelligent criminals. They own cars, villas, luxury. Even seem like honest people. They commit crimes. But when we have a look at them, they show us their hands; they are always clean white, immaculate."

Sam is also convinced there is a clue in a copy of a painting that is given to him by a rather effeminate antique shop owner, played by Werner Peters, who employed the first victim of the murderer. It seems the girl sold a painting to someone and Sam feels there is a lead. Once he gets home and puts the copy on the wall, his girlfriend Julia is instantly haunted by it. She comments, "It gives me the shivers." The painting is in a primitive style somewhere between a Currier & Ives holiday scene and a Grandma Moses, which Maitland McDonagh pointed out to me was "an interesting style to reference because it's so American."

Peters's character would be the first instance of Argento using a homosexual character in his films, but certainly not the last. In a way, he is a stereotypical "sissy," common to films in the 1930s through the 1950s, yet he is never derided or made the butt of a joke. It is interesting that Argento has Sam flirt with him to get the copy of the painting he has come to inquire about. Argento has always been very gay friendly and it seems Sam reflects this attitude. When questioned about the

girl who sold the painting, the shop owner says she was "peculiar, she liked women." But that doesn't bother me; I'm not a racist." Why would a clearly homosexual man be offended by lesbianism? And using the word "racist" in place of "homophobe" or another similar phrase is an odd piece of translation.

In a great scene that really doesn't do anything to advance the plot — only to put a bit of action into the proceedings — an unknown assassin targets the couple. Out for a walk one night and being tailed by someone assigned by Morosini, Sam and Julia are almost run down by a car, and a man in a yellow jacket (Reggie Nalder) jumps out and gives chase. Sam tells Julia to run away and get the police, which we assume she does. But, we follow Sam during this action scene to an overnight parking lot for city buses and trams, where the mysterious man in yellow finds him and nearly kills him. The tables are turned as Sam is soon following the assassin to corner him and find out who he is, and

Sam and Julia getting nowhere with Inspector Morosini. FROM THE AUTHOR'S COLLECTION/UMC PICTURES.

he tracks him to a hotel where a convention of amateur boxers have gathered. And of course, when Sam discovers them, they are all wearing the same yellow jacket as our man. Deeper into the plot, Sam is given a tip to visit a man named "Needle," and he goes to his shack of a home. While nosing around and looking for a clue, or even the man himself, it is revealed that he is our assassin in the yellow jacket. The setup is something Argento would later do in the end of *Tenebrae,* with one character concealing the other until a dramatic reveal.

According to film historian and journalist David Del Valle, Reggie Nalder really enjoyed living in Rome and the attention it afforded him by the artistic community there. Nalder had a role in Fellini's *Casanova* playing "Faulkircher" in 1976. Upon meeting Nalder with Del Valle during a party at Harmony Gold studio in Hollywood, Argento commented on what a wonderful face he had. Nalder's distinctive face is the result of a reported childhood accident, yet even without his burned skin, he has a very intense and interesting look about him. In the U.S., Nalder was mainly known for his appearance in Hitchcock's *The Man Who Knew Too Much* (1956), playing, not coincidentally I am sure, an assassin, and Argento was determined to use his distinctive visage to its fullest. Del Valle notes that Nalder was upset that he had no dialogue in the film, but the scene is so memorable and he enjoyed the film so much that his initial worries were quickly dispelled.

As the investigation continues, Sam is led from one bad lead to another, as these things are wont to do. The police do little to deter his meddling in the proceedings, even though he has been the target of a few attempts on his and Julia's lives. In the greatest scene of suspense the film offers, Julia is alone in their apartment and hears a noise outside the door. Thinking it is Sam arriving home from the train station, she opens the front door, only to discover a stranger standing there. She rushes back inside and attempts to call the police, only to have the phone cut off. In a panic, she bolts the door and tries to escape, but to no avail.

Reggie Nalder as "Needle," the assassin in the yellow jacket. COURTESY OF THE DEL VALLE ARCHIVES/UMC PICTURES.

In his very positive review of the film from October 14, 1970, Roger Ebert says:

> *Thrillers employ anticipation, fear, and a feeling of impotence; they work best when we're afraid for the hero or his girlfriend and can't help them and they can't help themselves. One of the most effective scenes in 'Bird,' for example, comes when the hero's girl is alone in their apartment and the killer starts hacking away at the door. The lights are out (again) and the phone is dead and the girl collapses into hysteria and crawls around on the floor. And we desperately want her to pull herself together and do something. But she doesn't. And the killer keeps hacking away.*

Not to impugn Mr. Ebert's work, but he gets this wrong. Sure, Julia is trapped in the apartment in the dark and she is alone, but she does make an attempt to escape through the living room window, only to find that it won't budge, and then the bathroom window is barred and much too small for anyone to climb through anyhow. After a brief panic, she collects herself off of the bathroom floor to run to the kitchen and grab a pair of scissors, which she dramatically wields at the camera and goes charging for the front door, where the killer has been cutting a hole. It is only upon her failure to injure her would-be assailant through the door that she "collapses into hysteria." And at this point, Sam is heard coming up the stairs, chasing off the killer. In a feminist statement of sorts, you could say that Argento is standing up for the modern woman to protect her home and her family.

This nighttime scene with Suzy Kendall being terrorized in the apartment is my favorite in terms of Vittorio Storaro's cinematography, especially in light of the fact that it was his first film in color. The film, which was made for a very low budget, is always lit well, whether we are in the bright gallery or this, the darkest of scenes. It is a job done by a complete professional at the infancy of his career, who would go on to do Academy Award-winning work in *Apocalypse Now*, *Reds*, and *The Last Emperor*. He was also nominated for the sadly underappreciated Warren Beatty film *Dick Tracy*, which ironically looks as if it could have been photographed by Luciano Tovoli, who would use a similar primary color palette in *Suspiria*.

Ebert's baseless assertion that Julia is merely a helpless wreck doesn't help the accusation that Argento is a misogynist. In this rare case in Argento's career, all the victims are women outside of Carlo. For the most part, the acts of violence are rather brief and tame, but some do have great impact — in particular the slashing of the woman in the elevator that Brian De Palma would recreate in *Dressed to Kill*, with Angie Dickinson on the receiving end of the blade.

As the film draws to a close and the team comes closer to solving the crime, Carlo has discovered a vital clue in a phone conversation that Sam has recorded when the killer called his and Julia's home. It seems there is a rare bird that was squawking in the zoo that sits below Ranieri's apartment. This begs the question that if Sam did such great research and this book he wrote is so well regarded by the experts, wouldn't he be able to identify the sound on the phone recording as that to belonging to a bird? Surely he must have listened to birdcalls and visited that very zoo that sits right below the Ranieri apartment? This rare bird is called "Hornitus Nevalis" according to the plaque on the cage, which Carlo says is a native specimen from Siberia, but in actuality is an African Crowned Crane.

When Sam, Julia, and Carlo run up to the apartment after hearing Monica screaming, they discover Ranieri with a knife and Monica again struggling for her life. This mirrors the earlier scene in the gallery and leads us to believe that he is indeed the killer. And he does confess to the murders, once he falls out the window accidentally and lies dying on the sidewalk. With everything wrapped up cleanly, Sam notices that Julia is missing and goes looking for her, wandering around town, asking various people, "Have you seen a blond girl with a long coat around here?"

Sam finds his way to a building and goes inside to find Carlo sitting in a chair, stabbed to death. Monica Ranieri enters the room cackling maniacally and enjoying the damage she has inflicted upon this poor, broken man. In the original script that Musante read, this scene was to have Monica up in a loft area of the room and she was to be revealed when Julia's decapitated head is thrown down to his feet. Musante told Argento that he wanted to do the film, but would not if Julia died, and particularly in this fashion.

The film wraps up in the art gallery where Sam was introduced into this ordeal. He ends up stuck underneath a sculpture of spikes and Monica is gleefully leaping up and down on top of him, impaling him. Argento would use this impalement by art motif later, with Anthony Franciosa in *Tenebrae*. The police arrive in time to save Sam, and Monica is taken away. A nod to *Psycho* ends the film, where Morosini goes on

Angie Dickinson is slashed to death in an elevator in Brian De Palma's Dressed to Kill.
COURTESY THE DEL VALLE ARCHIVES/FILMWAYS PICTURES.

De Palma's take on the black-gloved killer in Dressed to Kill. COURTESY THE DEL VALLE
ARCHIVES/FILMWAYS PICTURES.

a television show to explain the details of the case to a live audience. This overly explanatory scene is intercut with Sam and Julia on a plane, finally leaving Italy. Is he going back to The States to write a book about his adventures in Rome? From one fictional American writer to a real one…

In 1949, Frederic Brown published the novel *The Screaming Mimi* in the United States. The title is a clever play on "the screaming meemees," or a severe nervous attack, as well as the name of a WWI bomb that was known for its high-pitched squeal as it landed aground. The story is a classic crime thriller of the period, but the detective is replaced by a reporter involving himself in the investigation of a series of murders in Chicago. It is told by a narrative voice that breaks the action of the story every now and again, to interject with things like:

> *"It's got murder in it, and women and liquor and gambling and even prevarication. There's murder before the story proper starts, and murder after it ends; the actual story begins with a naked woman and ends with one, which is a good opening and a good ending, but everything between isn't nice. Don't say I didn't warn you."*

This bit of narrative description by the omniscient voice, which guides Frederic Brown's novel, could very well describe the giallo films of Italy in the 1970s. Interestingly, it would be Argento's colleagues that would swarm to the genre en masse after the international success of *The Bird with the Crystal Plumage*, with titles like *The Case of the Scorpion's Tail* (dir. Sergio Martino), *Seven Deaths in the Cat's Eye* (dir. Antonio Margheriti), and *The Black Belly of the Tarantula* (dir. Paolo Cavara), to name a few, which would really encapsulate the sleazier elements of these pulp crime novels.

Much in the way Argento's film showcases Rome in a very familiar fashion from someone who lives there, *The Screaming Mimi* shows us a Chicago that only someone very familiar with its geography and character can. "Bughouse Square has another name, but the other name is less appropriate. It is between Clarke and Dearborn Street, just south of the Newberry Library; that's its horizontal location. Vertically speaking, it is quite a bit nearer hell than heaven. I mean it is bright with lights, but dark with the shadows of the defeated men who sit on the benches, all night long." There are no mentions of famous landmarks or anything akin to a travelogue here. It is the dark, seedy side of the city that Brown is interested in. And why shouldn't he be?

It's far more interesting, and anyone can write a visitors' guide to Chicago. It takes someone who really likes a place to dare show it in such ugly detail.

The main character is William Sweeney, a down-on-his-luck reporter who is described early in the novel thusly:

> *You can never tell what a drunken Irishman will do. You can make a flying guess; you can make a lot of flying guesses. You can list them in order of probability. The likely ones are easy. He might go after another drink, start a fight, make a speech, take a train…You can work down the list of possibilities; he might buy some green paint, chop down a maple tree, do a fan dance, sing "God Save The King", steal an oboe…You can work on down and down to things get less and less likely, and eventually you might hit the rock bottom of improbability: He might make a resolution and stick with it. I know that's incredible, but it happened. A guy named Sweeney did it, once, in Chicago.*

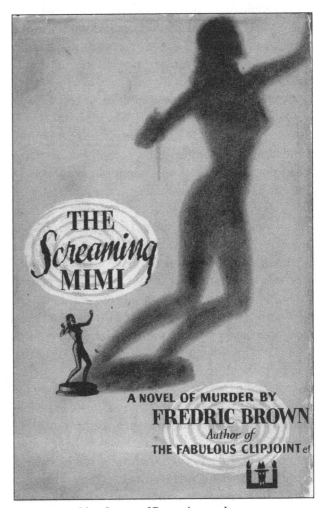

The original hardcover of Brown's novel.

Unlike Sam in *Bird*, William Sweeney has a drinking problem. He has recently left his job without telling his boss, as he is prone to do when he is on an extended bender. For Brown to have such an unsavory fellow as the protagonist of the story is pure noir/pulp, but also quite brave because there really is nothing redeeming about him or even likeable until he starts to "do the right thing" and help in the investigation into the murders that are to come. Sam Dalmas is his complete opposite: he is handsome, has a beautiful girlfriend, and had a bit of good luck with this new book he has just published. William Sweeney, on the other hand, is quite feckless; he spends his spare time in some place called "Bughouse Square" with his friend "God" Godfrey, a vagabond of sorts whose only function is to act as a voice of reason for our main character. Much like Sweeney, Godfrey also has an unflattering introduction in the novel:

"Sweeney sat on a park bench, that summer night, next to God. Sweeney rather liked God, although not many people did. God was a tallish, scrawny old man with a short but tangled beard, stained with nicotine. His full name was Godfrey. I say his full name advisedly, for no one, not even Sweeney knew whether it was his first or his last."

One major omission from Brown's novel is the character of "God." He would materialize in Argento's third film in the animal trilogy, *Four Flies on Grey Velvet*, portrayed by Italian Western star Bud Spencer. Spencer had appeared previously in the film *Today We Kill, Tomorrow We Die!*, which was written by Dario Argento and the film's director, Tonino Cervi. I asked Luigi Cozzi why the character isn't present in *Bird*, and he told me that Dario couldn't figure out how to make the character fit into the script; yet in his place, we have Carlo, Sam's agent, as a sort of substitute. It's interesting that when he appears in *Four Flies on Grey Velvet*, "God" is basically the exact character from the novel. Only "God" now has his own sidekick, "The Professor," who helps Roberto with his investigation.

One night, Sweeney is roaming around looking for his next drink when he comes upon a crowd of people surrounding the entrance to an an apartment building. Through the glass doors, he sees a woman lying prone on the ground. She has been stabbed in the side and is bleeding. A large dog stands guard over the woman and conveniently keeps anyone from coming to her aid. The police come eventually, but are also helpless to assist the

woman due to the large animal. They soon have the situation at hand, and Sweeney runs off to call the story in to the overnight desk at the newspaper where he works.

This is, of course, the novel's version of the art gallery murder, and is much more "provocative" than what Argento shows us in the film. As Yolanda stands up at one point, her white dress falls from her body to reveal her nude figure to the gathered crowd. For Argento to not use the scene to its sleaziest and perhaps "sexiest" potential shows restraint from a young filmmaker who could have easily strayed into baser territory. The film's only nudity is used to great impact in the scene where the killer enters a woman's home and attacks her while she is in bed. Her nightdress is torn from her body, exposing her breasts as she screams, a black gloved hand covers her mouth…and her panties are cut from her waist, the killer clutching them in his hand like a prize.

Sweeney quickly gets in good with his boss again once he presents this story of the "Ripper," as the murderer is referred to. He manages to visit Yolanda in the hospital briefly and finds out that she works at a nightclub as a dancer. Naturally, he goes to El Madhouse to watch her perform one night. He is easily swayed by this woman's beauty and form — of which he has seen more than she realizes — and he speaks with her after the performance to inquire as to her condition.

During this conversation, Sweeney, as well as the reader, are introduced to her agent, a repugnant fellow by the name of Greene, who is very protective of his client. With this set up, all the pins are ready and waiting to be knocked down. Our not-so-loveable hero quickly becomes involved in trying to figure out who almost killed Yolanda — who he is quickly becoming obsessed with — and just who has been killing several women in the area — the person dubbed "The Ripper" by the press.

His investigation next leads him to a gift shop, where the first of the victims worked, and he is greeted by Raoul, the shop's owner. Raoul is referenced in the novel as "that queer" and "the fairy." Raoul tells the tale of the former employee who, it turns out, was selling merchandise at the store and then pocketing the money herself. On the day she died, the poor girl only "sold" one item, a black figure of a woman standing erect and screaming. The "Screaming Mimi" referred to in the title of the novel. Sweeney asks if he can see the item in a catalog, and Raoul does him one better and shows him the other one they had in the shop. Sweeney inquires to whom the piece was sold, but turns up nothing.

In an interesting scene that is not in Argento's or Gerd Oswald's film, titled *Screaming Mimi*, Sweeney goes to Raoul's apartment to see the other Mimi the store had, as Raoul decorates his home with antiques and merchandise from the store when he gets "bored." Upon seeing the Mimi, Sweeney is compelled to inquire about buying the figure — it haunts his memory much like the painting Sam encounters in *Bird*. In this instance, Sweeney does not flirt with the man as Sam does, but the man offers him the Mimi, and Sweeney pays him the value of the other for his troubles in the matter and because he genuinely likes the guy, unlike the other characters in the novel, who refer to him so poorly and looks at him as a social miscreant.

With a little leg work, he finds out through the manufacturer of the statue that only two of the "Screaming Mimi," as the company accountant calls them, were ever sold in Chicago. Sweeney has one; could the killer have bought the other? Armed with the necessary information, Sweeney goes to Wisconsin to visit the home of the artist who sculpted the statue, Charlie Wilson, who sells his work under the name "Chapman." Charlie lives alone in a small house in a nowhere town where everyone knows everything about everybody. Sweeney learns that Charlie sculpted the "Mimi" after his sister Bessie was attacked at his home and he shot and killed her assailant. He further explains that his sister lives in a psychiatric hospital and will likely never get out.

Back in Chicago, Sweeney asks the head of the paper if they can run a story on a hunch about the "Mimi" and try to ferret out the killer. The trap leads Sweeney and the police to Green, who confesses to everything. And, as it turns out, he was Yolanda's psychiatrist. Thinking the mystery is wrapped up, the

police and the newspaper run the story about Green's confession, but something doesn't sit right with Sweeney. He follows Yolanda through town one day while she is walking Devil; he goes to a boarding house where she had been hiding out. While going through the empty apartment after she has gone, Sweeney spots the other Mimi and confronts Yolanda when she gets back. It turns out Yolanda is Bessie Wilson, the woman who was attacked by Doc Green to deflect the truth that she is the killer. It seems seeing the woman in the shop where she bought the Mimi and seeing herself in the Mimi compelled her to strike out at women who resemble her. It's very convoluted pop psychology stuff here. And the explanation doesn't make much sense, but there you have it.

The novel's publishing history in Italy is strange considering its pedigree in Italian cinema and the popularity of the giallo. According to WorldCat.org, the first Italian publication of *The Screaming Mimi* wasn't until 1997 under the title *La Statua che Urla* (The Statue that Cries). This translation is credited to Gianna Tornabuoni and was part of a series titled "Classici del giallo Mondadori." In 1975, there was what I assume is a loose adaptation of the story — at least the cover art and title recall the Anita Ekberg film — for the comic series *Jacula* (issue 154), an erotic comic about a female vampire. Exactly how *The Screaming Mimi* figured into anything is beyond me and perhaps this was used only for the cover. I cannot find any photos of the actual interior of the comic to verify what is or isn't in the story.

The plot and character similarities between *The Bird with the Crystal Plumage* and *Screaming Mimi* are slim; having a female killer has indeed stuck as well as the MacGuffin of the statue/painting. The scene in the gift shop has become the scene in the antique store where

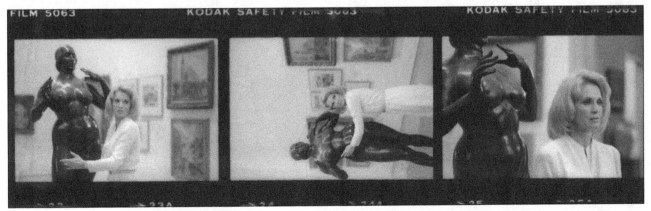

Angie Dickinson finds her own "Screaming Mimi" in a production still from Dressed to Kill. COURTESY OF THE DEL VALLE ARCHIVES/FILMWAYS PICTURES.

Sam meets the gay owner, who Sam shamelessly flirts with to get his way. It is also interesting that Argento chose to stick with Ranieri/Doc Green lying to protect Monica/Yolanda, because he would use this same idea again in *Deep Red* with Carlo covering for his mother, and again in *Trauma* with Piper Laurie's character manipulating the man she loves, Frederic Forrest, into lying to the police about his guilt.

According to Luigi Cozzi, Bernardo Bertolucci gave Argento the novel *The Screaming Mimi* to read. Argento liked it and decided to write a script based on it, but used the story beats and not the characters, which I think works in its favor, since the story had been told before. Brown's novel is fine on the page and works as a piece of detective fiction; yet when translated to the screen in 1958's *Screaming Mimi*, directed by Gerd Oswald, it becomes a limp psychosexual drama with none of the intrigue and suspense.

The film opens with a scene that is taken from the back end of the novel where Anita Ekberg's character,

Virginia Wilson, is attacked while taking a shower outdoors after a swim. A man who has presumably been lurking in the bushes jumps out and attacks her with a knife. Conveniently, her brother Charlie rushes out of the house with a shotgun and blows the guy away, leaving poor Virginia in a state of shock, which of course only a stay in the local mental ward can cure.

While poor Virginia is in the booby hatch, her brother, a local artist, is busy sculpting a likeness of Virginia during the attack. The figure is standing rigid with fear, her arms up to her face and her mouth wide open in a silent scream that nobody will ever hear except poor Charlie. Over the course of Virginia's stay at the hospital, the psychiatrist assigned to her, Dr. Greenwood — the excellent Harry Townes — develops an unethical and unhealthy attraction to his beautiful patient. Naturally, he has a plan to move her back into society under his watch. The good doctor's plan is to act as her talent agent while she wiggles at a night club called El Madhouse, which so happens to

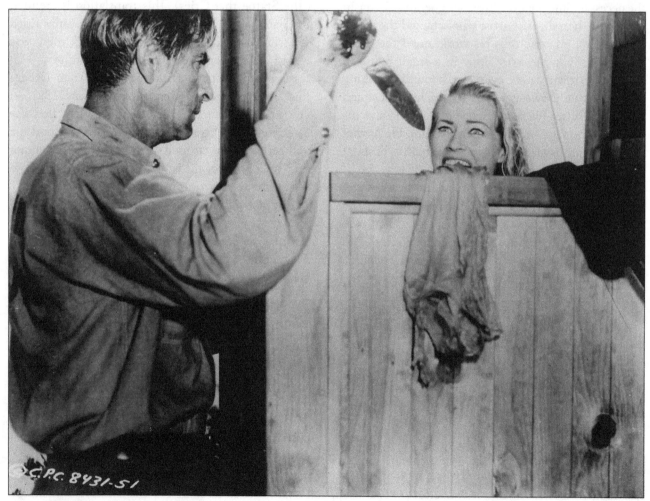

Anita Ekberg is terrorized at knifepoint in the shower in Screaming Mimi. COURTESY OF THE DEL VALLE ARCHIVES/ COLUMBIA PICTURES.

Yolanda does her S&M number for an adoring crowd in Screaming Mimi. COURTESY THE DEL VALLE ARCHIVES/
COLUMBIA PICTURES.

be run by none other than Gypsy Rose Lee playing a character named Joann "Gypsy" Masters.

It seems this film was built around having Lee play this role and Ekberg playing the "larger than life" dancer, as everything else is incidental. Lee's performance is an embarrassment, to be honest, and seems to be there only to cash in on her previous life as a stripper. When she hits the stage to perform outside of her managerial duties of the club, she sings "Put the Blame on Mame," the song Rita Hayworth made famous in *Gilda* to much better effect. Oswald and company seem fine having Ekberg writhe around scantily clad, but don't take advantage of having one of the most famous burlesque performers the country has ever seen do what made her famous.

William Sweeney, played by Philip Carey, is a journalist for the local paper who frequents El Madhouse and is there to watch Virginia's dance act, done under the name "Yolanda Lange," sometimes accompanied by her enormous dog named Devil. Wearing appropriately slinky costumes over that Amazonian frame, Ekberg is more camp than vamp. The most "famous" of the dance sequences involves Yolanda and Devil in a bestial ballet that is begging for a canine-loving drag queen to imitate for the three people in the audience that would get the reference. Anita Ekberg was only a few years away from the famous dance in the Trevi Fountain in Fellini's *La Dolce Vita*. Her opening dance number involves her hands being shackled together while she dances around in, basically, a big-fringed bikini. Two ropes have been suspended from the ceiling, and every now and again she twirls them around to not much effect, only to end up grabbing them at the end of the number and lowering herself to the ground to lie on the floor as the finale. It must be noted that Ekberg is not a good dancer by any stretch of the imagination, and she was clearly hired for her rather impressive chest. She is such a big woman, it is difficult to take her seriously as a dancer at a nightclub, or any other setting, as there is nothing demure about her.

Sweeney and Yolanda/Virginia meet after "Yo" does her chain dance, and they have some witty banter, only to be interrupted by Dr. Greenwood/Mr. Green. That night, Yolanda is found by a group of strangers lying on the floor in the lobby of her apartment building. As they stand outside the glass doors looking in, Devil is standing guard. Naturally, Sweeney just so happens to be one of the bystanders, and he rushes to phone the story in to the paper to make sure it's in the morning edition.

The rest of Oswald's film follows the novel fairly faithfully, omitting the controversial-for-the-time-in-cinema gay gift shop owner and his role in the plot. As the novel was a fairly big success and has proven so over the years, it is interesting that this film has fallen into obscurity outside of certain circles, even with Anita Ekberg and Gypsy Rose Lee in the cast. Perhaps my largest issue with the film is that it negates its central dramatic mystery by revealing to the audience that Yolanda and Bessie are the same person from the outset. It is fine to give the audience more information than the protagonist of your film, but when a major twist in the plot hinges on a case of dual identity, it only harms the film for the audience to be that much further ahead of the hero, as it diminishes the complexity of the plot machinations. And in a murder mystery, you need all of them at your disposal.

Argento, on the other hand, removed this idea of the dual identity completely from *Bird* and chose to focus entirely on the mystery of who the killer is. It could have been a case of just piling on too much in a film. Whatever the reason, it works. However, upon its completion, Dario had stated that nobody much liked the film and that the producers just wanted to unload it. Luckily, Salvatore Argento stepped in and defended his son's project, because they released it as planned. It was internationally very successful and was released all over the world, even being rereleased in the United States in the early 1980s under the title *The Phantom of Terror*. The film would be released under many names: *The Gallery Murders* (UK), *Killing Birds* (Finland), *Black Glove* (Sweden), and what Argento told me was his "favorite" alternate title, *The Sabre Tooth Tiger*.

U.S. re-release poster for The Bird with the Crystal Plumage *under the title* The Phantom of Terror. COURTESY THE DEL VALLE ARCHIVES/21ST CENTURY.

TONY MUSANTE

(Sam Dalmas, *The Bird with the Crystal Plumage*)

A versatile actor, having starred in everything from *A Streetcar Named Desire* on stage to *The Last Run*, directed by John Huston and Richard Fleischer. Audiences in the U.S. probably know him best from a short-lived television show called *Toma*, in 1973, which was reworked into *Baretta*, two years later for Robert Blake. Musante made his film "debut" alongside Martin Sheen in *The Incident*, a little seen, but fantastic film in which the pair play a couple of bored thugs out for a night of "fun" terrorizing passengers of the New York City subway. Tony also starred in the *DuPont Show of the Week* episode 'Ride With Terror' in 1963 on which the film is based.

DB: I know we're here to talk about *The Bird with the Crystal Plumage*, but I wanted to go back a little further. Can you tell me a little bit about *The Incident*? It's a great film and sadly overlooked and relatively unknown. And I think it could be a fantastic stage play.

TM: It was originally done on television. It was done for what used to be called "live on tape." In essence, it is a theater piece, but done for the camera. It was done as a sixty-minute piece for television on the *DuPont Show of the Week*. Then when we did the film, which was four years later, it became a ninety-minute film. In essence, what was done was simply to put back everything that had been cut to make it sixty minutes. To answer your comment about it being a play, it was done as a play about ten or fifteen years later after the film. So it did actually make it to the stage. They used the script from the film, so it didn't come from the theater, but it made it to the theater. Someone who played my role, his name is Dondi Bastone, he is now a successful film music supervisor. I saw his credit recently for the Alexander Payne film *The Descendants* with George Clooney. I haven't seen him since I saw him onstage playing my role. And I occasionally see his name on films; it's great he has a thriving career in the industry. He was a great actor.

DB: The credits in *The Incident* read "Introducing Tony Musante." Was this your first feature film?

TM: Well, it was my first leading role in a movie. The first feature film I did was *Once A Thief*. And it was shot in San Francisco...it was a film starring Ann Margret, Jack Palance, and J.D. Chandler. It was a very nice cast and it was shot black and white. And we shot it in San Francisco. That was in '64. *The Incident* was '67 and *Bird* was in '69. *The Incident* was my first leading role in a film.

DB: So how did you begin working in Italy?

TM: I won the best actor award at the Mar del Plata film festival in Argentina for *The Incident* and there were some Italian producers there. I did a film for them called *The Mercenary* in 1969. That was an Italian film shot in Spain with Franco Nero and, again, Jack Palance. Sergio Corbucci was a friend of the producers of *Metti Una Sera a Cena* [One evening over dinner/Love Circle], my first film shot in Italy. Dario was the co-author of the screenplay of *Metti*. And this led to the role in *Bird*.

DB: I wanted to ask about working with Sergio Corbucci. How was his directing style different from the American directors you had worked with?

TM: He was very imaginative and very Italian in the sense that he was improvisational. That doesn't mean American directors aren't, but the Italian directors at that time, to an extent even to this day, will be very inclined to say, in my experience, "Hey this is working at the moment, let's go in this direction." Even though the script may be taking the character somewhere else. I would say that's the biggest difference. At the time, also, and it's still true, Italian directors tend to have the final cut on their pictures. Americans typically don't. Even today, American directors don't get final cut unless they are producing the film. Also, Italian directors can be quite imaginative, but they have the advantage that the producers are telling them, "This is your picture, do what you want."

DB: Were all these Italian films you worked on post dubbed?

TM: When I first started in the late '60s until I would say the mid '80s, most films in Italy were not shot in direct sound. The last few films I made there were all shot with direct sound in Italian. At the time we shot *Bird*, which was in English, it was dubbed into Italian and English, but the guide track was obviously English.

The U.S. Poster for The Incident. COURTESY THE DEL VALLE ARCHIVES/20TH CENTURY FOX.

DB: You worked with John Huston, who was replaced by Richard Fleischer on *The Last Run*. What can you say about them?

TM: First of all, Dick Fleischer was about five foot one and Huston was almost six feet tall. That's the big difference! I don't say that lightly because I had never met Fleischer. I only knew him from *Tora! Tora! Tora!*, *The Boston Strangler*, and a host of other pictures. But I imagined this great big guy! I never imagined the director of *Tora! Tora! Tora!* being a tiny little guy. They were both very strong-willed and I was surprised, in retrospect, that Fleischer would take over the picture because he had very distinct views about what he was doing. They were both working from the script by Alan Sharp. Alan's script was shot twice, basically. My guess is the final version is probably seventy-five percent Fleischer and twenty-five percent Huston. As a young actor, I was just excited to work with either of them and nobody asked me who I liked better. I was happy to be doing the picture! I would say Huston was, probably, and this is just from my brief experience with him on that picture. I would say he (Huston) was more instinctual and Fleischer more script-oriented as a director. I think George C. Scott was probably the driving force behind the film. I don't think the film would have been made if it weren't for Scott. He had just been nominated for *Patton*. It was his name and reputation that was getting the film made. But you couldn't knock doing a picture with either director, but it was George who got the thing done.

DB: Do you know why the changeover happened with directors?

TM: The producers at MGM didn't like what Huston was doing with the project. He had one idea of how it should go and they had an argument and Huston lost.

DB: It's strange that someone so revered could be cut from a project. Huston isn't a first-timer here.

TM: I haven't the slightest idea. You'd have to be in the boardroom to know what went down. But there I was in Spain as a young actor and these two venerated directors and MGM and George C. Scott did their thing and how it turned out is how it turned out. But I maintain that I don't care if it's Coppola, Fleischer, Huston, American directors just don't have final cut typically. What's funny is I don't think MGM

or Huston lost out on the deal. I happen to really like the movie, but again, I was in it.

DB: A little bit of bias there?

TM: Just a little.

DB: Let me ask you about working with Sven Nykvist on that project *(The Last Run)*.

TM: Sven was wonderful. He was just one of the greatest cinematographers. When I say this, it's not to say anything regarding any of the others. I'm sure you've heard this before. The cinematographer says film is his medium and his canvas, like a painter. He really had this feeling about how he shot a picture. But until he passed away, I would see him every five or ten years either in New York or Europe. And he was a very gentle person. And he was very, very proud of his work. He would listen to a director and subvert his vision to the director's desires. But it was always Sven's artistry that came into play. He told me one story, which has nothing to do with shooting a picture. But it has to do with the way he liked to work. He did a lot of work with Bergman and he said during the film, "I know one thing: September ninth at nine a.m., we are going to get together in Stockholm with the cast of Bergman's next film and have a complete read through of the script with the cast." Well, this doesn't happen very often with American films. I don't know if on September ninth they did get together, but he was convinced they would. But this was what he told me about working with Bergman.

DB: What can you tell me about Robert Aldrich?

TM: One of the best! Contrary to what I just said about American directors…I like American directors, especially when they hire me. But Bob Aldrich, I only did one film with him, *The Grissom Gang*. Half of those major roles and about a dozen supporting party…Bob had every one of those people out to Los Angeles in his studio around a table for two weeks rehearsing the script. Now that may seem to you a good way to do it.

DB: That's quite a luxury!

TM: No kidding! And guess who paid for it? He did! Aldrich was great. He had everyone, no matter where they were from, at his expense in his offices around that table reading the script and going over it for that time. We rehearsed the entire film as though it was a play. He taped out the set for each scene and we rehearsed it. Then everyone went home and he started shooting in whatever order. However, all the actors had gone through the entire script from start to finish as though it were a play. And I'll tell you, in my opinion, that's the way all films should be made. The problem is it costs a lot of money to do a film that way. But that was Aldrich. I'll tell you another story about him. His company was known as Associates and Aldrich. Most companies would be Aldrich and Associates. He had the feeling that everyone involved was important. Of course, as the producer and director, he could afford to be, how should I say this, considerate of everyone. And he could afford not to be as long as they had a job. However, from the first assistant director to the greens man, I learned over the three months I was involved with the project, anyone who had worked with him before expected to work with him again. And Bob never knew when he was going to do his next picture. But any of the people I've mentioned would always call him and say, "I have an offer to do another film. Do you have anything coming up? I'm available." That kind of camaraderie and devotion to a director pays dividends in the final product, at least on the set. Whether the film is successful depends on how many people buy a ticket. I'm sorry he's not with us anymore. If he called me tomorrow, I would say, "I'm available." That's just the kind of guy he was.

DB: It's nice to hear that he fostered such loyalty. On an unrelated note, do you mind talking about the *Toma* "incident"?

TM: No, it's fine. What did you want to know about *Toma*?

DB: Well, the most popular story I have heard is that there were problems between you and the producers of the show and you were let go and replaced with Robert Blake and *Baretta* took its place.

TM: *Toma* was offered to me as a movie of the week. Interesting you should bring up *The Last Run* because about eight or nine months after that was finished, I was back here in the states doing a production of *A Streetcar Named Desire* at the Hartford Stage Company in Connecticut.

DB: I assume you were playing Stanley?

TM: Yes, it was very exciting.

DB: I would have liked to see that.

TM: I'm sorry you didn't get to. And it would be great to have that on film. Anyhow, I received the script for *Toma* on my doorstep one day during the run of *Streetcar*. It was literally propped up against the door wrapped in brown paper. Now, you don't turn most things down if they are literally hand delivered to your door. I read it and liked it a lot. I never thought anyone would want to hire me to play a cop, but shoot, why not? I thought it was excellent. I flipped back to the title page and for the life of me, I will never know why I didn't think of this at the time. It had been written by a fellow named Ed Hume, who was a very successful writer and creator of *The Streets of San Francisco*, and we had gone to college together! Here's an old college friend sending me a script! Well, of course, not literally. Between the time, I said I would love to do it and the time that we went into production was about a week. At the time, it was offered as a series, take it or leave it. At the time, doing a television series was not what actors did if you were seriously interested in doing anything other than television. This is very different today. But at that time, if you took a series, it was pretty unlikely you would ever do a feature again. Be that as it may, I said I would love to do it as a movie, but not as a series. So Universal and I had a discussion and I told them this. They said there was no guarantee it would become a series, but if it did that I would only do it for a year. And then go off and do whatever you want to do. So that's why it only ran the year. I enjoyed the show immensely. We shot 23 episodes and we were very successful. At the end of the year and a half, I said, "I'm going back to New York." And they said I couldn't, but my contract said I could. Unfortunately, there were other avenues to the contract that weren't explored. I had agreed with Universal if they wanted to do six or seven ninety-minute shows. Or if they wanted to do two-hour episodes, that was fine. But since we had a contract, we parted company. *Baretta* did come from the concept of *Toma*. Are you familiar with the show *NCIS*? I'm just passing this along. The executive producer, Charles Johnson, he was the casting director on *Toma* and it was his first job in L.A. in that position. And we have stayed friends through the years. As a matter of fact, my wife wrote two scripts for *Toma* and Charles, as casting director, because he knew us, got two jobs as an actor on the show.

DB: So, on to *Bird*, finally…The novel the film is based on, *The Screaming Mimi* by Frederic Brown, did you ever read it?

TM: No! I didn't know it was based on a novel. Oh, wow, I would love to read that. Dario never told me it was based on a book.

DB: It was an unofficial adaptation and the story goes that Bernardo Bertolucci gave Dario a copy of the book to read.

TM: That could very well be true. One of the producers of *The Love Circle* was Bernardo Bertolucci's cousin.

DB: When you initially read the script for the film, do you recall what appealed to you?

TM: Yes, it was a young leading man who is not a detective and who just happens to get involved in this crime. And for no reason that anyone can discern, he helps solve the thing. This is the kind of movie I used to go to as a kid. So I loved it.

DB: Can you tell me about your first impressions of Dario?

TM: Well, first off, he spoke no English and I spoke no Italian, so we just smiled a lot. I'm serious. Obviously, we communicated through translators. And we were both about the same age. I loved the script and I wanted to do it, so we did it. Unbeknownst to me, although he smiled a lot, he didn't really appreciate that I as an American actor would have my own ideas for the character and motivation for the story. I'm used to American directors, where the actor would say, "I think we should do something different here." And the American directors would say yes or no, but they would listen to you. Dario would smile and I thought he was saying yes, O.K. I subsequently learned there were many times he disagreed with me completely, but he went along with it. But we had a very nice time shooting in general. Also, the cinematographer, Vittorio Storaro, and that was his first film in color, I must add. So here was Dario and Tony and Vittorio and the American author Don Dunaway; we were all

in our late 20s, early 30s. I thought this was a very exciting project, which it was. So I thought this should be the first of many. Well, it wasn't, but it was a very exciting thing to work on at the time. Dario and I had been in touch over the years and he did offer me another script, oh, ten or fifteen years later, but it never got made. You're going to ask me what the project was and I don't remember anything, really. It wasn't a horror film; it was more of a mystery. But it was a good script. I said yes and he said yes and at that time, producers were more important and money was harder to come by.

DB: Is it true that Dario didn't like that you were more of a "method" actor and that you would ask him about character motivation? I've heard stories that you used to call him at all hours asking about character motivation and that this really annoyed him.

TM: Well, I can tell you it's not true because I never ask a director anything. I just don't. What I do is to come in with my ideas and if the director doesn't like them, he can tell me. But Dario smiled a lot, so I assumed he liked my ideas. But no, I'm sorry to say it's not true. It makes a good story that I would show up or call his apartment and ask him questions about the character, but no, that never happened.

DB: I asked him once myself about how you two got on and he said in the beginning, it was fine, that there was a little tension, maybe. But from some of the stories going around, it sounds like you two came to blows almost at times.

TM: No, the truth is, as I said, he was speaking Italian and I was speaking English, so I thought we were getting along just fine. And so the picture came out and it was very successful, so I assumed that we got along fine. It wasn't until, oh, two or three years later that I became very good friends with Don Dunaway, who was the English writer on the script, who, by the way, I had brought to the U.S. and he wrote four episodes of *Toma*. Don said, "You have no idea when Dario was smiling, he was smiling because he was so happy that you would go ahead and shoot. He didn't want to know that you disagreed with the scene or anything." But that's crazy. We shot the picture and I had no problems with anyone.

DB: So tell me a bit about working with Suzy Kendall…

TM: That was a dream. She was wonderful to work with. As a matter of fact, here's a story: did Dario tell you about her head being chopped off?

DB: No, what?

TM: In the original script at the end when my character finds Suzy's character trapped in a loft, but her head has been chopped off. I'm telling you her head is chopped off in front of me and rolled down the floor. And I did disagree with this and I said to Dario that I didn't want to do the picture if this was in it. The next time I read the script, the scene had been changed. However, when it was sent to Suzy, whom I knew personally through a mutual friend who is a director, she said she read the script with that scene in it. At the time, she was married to Dudley Moore and read it in the bathtub! And she got to the page where her head gets chopped off and she laughed and called out to Dudley, "Do you believe this scene?" And she read it to him. She told me later, "I knew you wouldn't do a picture where your girlfriend's head gets chopped off and rolled down onto the floor." And she was right because I had recommended her for the film!

DB: I've never heard of this ending to the film.

TM: Well, it doesn't end that way!

DB: I mean, I didn't even know there was ever a version of the script with this ending

TM: You remember at the end when Suzy is trapped behind the sofa, tied up, and I meet my old friend sitting in the chair and it turns out he's dead. That's when her head was supposed to be cut off and rolled down the floor.

DB: That's pleasant.

TM: It was never shot! But that's just a footnote on the screenplay.

DB: Do you have any stories about Reggie Nalder?

TM: He really was one of the nicest guys you'd ever meet; that's all I can tell you. We didn't have any dialogue scenes, so we never spent much time together. I knew him from the Hitchcock film, but he was just so nice. I was very sorry when he passed away. He was

in Rome every so often and we would see each other after we shot the film. We never worked together after that, but we talked when we saw each other over the years.

DB: Back to your and Suzy's characters in the film. I have always thought it interesting in thrillers and what horror movies became with a lot of stopping of the action of the film for the couples to have a sex scene. I find it interesting that in this and many of Dario's films, characters don't have the most successful or healthy sex lives. And your character in the movie, outside of the one time having sex with the metronome, never successfully beds her again. I find it funny.

TM: Well, I've never thought about that. You'd have to ask Dario if this was something intentional or not. I just saw it as a boyfriend and girlfriend going about their lives and the only interruption I saw was that I was being accused of murder!

DB: Is there any one scene that you really love or are proud of in the film?

TM: Not really. As a whole, I just really enjoy that it's a classic mystery about a guy who's trapped in this situation that he knows nothing about. In the best ways of filmmaking, he solves or is responsible for helping solve the crime. To me, it was such a classic non-leading man role. And I thought it was a great character piece. And they didn't chop Suzy's head off at the end! There were people who asked me why I wanted to do something in this genre and not make a "serious" picture because I had other offers. I told them because it's a nice, fun story. And Dario asked me to do it and it was as simple as that.

IL GATO A NOVE CODE
THE CAT O' NINE TAILS

Winter of 1998: I remember a package from my Argento dealer. I should explain…Earlier that year, I met a guy online, named Henry, on the old Yahoo message boards, where we would discuss all kinds of movies that we loved, hated, loved what other people hated, and vice versa. We quickly discovered our life-long love of horror movies, and we reminisced about some of our favorites that we grew up watching, as we were around the same age. One night, we were discussing some "obscure" horror movies, and I mentioned I watched *Suspiria* a few years back and that one really put me on my ass. Henry countered with, "I have a lot of Dario Argento's movies on tape if you'd like to see them." Like any respectable film geek, I couldn't say no. And, really, how else was I going to watch these weird movies that my friends all made fun of me for liking?

Henry started sending me VHS dupes of several of Argento's films and *The Cat O' Nine Tails* was the first one I watched. And, like any worthwhile pusher, he kept 'em coming until I was hooked. I was intrigued because I had been a fan of Karl Malden's for years and the title made no sense; naturally, I was in. This was my third Argento film, *Tenebrae* being the first under the U.S. title *Unsane*, and *Suspiria*, as mentioned above. I recall being entertained by the dark humor in this film, unlike *Suspiria*, which is so downright bizarre, I never knew what was intended to be humorous and what was just weird.

The scene in which Dr. Calabresi is murdered at the train station still makes me laugh, as the photographers and journalists are assembled to meet some young movie star when she arrives at the station. Instead of that story, they get another first, as Dr. Calabresi is pushed in front of a train and the paparazzi can barely be bothered to pay attention once the starlet appears, standing in the door of a train car waiting to be adored. "That's right, smile, smile. A man is dead," a photographer intones with a delicious deadpan.

Argento has gone on record as saying he feels this is the least successful of his films, although the budget allowed him was roughly four times that of the first, and he was working with a major star with Malden. I don't see why he would be so unhappy with the film, as he has made movies of less quality and never claimed them to be the least of his output. As far as I can gather, Argento insists the film has too much of an American flavor to it. Whether that is the cast, some meddling from producers, or just something he didn't like about the plot, he has been rather vague about his reasoning. After all, Argento has never been one to talk at great length about his work and certainly not about the backroom dealings.

As a second effort, the film doesn't suffer the dreaded "sophomore slump" many artists fall into after a successful first run. Rather, it feels like a natural progression from its predecessor. The second film in the animal trilogy, *The Cat O' Nine Tails* is every bit as good as *Bird* and in some ways thematically richer than its predecessor. Certainly Argento's visual style is expanding with this film, and his obsession with the human eye and all things related to sight are on prominent display.

After the international success of his first film, Dario went back to the giallo for his second feature. This is the first of Argento's features to be shot in Turin, Italy, a city he adores for its odd architectural angles and collision of old city and modern industrialization. The city boasts the Museo Egizio, with the largest collection of Egyptian artifacts outside of Cairo, and the Alfa Romeo and Fiat factories call the city home as well. Over the course of his career, Argento would return to the city many times, most famously using it as the backdrop for *Deep Red*.

As with *The Bird with the Crystal Plumage*, this film also has antecedents in the Frederic Brown novel *The Screaming Mimi*. James Franciscus's character, Giordani, is a reporter, much like William Sweeney from the novel. There is a scene lifted directly from the book where Sweeney goes to a barber for a shave, they very comically discuss the murders taking place, and the barber notes that the police think the murderer may be a barber. Likewise, in the film, Giordani sits in the barber chair reading a newspaper article about the murder of his friend, the photographer who was killed while trying to get Arno and Giordani a copy of the original photo that he had taken of the train murder. The headline asks if the murder weapon was a razor, which causes the barber to go on a rant about how he would slit someone's throat, all while shaving Giordani, to great comedic effect.

The influence from Brown's novel also seems to appear in a nice bit of ironic humor in the scene when Giordani tracks down an informant and petty thief by the name of G.G. to help him break into the Terzi home. William Sweeney in *The Screaming Mimi* also used his pull as a reporter to parry with the less-than-desirable citizens of Chicago when he needed information. Once they get inside the house, G.G. tells Giordani he can't open the door of Terzi's home office after they have gotten in and closed and locked the door behind them. Now they have to break out of the home they broke into…G.G. the loser, indeed. While looking for incriminating evidence against Terzi, they discover Ana Terzi is adopted, and Terzi's diary makes clear what the film had been hinting at: that Terzi has more than paternal feelings for his charge.

Dardano Sachetti, who cowrote the story for the film with Argento, had also written another script with him previously that was never produced, titled *Montesa*, named for the Spanish motorcycle maker. The film told the coming-of-age tale of two young men who hitch-hike from Rome to Spain to buy a motorcycle. Sachetti

Argento surveys the scene while Malden confers with the crew. COURTESY THE DEL VALLE ARCHIVES/TITANUS.

told me it was written in response to the massive cultural upheaval that was taking place in Europe in 1968, which mirrors what was happening in the United States. In fact, the film seems to be an Italian version of *Easy Rider*, with its "sex, drugs, and rock n' roll" attitude, in Sachetti's words describing the tone of the film.

Sachetti said the initial treatment he handed to Dario for the film was seven pages and was built around the concept of the XYY chromosome abnormality he had seen written up in *Scientific American* magazine. The article purported to have some evidence of prisoners in America who had an abnormally large ratio of having this anomaly, which they called "The Evil Gene." This genetic mutation was alleged to be responsible for these individuals being violent criminals, thus landing them into a life of crime and, in some cases, to prison, where such research would take place.

After working with Argento on this film, Sachetti went to work for Mario Bava cowriting *Bay of Blood*. Sachetti said, "Dario and I had an argument, which was caused by a misunderstanding. I was young and impetuous and this left a mark. An echo of my argument with Dario reached Mario, who was looking for somebody to write a story for him. We met; I wrote a story he liked; and we started working together immediately."

In this, his second film, Argento has given us a script every bit as tight and entertaining as the previous. His writing had gotten sharper in terms of plotting and even in terms of dialogue. The scene where Arno and Giordani are "explaining" the title is a little silly as the title is a complete non sequitur. I can forgive it because unlike *Bird* and its literal bird in the zoo that provides a vital clue to the plot, there is no visual to show a "Cat with nine tails" per Giordani. It would be goofy as a visual metaphor: a mutated cat? But it could work perhaps in an S&M scene with someone having rough sex using a cat o' nine tails and beating someone with it. Unfortunately, or fortunately, this isn't a Jess Franco film. So we are never privy to that scene.

Franciscus and Malden on the path of a killer. FROM THE AUTHOR'S COLLECTION/NATIONAL GENERAL PICTURES.

Casting Malden and Franciscus was a coup for the film and lent the project much needed cache after the fairly unknown cast from *Bird*. Karl Malden had been a very well-respected actor in Hollywood for years. He was nominated for the Academy Award for *On the Waterfront* in 1955 after winning for *A Streetcar Named Desire* in 1952 playing Mitch, a role he reprised from the Broadway production of the play. James Franciscus was probably mostly known for his TV show *Mr. Novak* and would later have a starring role in *Beneath the Planet of the Apes*.

Karl Malden plays Franco Arno, a blind retired journalist who lives with his young orphaned niece. He teams up with a journalist named Giordani, played by James Franciscus, to solve a series of murders linked to an experimental procedure at the institute. As the film opens, Franco and his niece are walking down the street for an evening stroll; Franco overhears something being said in a parked car as they pass it. "I'm not interested in blackmailing you. I have to pass on the information," one of the men says. Not wanting to alarm the girl, he stops to tie his shoe and asks her to describe what the men look like. She gives him a very vague description of one of the inhabitants of the car, but cannot see the other.

In what could be read as a simple scene that is setting up a murder mystery plot, there are a few more things going on for those who wish to see them. Of course, playing a blind man who uses his niece to "see" the men in the car cements a long-standing Argento theme of sight, sightlessness, and the visual motif of the human eye. After putting Lori to bed, Arno turns out the light to sit at his table to build a crossword puzzle. It is a great grid of block letters and slides. During his work, he hears something out the window and so he gets up to "see" what it is. In a brilliant bit of editing and camera work, we witness what he is only hearing. And yet, we don't know how much he is privy

Franciscus and Malden search high and low for a clue and all they find is a crew member in the corner. FROM THE AUTHOR'S COLLECTION/NATIONAL GENERAL PICTURES.

to from the top level of the building in which he lives that overlooks the Terzi Institute, in which a crime is taking place.

It is in this sequence with this robbery that we are introduced to Argento's love — or is it an obsession? — of extreme close-ups and, beyond that, the human eye itself. We are shown one of what we presume to be the killer's eyes in extreme close-up, often accompanied by a sound effect when he blinks. It suggests a camera shutter. A similar tactic is used in *Opera* whenever the killer, we presume, gets the "urge" to kill, and a shot of a throbbing brain is intercut with the main action.

The next morning, Arno and Giordani meet outside the institute. Ironically, it is the sighted man who cannot see and runs right into Arno, knocking his cane out of his hands. Giordani is there to unofficially cover the story, where we learn about the scientific espionage that may or may not be going on. Ana Terzi, the daughter of the head of the institute, breezes onto the scene, all hair and crazy couture. Catherine Spaak is an interesting actress for this role, as she appears to have been manufactured in a scientific laboratory herself: her beauty is almost unnatural. Added to this ethereal beauty, her costumes and hairstyle are reflective of haute couture, almost futuristic against the "off the rack" fashions of the day that everyone else wears.

Both of the leads give solid performances, and I am sure playing opposite Malden, Franciscus couldn't help but be good. I would imagine it being akin to a short master class in acting, as Malden was a member of the Actor's Studio and had studied, worked with, or taught everyone of any importance well into the 1970s. Franciscus is a cool personality who is just so slick that he could probably get away with murder and nobody would bat an eye. My favorite scenes with Franciscus, however, involve the flirty banter between him and Catherine Spaak. Their big romantic scene where Spaak tears away her clothes like they are made of Velcro is very strange. There's a dash of Hitchcock's *Suspicion* with the possibly poisoned glass of milk. The shot with the glass of milk "floating" in the air toward Catherine while she is reclining in bed is repeated in *Suspiria* with Jessica Harper and a glass of wine. Their romantic roust is almost a parody of sex scenes in movies that were becoming more common at the time. Throughout his career, Argento has made very little use of sex scenes, so they stand out when they're there.

During a scene where Ana Terzi tells Giordani everything he needs to know about the cast of characters at the institute, she also tells him that Dr. Braun is

gay. The next thing you know, Giordani is in the most ridiculously posh gay bar you will probably ever see on film. The velvet patterned sofas and chairs look like an exclusive hunting club somewhere, not a gay bar where "peculiar men," as Ana referred to Braun, would hang out to pick up a trick.

The bar is called "The Saint Peters Club," which is a great pun. Does this infer these men are all cock worshipers? What would that Saint card look like? And how would you get a figure on your dashboard? In a very Catholic country, for Argento to make such a blasphemous joke really does take some nerve. Argento was educated in a Catholic school as a child, but never seemed to carry it any further than that, and from speaking with him, I don't get the idea that he is religious in the least as an adult.

Whereas *Bird* only has one gay character, this film has a room full and beyond. Some of them are badly accoutered drag queens, others swishy stereotypes. Of course, when Giordani walks into the bar, all eyes are on him. He spots Dr. Braun and his young companion, Manuel, at a table and asks to speak to Braun alone. This immediately puts his young charge on alert. Seated at the bar, Dr. Braun flirts with Giordani, telling him, "You have beautiful eyes…stupendous. Blue with a touch of red, very rare." Once Giordani tells Braun he is a reporter, Braun attempts to leave, causing Giordani to grab his arm in protest. This catches the eye of Manuel, who jealously and protectively gives the supposed interloper the stink eye only to be sent away by Braun. Giordani proceeds to tell Braun that he thinks he has some information about the murder at the institute. This scene recalls *Bird*, where Sam flirts with the antique shop owner to get something out of him that he needs. Giordani is completely nonplussed by Braun's advances, and I genuinely feel this reflects Argento's attitude toward gay people. They are nothing to be feared; they are just as flawed and weird as everyone else, but the fact they are gay has nothing to do with anything.

Later in the film, Giordani has an encounter with the ex-boyfriend of Manuel, Dr. Braun's young plaything. The man is upset with Braun for "stealing" Manuel away and is willing to blackmail Braun him to get him back. So he comes to Giordani with the whereabouts of where Braun and Manuel are hiding out to expose him, in the hope that Manuel will come back to him. The man acts like a lovesick teenager and proclaims that if Manuel doesn't return, he will kill himself. In a film populated with men and only one female adult character, of course the bulk of the relationship drama would be between gay men.

Argento has never been seen as a sentimental filmmaker, but in this case, it is right upfront in the opening scene with Arno and Lori. You can feel the affection they have for one another. They are out for a nice leisurely stroll, holding hands, and it's very clear they have a dependent relationship. He takes care of her the way any parent would, and she helps him to see the world around him. She affectionately calls him "Cookie" because "Cookies are sweet. And I like them with chocolate milk." Familial bond is paramount to Argento and many in the Italian film industry, as his father produced his films up until *Opera,* leaving brother Claudio to take his place. And now his nephew Nilo has been working with him for the last few films, having started as the production secretary on *The Card Player.*

Even in these early films, Argento's visual aesthetic is evident, but it's not until the next film, *Four Flies on Grey Velvet,* that his eccentricities as a filmmaker would really start to find their home. There is an interestingly edited scene in *Cat* when Malden, early in the film, is recollecting meeting Franciscus, and the audience sees him in his office, where they will be going shortly, even though Malden has not been to this office and could not possibly know what it, or Franciscus, looks like since he is blind. In *Four Flies On Grey Velvet,* there is a scene where Michael Brandon is driving to meet a private investigator for the first time, and he is literally driving up to the office via several flights of stairs and galleries along the sidewalks in a similar editing technique. This visual theme ties these two films together in a way that leaves the first film to stand alone in its style.

The Italian poster for Cat O' Nine Tails.

QUATTRO MOSCE
DI VELLUTO GRIGIO

FOUR FLIES
ON GREY VELVET

The final film in the animal trilogy, *Four Flies on Grey Velvet*, is in a way my favorite of the three, due to its contribution to the language of the amateur detective thriller Argento had impressed upon the viewing public with the first two films, and the advances he would make within the neo noir. This was another film I was exposed to by way of a bad VHS dupe, courtesy of my friend Henry. Imagine sitting and watching the film on a tiny nineteen-inch television in all its Technicscope glory on a who knows how many generations down videotape and trying to make out what is going on. These weren't optimal viewing conditions, but it's all I had at the time, and I relished it. The grunginess somehow made it special, like it was something secret and sacred only to me. I didn't know anyone for years that had seen any of Argento's films, and this was one of the most rare of his filmography. So in experiencing it, I felt like I had something holy in my grasp.

The only footage of the film I had seen prior, was part of the Skinny Puppy video for their song *Worlock*. I wasn't a fan of their music, necessarily, I just wanted to see anything from Argento's films that I could get my hands on. I had heard Ennio Morricone's improvisational-sounding jazz/rock score before I even saw a single frame of the movie, and I was excited to see how the music and the film complimented each other. I wasn't disappointed, as the music is just as effective and haunting as the previous two. Joseph Bishara, composer of James Wan's *Insidious*, commented, "Of the earlier films that Morricone scored, *Four Flies* really stands out because it's so strange and it really compliments the

oddness of the film. It sounds like a lot of his experimental jazz he was doing at the time. It's a great score. But he never wrote a bad one."

Roberto Tobias (Michael Brandon) is a musician in a progressive rock band who is being followed by a mysterious man in a fedora and black sunglasses. One night after rehearsal, Roberto becomes the stalker as he follows the man to an empty theater. After a brief exchange and ensuing struggle, which ends with the mystery man stabbed, assumed dead, and landing in the orchestra pit with a blinding ray of light shining on him, Roberto looks up to see a man in an eerie cherub-faced mask in the upper stalls of the theater photographing him.

Instead of going to the police, Roberto goes home to his quite cold marriage bed, and it isn't until he is threatened with exposure for murdering the man that he tells his wife, Nina (Mimsy Farmer), what has happened. She dismisses his fears, telling him perhaps he just had a nightmare. Over the next few days, Roberto discovers someone has left photographs of the fateful encounter in his home and is blackmailing him into further silence. Roberto must now fight to stay alive, while keeping his rocky marriage afloat and trying to figure out what really happened that night.

When Nina asks if Roberto is OK after that first attack in the apartment, when he is strangled with a wire garrote much like in *The Cat O' Nine Tails*, she won't let up until he is yelling at her. As we will learn later, she is only serving her own selfish and twisted need to know that this disturbs him, in acting out her revenge against her father, whom, she explains in the finale, Roberto reminds her of. This angle with the demented wife torturing her father's surrogate and husband was the idea of Mario Foglietti, who contributed to the story along with Luigi Cozzi.

Afraid for his life and having no desire to involve the police, Roberto hires private detective Gianni Arrosio (Jean-Pierre Marielle) at his friend God's behest, insisting he needs a "private dick" to tail him. He describes him as a "bit eccentric, but cheap." It doesn't take long after meeting the detective to figure out that "eccentric" is simply code for homosexual. After the somewhat stereotypical approach to portraying the male gay characters as nothing more than set dressing and, in the case of the antique dealer in *The Bird with the Crystal Plumage*, the classic "sissy" from the earliest days of film, Arrosio is an interesting sort of hero character that does more to solve the mystery than the film's "traditional" hero figure in Roberto. During their first meeting, when it is clear that Arrosio is gay,

Roberto assumes he has the wrong guy, and in a great moment, Arrosio says, "And you're thinking this fairy is going to jump on a table when he sees a mouse. Oh, you heteros. I don't suppose you've ever had a homosexual experience? We're men, too, just a little different."

Marielle imbues the character with a good deal of compassionate charm, and the audience goes along with Roberto in really getting into his corner to not only figure out what is going on to solve the case he has been entrusted with but also to finally "win one." With his admission that, "In three years, I haven't solved a single case. Eighty-four failures…a fantastic record! It couldn't possibly last. I could just sit in my office and wait for the criminal to show up!" he is charming Roberto with his honesty and enthusiasm and, in turn, the audience as well. In a way, he is the most likeable character in the entire film. Argento has no interest in carving out the same stereotypes witnessed in *The Cat O' Nine Tails* with the collection of transvestites and

Michael Brandon and Mimsy Farmer experience anything but connubial bliss. COURTESY MAITLAND MCDONAGH/ PARAMOUNT.

surly closet cases at the St. Peter's Club, and instead gives us a nicely progressive portrait of a loveable loser who just happens to be gay.

As his clues begin to stack up, Arrosio comes to a point where he is led to an apartment building, where he meets another gay man roughly his age and decides to flirt with him to get information from him. This is a clever play on the typical vamp in any film noir using her feminine wiles to pump a man for the goods. Strangely, this is the scene where Argento does go for the cheap effeminate stereotype, as the landlord sits in a chair fanning himself like Sister Woman in *Cat on a Hot Tin Roof* at Big Daddy's birthday party or Sydney Greenstreet in *Flamingo Road*. In the end, Arrosio gets what he needs, but only after telling the stranger he will call him for a date.

The true hero in the film comes to a tragic ending when he is murdered in a train station bathroom. Staging the scene in a train station lavatory, where gay men have been known to cruise for sex, can be read as insulting to the character because it suggests he would naturally go into the bathroom in a train station for no reason because it is "in his DNA" as a promiscuous queer. We are never given any clue as to why Arrosio decides to go into the bathroom instead of following whoever he is after out of the station, being a more logical exit. That being said, Argento gives him one last moment of dignity and satisfaction in knowing he solved the crime, as he lies dying on the floor of a toilet stall and smiling at his own cleverness. His unlucky streak has been broken, but at what price? Interestingly, Roberto is not afforded the same treatment, for it is God who sweeps in to save the day to rescue him, thus turning him into the damsel in distress the fey detective would logically be cast into if the heterosexual male and his homosexual counterpart were given "roles." Nina's absent father limns Argento's need of exploring childhood trauma and the terror it wreaks in adulthood, with this refrain: "If you get hit once, you hit back twice. I don't want to hear you crying! You idiot!" Argento's parental trauma and pursuant psychology is in full force with the memories of the killer.

The "private dick," detective Arrosio, is on the case and won't stop until he's solved at least one! COURTESY MAITLAND MCDONAGH/PARAMOUNT.

The whirling shots of the padded walls of a cell predict the tortured screams and silhouettes in *Tenebrae,* along with the shots of water glasses and pills to calm the psychotic mind. In remembering a past and reliving it and medicating either with pills or violence, can one move beyond the pain of the past? The parallels with *Tenebrae* don't end there, though. When Nina kills the hired man, he shows the audience the fake knife that dispenses blood, which coincides with Peter's razor in *Tenebrae.* He also spits blood in her face after being hit in the head, just as the woman on the beach spits blood on Peter Neal in the flashback. This scene also predicts the noose-o-matic in *Trauma,* while referencing the garrote wire of *The Cat O' Nine Tails* when the hired man is killed with the wire being twisted around his neck until he is dead.

Roberto is an interesting figure as the poor put-upon husband of the manipulative Nina. In another of Argento's weak male characters, he is feckless at every turn. Brandon is powerless against his desire for

his wife's cousin, who doesn't take long to warm to his advances, in which we witness the only act of lovemaking. He can do nothing to warm up his rather frigid wife, to which point we never see them embrace or kiss as any loving couple would. They seem more like roommates who tolerate each other than a young, attractive couple who most would envy from the outside, a stark contrast to Sam and Julia in *The Bird with the Crystal Plumage,* who are making love at any opportunity, even if it is almost always timed badly.

In what should be called the "Screaming Mimi trilogy," there is yet another reference to Frederic Brown's novel with the character of "God" (Bud Spencer). He comically objects to being called "God" and insists that Roberto refer to him as either Godfrey or something "not so appropriate" as "God." He suggests "God Almighty" with much mock humility. Much as in Brown's novel, God is a lovable drifter to whom our lead character goes to for advice and help when he's in a tight spot. Argento takes this character from the

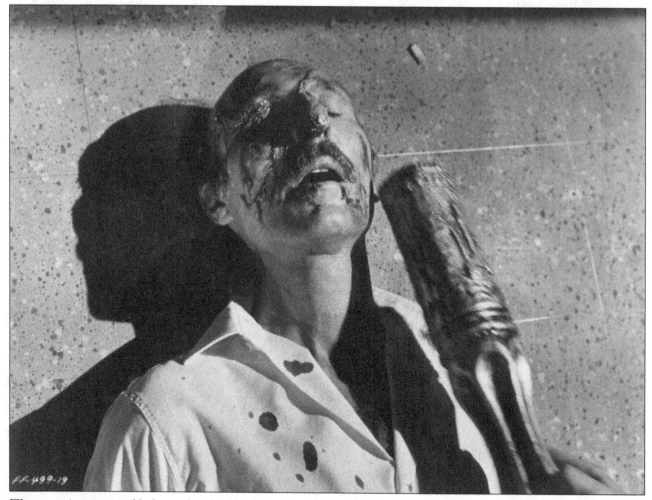

The mysterious man is bludgeoned to death by his even more mysterious employer. COURTESY MAITLAND MCDONAGH/
PARAMOUNT.

Argento perched to view the setup of the climactic car crash. COURTESY OF INDEPENDENT VISIONS.

novel and splits him in two here and offers another odd fellow by the name of "The Philosopher," a close friend of Godfrey's who spends his days lounging around and spouting biblical phrases. God also has a pet parrot, which he spends his days talking to, named "Jerk Off." Much like Max Von Sydow in *Non Ho Sonno*, these lonely deep thinkers need someone, a bird in both cases, to bounce their philosophies off of.

Argento's most stylish film up to this point, *Four Flies on Grey Velvet*, is a visual and aural bridge between the earlier detective thrillers and the more abstract treatises of *Deep Red*. There is a direct line from *Four Flies* to *Deep Red* in that Luigi Cozzi informed me that the original opening to the film was to be similar to the opening that opens *Deep Red* with the parapsychology conference. According to Cozzi, there was still the talk of insects, thus tying in the insect motif of the title and Mimsy Farmer's necklace that acts as a vital clue to the mystery in this film. Strangely, Cozzi also informed me that Argento came up with the title of the film before he had any idea what the story was going to be, and that in grand AIP tradition, the story had to serve the title somehow as it had come first .

During production, according to Mimsy Farmer in an interview given for Video Watchdog, issue 161, we get a rare glimpse of Salvatore Argento:

> *His father was the producer; now he was a terrible guy. They were shooting the car crashing into the truck and it was going to be done by remote control. I don't know why it happened, but the person responsible for it had the remote control in his hand and something triggered it. He was near the car and the car blew up and the guy was in flames. The producer, Dario Argento's father, was up on the ladder, screaming, 'This is costing me money, what's happening? We have to shoot this scene, it's four in the morning!' I was there hearing all this; I was really a witness and he couldn't have cared less about this poor man who was in flames. They finally rushed him off to the hospital and he didn't die, thank God… but the whole episode was indicative of the father's attitude, you know—very, very cynical. That is the only experience I've had like that, thank goodness.*

Musically, the film branches out into acid rock, courtesy of Ennio Morricone's trippy jazz/rock score that prefigures what Goblin would offer in *Deep Red* in 1975. The music is introduced in the opening credits by way of Roberto Tobias's band, where at one point, the camera is inside the sound hole of a guitar being strummed awkwardly. Morricone's score for this film, while effective, did not please Argento, and the two would have a falling out. They wouldn't work again until 1996's *The Stendhal Syndrome*, where I think Morricone made up for any "missteps" with this score in Argento's eyes. However, it would be Argento's next giallo, the truly groundbreaking *Profondo Rosso*, which would fantastically blend the giallo, the supernatural, and a pulse-pounding progressive-rock score by Goblin, into a meditation on what the giallo could and should be, while influencing contemporaries at home and abroad for years to come.

STUART GORDON

A native of Chicago, Gordon ran the Organic Theater, where he directed counter culture comedies and some early work by playwright David Mamet. *Re-Animator* (1985) was Gordon's first film to make a lot of noise, and he's been in the horror game ever since. With an impressive range of work from the Sci-Fi actioner *Robot Jox* (1989) to the bizarre horror-noir film *King of the Ants* (2003). Stuart is harder to stereotype than one would think: he even co-wrote the Disney film *Honey, I Shrunk the Kids* (1989). Gordon has made several adaptations of H.P. Lovecraft tales including *Dagon* (2001), *From Beyond* (1986), and "Dreams in the Witch House" for the TV series *Masters of Horror*. He has also worked in Edgar Allan Poe territory with *The Pit and the Pendulum* (1991) and "The Black Cat," also for *Masters of Horror*.

DB: Did you have a particular first impression of Dario as a filmmaker?

SG: Well, the first film of his I remember watching was *Suspiria*. I may have seen *Four Flies on Grey Velvet* and not realized it was one of his movies until later. My biggest impression of him is that he really captures the unconscious and dreamlike potential of film unlike anyone else. And besides John Carpenter, he's really the only horror film director who looks like he should be making horror movies. He has thinning hair, deep-set eyes, a very prominent skull, he looks like a character out of something…like the crypt keeper or something. People, when they see me, I think, are disappointed because they expect me to have blood on my hands. But I'm just a very normal-looking person.
I've also heard a few stories about him…I made a few movies in Italy and was told that he only works at night. He would begin at 6 p.m. and stop at 6 a.m. like a vampire or something.

DB: Sorry to say, it's not true, at least not in my experience. I've been on one of his sets and the noonday sun was blazing.

SG: It may have been true then; this was in the 80s that I heard this, so maybe things have changed. He was working at De Paolis Studio, where I think he shot *Suspiria*.

DB: That would be great if it were true. Maybe it was.

SG: The strongest impression I have of him was at a festival screening of *The Stendhal Syndrome*. It was a packed audience and it got so hot in there, during that rape scene, I felt like I was going to pass out. I felt like I had The Stendhal Syndrome myself. I had to leave the theater to get some air. I saw him later doing some interviews and I bowed to him and said, "You are the master." And ya know, he is a true master.

DB: *The Stendhal Syndrome* is one of my favorites of his.

SG: I think it's one of his best.

DB: Do you find any of his work inspiring you? Maybe even on a subconscious level that you don't recognize until after the fact?

SG: I don't think you can really imitate or be inspired by him; his work is so unique and personal. He has such a unique approach to things. I was invited to a symposium in Vienna last year on dreaming and it was in honor of the 50th anniversary of the discovery of R.E.M. sleep. I couldn't understand why I had been invited. It turns out they wanted me to discuss dreams in film. And so the very first clip I showed was from *Inferno*. And it was the sequence where the woman drops her keys and goes into the puddle. There's the room…it's very surreal and dreamy. But when you're watching it, it feels like it could happen. The scientists were blown away by this and they said, "This is a dream that has been captured." They [the scientists] are trying to find a way to do this, to capture a dream. And Dario managed to do it.

DB: That's great and a shock that scientists would say that. It's just a movie!

SG: Well, they had a debate about it. Scientists have to qualify everything, you know, and so they started debating right there. This one guy said, "Well, this could never happen; in your dreams you never see yourself." But the way it's shot, it has the logic of a dream. They say artists are trying to capture the unconscious consciously. And I think that's very true in this case.

DB: I read a quote that Argento said that even his realistic films aren't very realistic. Do you have any thoughts on the thrillers and this mode of thought?

SG: I don't think any of his films are completely realistic. *Stendhal* isn't realistic at all. In the end, he pulls the rug out from under you and you realize you've been watching the movie through the eyes of somebody who is deranged. There is a reason that it's as bizarre as it is. All his movies, the style isn't reality we're looking at. In *Opera*, there are ravens flying around everywhere, which could never happen. But it seems right when he does it in his films. It's not logic in terms of intellectual; it just is what it is.

DB: What would you say his biggest mark is in genre?

SG: It's funny, he is called "The Italian Hitchcock," but in a way, I think that's doing him a disservice. Hitchock was great, don't get me wrong, but Dario has his own sense of style. But Hitchcock wasn't realistic, either. Dario's approach is so different from Hitchcock. I think the only thing they have in common is they are stylists and they love suspense. But the approach is very different. I think Dario is very unique. You could say that Hitchcock is the British Dario Argento.

DB: Is there something thematic, a particular visual sequence that really blows you away?

SG: That underwater scene in *Inferno* is brilliant. In *Stendhal*, the sequence where she goes into the painting and kisses the fish is very dreamlike. The other thing in terms of themes…you have the Three Mothers. Those movies are very powerful. I saw *Inferno* in Italy; my Italian is not very good, but that's fine. It speaks to you in images. I had a very fitful night after watching that. The idea of the three mothers, it's a very Jungian archetype that he creates there. You almost believe that it's real, although it's completely fantastic.

DB: You mention *The Stendhal Syndrome*; the use of art in that film and in a lot of his movies really stands out. They way he alludes to other artists. Do you have any thoughts on this?

SG: He was really making a statement about the power of art, but showing it in such a way that he created his own Stendhal Syndrome, really, within the movie. It was not just an intellectual exercise. It grabbed you visually and viscerally. That is true art. That's why he's the master!

DB: I was watching *Suspiria* and it made me think of your film *Dolls* in that they both deal with these fairy tale archetypal themes and characters. In *Dolls*, you have the father, the stepmother, the daughter. In *Suspiria*, you have this girl going to live in a strange place and she is surrounded by these maternal figures that are supposed to take care of her, but have other plans, much like the wicked witch or evil stepmother or just a terrible mother figure. Would you agree with this commonality between the films?

SG: Completely; in fact, in the fairy tales and often the characters, these archetypes, don't even have names. It's 'the girl,' 'the prince,' and 'the wicked witch.' In his films, you have those kinds of characters. And in *Dolls*, you have the doll maker…we were drawing a lot on *Hansel and Gretel*. And like you said, there is that similar feeling in *Suspiria*.

I read a book right before I worked on *Dolls* called "The Uses of Enchantment" by Bruno Bettelheim and he says that why fairy tales are violent is because they are tools to teach kids about life and that the world can be a scary place. And you have to deal with it.

He talks about *The Three Little Pigs*, basically identifying with the kids by calling them little and telling the children they can defeat the Big Bad Wolf even though they are little themselves. They really are life lessons for kids. If you take out the scariness, in fact, you take out the whole purpose of them. What was fun with *Dolls* is we made a fairy tale where we could emphasize this, the scariness.

DB: A lot of people say Dario's films are exceedingly violent. It makes me think, well, he's making horror films, but they're so stylized that the violence isn't even scary, it's just beautiful and graceful.

SG: That scene in *The Stendhal Syndrome* where the bullet goes through the woman's face, it's in slow motion, it's very graceful. I don't think his movies are that gross…or bloody; he sort of suggests things to you. In *Opera*, where the needles are taped to the girl's eyes, it's so powerful, but you don't see that much, it's just the suggestion of it and my God, what's going to happen if she opens her eyes? He really lets your imagination do the rest.

LA PORTA SUL BUIO
DOOR INTO DARKNESS

"This series is very important because it turned Dario into a star here," Luigi Cozzi told me via e-mail. "When it was aired, it got rave reviews and was an enormous hit. Dario starred as host at the beginning of all four episodes and so he became well-known immediately. Dario said that my episode (*Il Vicino di Casa/ The Neighbor*) was the best of the series and actually, it's the one which got the highest ratings."

As Cozzi mentioned, the first episode to air was *The Neighbor*, about a young couple, Luca and Stefania (Aldo Reggiani and Laura Belli), who are moving into a new apartment in a seaside building. Their first night there, with no electricity or phone installed, the upstairs neighbor (Mimmo Palmari) greets them less than warmly.

The episode opens as they all do, with Argento introducing the episode, yet in this one, he takes an active role in the opening scene by hitchhiking with the young couple, the camera taking his point of view and making the audience the third passenger in his car. He tells them of a house by the ocean that would be perfect for them and their newborn son because, "I live in the country and I can assure you nothing ever happens," nodding to Sam's dialogue in *The Bird with the Crystal Plumage*: "Go to Italy, they say, nothing ever happens there."

Throughout the episode, Cozzi pays homage to films that he loves. Luca even writes for a *Famous Monsters of Filmland* style magazine. Upon arrival at the house, he comments, "From here, it really does look like Dracula's castle." To which Stefania responds, "And we're his snack." Once they're a bit settled, he insists on watching *House of Frankenstein* on a portable TV, even though his wife is scared, to which he boasts, "It's practically a comedy."

Cozzi wrote the script using inspiration from *Rear Window* and the American author Cornell Woolrich. The influence of *Rear Window* and Raymond Burr as the villain of that film would extend so far as to have Mimmo Palmari outfitted with gray hair and a beard, so as to resemble Burr in Hitchcock's film all the more. Overall, it's a tense and nicely paced story, yet the element of the baby becomes a problem. It's not in the least believable that a baby that young would never wake up during everything that is going on. So to have the child begin crying only to serve the dramatic arc of the story feels false. And why not have the baby in the episode more as something to heighten the terror? In fact, I forgot about the child for a while when the parents were in danger because he's never brought up again until the very end.

This first segment of the series has an interesting editorial nod to Argento's previous films, with some of the editing of the water stain and the couple looking up the stairs; in both instances, the images are flash cut, similar to the jarring editing in *The Cat O' Nine Tails* with Arno "seeing" Giordani at his office. The episode prefigures Cozzi's first feature film, *The Killer Must Kill Again*, in that both have a male character named Luca, and a cigarette lighter plays a role in the plots, as well as a murderer who is "forced" to kill more than he originally planned in order to try and cover his tracks. Cozzi said of the killer in the episode, "You almost feel sorry for him…He had to kill her [the wife] to shut her up."

The first episode that Argento wrote and directed (under the name Silvio Bernadotte), *Il Tram/The Tram*, is taken from a sequence taken out of the screenplay for *The Bird with the Crystal Plumage*. While cleaning the trams in Rome one morning, a worker comes across the body of a young woman shoved under a row of seats. It's up to Commissioner Giordani (Enzo Cerusico) to solve the murder with the help of a re-creation of the crime, involving the passengers who were aboard that fateful night.

Argento packs the vehicle full of allusions to his previous work. The sequence in the train bay with Giulia running under and in between the train cars is reminiscent of Sam eluding the assassin from *The Bird with the Crystal Plumage*; the elderly woman on the tram is Maria Tedeschi, the "old woman in the fog" in *The Bird with the Crystal Plumage* when Sam is almost hit with a cleaver. Gildo Di Marco, who played "Garullo" in *The Bird with the Crystal Plumage* and the "Postman" in *Four Flies on Grey Velvet*, is another of the passengers. Giulia (Paola Tedesco) shares a name with Suzy Kendall in *The Bird With the Crystal Plumage*, and Commissioner Giordani shares a name with James Franciscus's character in *The Cat O' Nine Tails*. The episode also has an appearance by Fulvio Mingozzi, as a

cop, who would go on to drive a few cabs for Argento in *Suspiria* and *Inferno* and who had been in all three of his features up to this point. Even the victim, Monica Rini, echoes Monica Ranieri from *The Bird with the Crystal Plumage*. When Monica's body is found, she is lying face up, her eyes wide open, much like several of the corpses in *Blood and Black Lace*, *The Evil Eye*, and, most eerily, the dead woman who haunts Jacqueline Pierreux in "The Drop of Water" episode of *Black Sabbath*. Argento seems to be carrying on the tradition of the "awake" dead, suggesting the deceased knows who killed them and they would talk if they could; something Argento would exploit later with the laser beam through the retina of the dead theory in *Four Flies on Grey Velvet*.

Testimone Oculare (Eyewitness) is the third episode in the series and was partially directed by Dario Argento after Roberto Pariante was dismissed of his duties, with Luigi Cozzi reshooting Pariante's unsatisfactory material. Argento recommended Pariante for

Argento hitches a ride into Darkness.

the job, after he had assisted on all three of Argento's features, allowing him to make his debut as a director. The script, based on a short story by Dario, which was written by the staff writers at RAI, was rejected because the changes were thought unsatisfactory. Ultimately, Argento and Cozzi quickly rewrote it in time to make their production date.

"Eyewitness" begins with Roberta (Marilú Tolo) driving home on a dark road when a woman runs out in front of her car. Thinking the woman is dead, Roberta goes to a bar and calls the police only to find, once the authorities arrive, the woman's body is gone. The remainder of the episode deals with Roberta trying to discover what happened that night, with everyone else, the police included, doubting her sanity.

Again, Argento reaches back into his earlier films for influence. In the scene with Roberta in the bar, a cup of coffee glides toward her like the glass of wine in *Suspiria* and the milk in *The Cat O' Nine Tails*. Thematically, there is also the shared vindictive and

murderous spouse reminiscent of Nina in *Four Flies on Grey Velvet*. The episode is quite tense and dark as the audience becomes the analogue for Roberta. As she becomes more and more paranoid and scared, so does the audience.

The last episode, *La Bambola (The Doll)*, is directed by Mario Foglietti, one of the writers of the screenplay for *Four Flies on Grey Velvet*, and Argento's style is all over it. Foglietti obviously learned a few things watching Argento on set and absorbed some of his style from watching the films. Luigi Cozzi says that Dario was the least involved in this segment of the series, and RAI asked him to act as a second unit director to Foglietti to help speed up the shooting process.

An unnamed patient has escaped a mental hospital, and the film follows a young woman (Mara Venier), as a handsome young man (Robert Hoffman), who is being tracked by the police, follows her. From the outset, the subjective camera point of view echoes the killer in *The Cat O' Nine Tails* and the mental hospital

Argento, Aldo Reggiano, Laura Belli, and Luigi Cozzi confer during shooting Cozzi's episode The Neighbor.
COURTESY INDEPENDENT VISIONS.

The dead awake stare of death.

Argento with star Enzo Cerusico, assistant director Roberto Pariante, and the series' script supervisor, also the wife of Elio Polacchi, cinematographer of the series. COURTESY INDEPENDENT VISIONS.

from *Four Flies on Grey Velvet*. Elena Moreschi (Erika Blanc of *Kill, Baby Kill*) works in a fashion house much like the one seen in *Blood and Black Lace*. The scene where she is attacked in the sewing room with the velvet-covered multi-colored mannequins and heads lined up in rows, recalls the mannequins in Bava's film as well. Out of the four episodes, this one is perhaps the most disappointing because it starts off well, has some interesting moments, but is far too long for the story being told.

Giorgio Gaslini was recommended to write the music for the show by Luigi Cozzi and he wrote a suitable score for all four episodes as well as the main theme for the show. There's nothing as memorable as the *Deep Red* theme, but you can see why Dario wanted him back to score *The Five Days* and *Deep Red*.

Dario Argento's first foray into television made him a national celebrity and continued to expand his audience in the wake of its broadcast. The show broke new ground in terms of what could be shown on Italian television. And, since there was only a single station, Argento had a captive audience, and luckily, they begged for more. This newfound exposure cemented his position as a "Master of Horror," which he would parlay into a duo of films for a series of the same name thirty years later.

LE CINQUE GIORNATE
THE FIVE DAYS

By 1973, Argento stepped out of the genre box he had placed himself into, with the release of a historical comedy about a citizen uprising in Milan during March of 1848. An unexpected and commercially and critically unwelcome follow-up to *Four Flies on Grey Velvet*, *The Five Days* is the odd man out in Argento's career, being the only "comedy." Despite being labeled such, it's so much more. For every ridiculous scene — the childbirth complete with haphazard enema — there is something not so funny — a baby

screaming and crawling off of its dead mother during battle is quite touching. Argento attempts to build an interesting paradox in tone through the film, keeping the viewer wondering what will pop up next, with very mixed results. The film fares better in its serious moments, which, for the most part, are surprisingly effective when set against the buffoonery of Cainazzo and Romolo's adventures.

Cainazzo (Adriano Celentano) is a prisoner who manages to escape his confines thanks to a cannonball

Expulsion of Austrians from Milan, March 22, 1848. Watercolor etching by Sienese and Scotto from the Central Museum of the Risorgimento, Rome.

being sent into a wall of the prison. Once on the outside, Cainazzo attempts to find an old friend, Zampino (Glauco Onorato), a fellow thief who owes Cainazzo a cut of their last job. While on his journey on the outside, he meets Romolo Marcelli (Enzo Cerusico), a baker from Rome. The two quickly become friends, get inadvertently involved in the ensuing revolution of the Milanese citizenry against the Austrian forces, help birth a child, and become involved in some very strange sexual encounters to boot.

This central relationship between the two strangers, who become partners in their journey for survival over the course of a few days, is reminiscent of many unlikely pairings in Argento's films, whether it is David Hemmings and Daria Nicolodi in *Deep Red* or Jennifer Connelly and Donald Pleasance in *Phenomena*.

Argento uses the humor that is organic to these pairings to lighten the proceedings when it arises and bring a bit of pathos to the characters. Many critics, professional or otherwise, have blasted Argento in the past for his lack of humanity or his perceived weakness as a writer when creating characters.

Visually, the film pulls many cues from the films Argento cut his teeth on as a writer, such as *Once Upon a Time in the West*, *Five Many Army*, and *Cemetery Without Crosses*. The film could easily be a "Spaghetti Western," were the script altered slightly and the location changed. Luigi Kuveiller's cinematography is a bit bland, but the film is supposed to look bleak and dusty, so it works. Kuveiller would be invited back to photograph what is arguably Argento's finest achievement, *Deep Red*. Reuniting with Giorgio Gaslini after

Vincent Price, Franco, and Ciccio in Bava's Dr. Goldfoot and the Girl Bombs. COURTESY THE DEL VALLE ARCHIVES/MGM.

their collaboration on *Door into Darkness*, who would also return to work on *Deep Red*, the music in *The Five Days* is as eclectic as the film itself. Some of the music sounds appropriated from *A Clockwork Orange,* and other pieces are akin to what is heard in a knockabout silent comedy.

In the film's reactionary violence there is reactionary sex. And this makes sense: When people feel troubled or threatened, they turn to the basic comforts and necessities of life — food, sex, shelter, etc. In the midst of the mayhem, Romolo stops to have sex with a beautiful, younger widow, and The Countess (Marilù Tolo) invites a group of revolutionaries to bed her en masse after becoming aroused when a soldier's blood splashes on her when he is killed in battle. During this rather intricate set piece, Tolo entices the group of men into her home as the camera follows her down a long corridor with torn curtains framing her in a moment that is pure gothic horror. Once she places herself on the ground and lifts her skirts for the group of anxious men, the camera moves overhead and moves back over the crowd to reveal Cainazzo at the back of the line.

The very moody set piece of the "gang rape" of The Countess isn't the only interesting and unexpectedly creative set piece. In a sequence where Cainazzo "crashes" a party for the wealthy citizens of Milan and is duped into becoming a server at it instead of a guest, he seizes an opportunity for food and crawls under a banquet table to avoid being caught, and he falls asleep. He later awakens to find the room full of people, and as he lays there listening to their conversation, the camera takes on his point of view of the people's feet moving as they speak.

In a film overflowing with the violence of war and the violence and desperation at times of people's sexual needs, Argento still manages to follow up the homosexual detective in *Four Flies on Grey Velvet* with some fairly overt homosexual content. Early on after meeting, Romolo has it pointed out that the ass of his pants is torn, and the ragingly homosexual architect who is helping The Countess laughs and teases him about being able to see, "Every inch of your little ass." Cainazzo tells Romolo, "Come on, Honey, he'll paint your picture later, you'll see." The two also have an implied homosexual relationship as well, as during the opening of one scene, the two are cuddled up together sleeping when a group of revolutionaries come upon them with guns drawn to wake them up and join forces with "Il Duce."

In a scene that can be seen as a stylistic and visual predecessor to David Hemmings's exploration of Villa

Scott in *Deep Red,* Cainazzo and Romolo walk through an abandoned building looking for loot, when they come across some strangers in a scene that would fit just as easily in a Ken Russell or Fellini film. An overweight man dressed in an ersatz toga sits in a large chair holding court with a butler and a feral woman whom he claims is his niece. This paragon then informs them that the revolution is for nothing and all this fighting will only give the wealthy more power, even if it does defeat the Austrian forces.

Once Cainazzo finds Zampino and realizes he's been a double agent of sorts, working on the side of the invaders and not fighting with his countrymen, Cainazzo realizes just how deep corruption runs, even spilling into your own backyard and home, as the two were friends. The entire film seems to be Argento's "love letter" to the Italian political system of the period and today. His constant swipes at the corruption and lack of any real leadership on any level of society is reflected again and again in his work, specifically his feelings of the elite and powerful.

Mario Bava had trod similar ground with a silly slapstick comedy, *Dr. Goldfoot and the Girl Bombs,* "starring" Vincent Price in 1966. The Italian comedy duo of Franco and Ciccio were the real stars, and Fabian and Price were merely brought in due to contracts with AIP. However, much like Argento's predicament, the comedic element simply didn't play outside of Italy, as it was a mode of comedy that was so specific to the region as well as being outdated at that point. Unfortunately, Bava's film was indeed a bomb, and neither Argento nor the distributors attempted to push *Giornate* into other countries with any real force, knowing it was "too Italian."

Upon release, *The Five Days* was greeted less than enthusiastically, as audiences and critics didn't want *this* Dario Argento in their cinemas. Rather than retreat back into the giallo that had made him a household name, Argento really stepped up to the plate with his next film, *Deep Red.* He reinvented the genre, fusing the "art" and thriller film in a fresh and wholly original way, utilizing rock music, graphic violence, and a stunning visual acuity. *This* was inarguably the film his audiences wanted, and they received it in spades.

The Italian poster for Le Cinque Giornate.

INTERVIEW

JOHN CARPENTER

Cited as the godfather of the modern slasher film in many circles due to his seminal film *Halloween* (1978), John Carpenter really needs no introduction. As a writer and director Carpenter has made such memorable films as *The Fog* (1980), *The Thing* (1982), *Christine* (1983), and *Prince of Darkness* (1987).

DB: You have stated that you first became aware of Argento through his work on *Once Upon a Time in the West*. Do you recall when or what your first film of his you saw?

JC: Well, that's a very stylized western…and later in the early '70s, I saw *The Bird with the Crystal Plumage* and again, it was very stylized. And I put the writer and director together. Then I became very familiar with him as a director when I saw *Deep Red* and *Suspiria*.

DB: Can you expand at all on your statement of Dario having "absolute courage" in what he does as a filmmaker?

JC: Well, it seems to me that a lot of us who make horror films or traffic in that area walk a fine line in what we present. And one thing that Dario has done and does is he takes sex and violence and combines them in a scene to the point where it makes you very uncomfortable. And he takes the beauty of violence to an extreme. And you have to have courage to do that because you are going to have people come after you. One thing he does in his movies: he frames these shots, these sequences like a painter. They're beautiful…but the content is just astonishing. I admire him, I admire his ability to do that, to pull it off in the way he does.

DB: With *Suspiria* in particular, I think, every element in so in sync. You could almost watch it without the dialogue. It's a silent film.

JC: I completely agree with you there. I think if there is one place Argento is weak, it's in his narrative. But I think that also is irrelevant. I don't think it matters because his movies are like nightmares. I don't think he cares that much about narrative. I don't think it's of interest to him. I think he wants to put you in this dream you can't wake up from.

DB: Speaking of this weak narrative, do you think there is a particular system of logic at work? Many people have compared Argento to Buñuel.

JC: I would point out that Buñuel's work is very narrative. His early movies, not so much, but the features for the most part have very specific, logical narratives. It's just that in the context of those stories, there are these absurd things. Surrealism isn't just about being bizarre, it's about the absurd and that ties together with the whole philosophy. What Dario is doing is a visual nightmare and his narrative structures, they involve a witch, a curse, and they are simply a pretext to explore a visual fantasy. You don't want to study the plot of *Suspiria* too much or you'll get a headache. It's not necessary to study that; it's not that primal. The primal thing is the effect. And I think that's true of all his work.

DB: *Phenomena* is a prime example of this in terms of, perhaps, Argento showing us the real world and placing ridiculous things inside of it, now that you bring it up. It's the real world, we identify with everything in it, but the murder plot, the razor-wielding monkey, and the murderous monster-child are all very surreal things.

JC: I think you're accurate in that. It has a lot of interesting ideas. Cohesive narrative isn't as strong for him as are the visceral issues. I can suspend disbelief…I don't care. Just give me a little plot; I'll go this direction or that. It's about Donald Pleasance and the bugs that are inside of you when you die. You can study it that way. Or it's about this child that's locked up or the ape that gets revenge in the end! It's hilarious and outrageously funny, but vastly different than Buñuel. Watch *That Obscure Object of Desire* and you can see the difference between them. The surrealism in Buñuel's films is hysterical, but is so contained within conventionality.

DB: As a filmmaker in the horror genre, do you have any thoughts on censorship in Dario's films?

JC: Well, my favorite, I mean, the funniest example for Dario would be in *Opera* and on TV, they edited the film down quite a bit and he says he still resents that one.

It's all just part of the game. My movies get edited for different reasons all over the world for whatever reason. And there's nothing you can do. It's just part of the game. I mean, if you want to work completely free of censorship and interference, you have to put up your own money and forego the usual distribution chain. But the minute you're in the capitalist business and collecting tickets, they're going to cut your film.

DB: I wanted to ask about your potential involvement in *Two Evil Eyes*?

JC: Well, Dario had contacted me, asked me if I wanted to be part of the project. But I was busy on a film of my own.

DB: Was there even any discussion of story ideas?

JC: I would have gladly done it because I love them both, but it never got further than me telling Dario I couldn't do it. And they didn't need me, anyway. I think the film is fine the way it is.

DB: Was there any discussion of any other projects together?

JC: Well, I did go to Turin back in I think 1999. And we were visiting the Egyptian Museum there and we discussed life, our projects at the time. And he was hoping that we would do something together. I don't know if it's ever going to work. He was just planning *I Can't Sleep* (Non Ho Sonno). I know he's planning on doing another giallo. I don't know that our styles would make a good match; we are so different. But my admiration for him is boundless.

DB: It's funny, speaking of different styles: you have said in the past, and correct me if I'm wrong here, but you've said in the past that you like the process of shooting the film more than writing, whereas Dario says he likes writing more.

JC: Yes, I would say that's true. So there you go. I mean, everyone I know that does this [directing], they all like different things. Some guys love to edit. Some like to write, to shoot. It's such a personal thing. I like to shoot more; writing is much more painful.

DB: I watched *Halloween* again recently in listening to the music and watching *Suspiria*. I noticed a similarity in the simplicity and repetition of theme. Is there an influence in the score to *Halloween* in *Suspiria*?

JC: Well, of course there is, but also the main theme from *The Exorcist*. One of the first rounds…I mean the repeating themes. That thing got in your head, too. And I think that the *Suspiria* theme resembles Tubular Bells. I love minimalism in music. My synth score for *Halloween* is all based on a rhythm my father taught me when I was younger in 5/4 time. I just rocked octaves. The biggest influence on me musically is Bernard Herrmann. He did very beautiful film music on very basic means, very low instruments. He had a certain progression I have always been drawn to.

DB: Where do you think Dario will end up in genre film history or even film history in general? He's had such a polarizing career.

JC: That's hard to say; we're all still doing it. I've always wanted to do something like Dario does, but I don't have the visual ability he has. He just sees things a different way. As do I. So I just have to be a fan.

PROFONDO ROSSO
DEEP RED

After the failure of *The Five Days*, Argento heard the call to return to his beloved giallo. However, I doubt he could have known how much he would change the subgenre with a single film. *Deep Red* is a culmination of the visual and psychological themes that Argento had explored in his previous films as well as being an ode of sorts to Antonioni's seminal film *Blow Up*. Melding elements of the classic horror film, chiefly the supernatural angle of the "haunted" villa with the distinct visual tropes of the giallo — the black-gloved killer, sexually tinged murders, and eccentric characters — the film was a game changer for the form. Its graphic and intricately choreographed set pieces of suspense and murder were hugely influential on the likes of directors from John Carpenter to Quentin Tarantino.

My introduction to *Deep Red* — possibly Argento's greatest film, although not my personal favorite — came courtesy of a muddy VHS dupe from a Japanese Laserdisc. At this point in examining Argento's films, I was so intrigued by everything I had seen that it didn't matter how awful the copy was in its visual or audio attributes; I just had to keep watching. Initially, the film struck me as a bit long, and that house hunting crawl of Marcus's still irks me. However, the film manages to do almost everything right, and I could easily forgive its lax pacing in favor of its amusing characters, intriguing plot, and excess of style.

Marcus Daly (David Hemmings) is a British pianist and composer living in Rome. One evening, after a pep talk with his perpetually drunken friend Carlo (Gabriele Lavia), the two witness the murder of Marcus's neighbor, Helga Ulmann (Macha Meril), who happens to be a famous psychic. After being interrogated by the police, Marcus meets Gianna Brezzi (Daria Nicolodi), a local journalist, leaving the two to team up in an attempt to figure out whodunit and, more importantly, to stay alive.

With this return to the giallo, Argento emerged invigorated with a new eye for the bloody proceedings at hand. This film looked nothing like *Four Flies on Grey Velvet*, his previous giallo. Neither did it resemble *The Five Days* in any considerable way outside of some of the tracking camera work through a few buildings that would be used to chilling effect here, courtesy of Luigi Kuveiller. Expanding upon the rather outré photographic styling of *Four Flies on Grey Velvet*, *Deep Red* plunges the viewer into a dizzying affair that is, at its core, a surprisingly intricate meditation on male and female relationships, gender roles, familial bonds, and, of course, the oddity of the creature that we call man.

Deep Red's psychological underpinnings are numerous, starting with the use and portrayal of Marcus as the prominent male figure. When we first meet Marcus, he is in control and in his element teaching his students. In his next appearance, he is lecturing Carlo on the errors of his drunken ways, still retaining an air of superiority and some arrogance. Although you can tell he cares deeply for Carlo, he refuses to give credence to any of his delusions, telling him in no uncertain terms that he must straighten himself out or pay the price. By the end of this scene, Marcus's plunge into the dark heart of the human soul begins, as he and Carlo witness Helga's murder and he finds himself being interrogated, with Carlo nowhere to be seen. At the end of the interrogation, Gianna bursts into Helga's apartment, eager to capture the story as it breaks. She takes a moment to snap a picture of Marcus completely unguarded, a visual metaphor for Gianna's presence in his life. When

Gianna takes this photograph of Marcus, it is a frame dominated by negative space with his image pushed off to the right side of the frame. Later, near the end of the film when Gianna and Marcus are exploring the Da Vinci School, there is a similar shot of her with the reverse composition. She is in a pitch-black room with only a small rectangle of light illuminating the space. With relish and affection, she creates turbulence in his very existence, unseating his ideas of man as the stronger, more dominant of the sexes and every hoary cliché of manhood that this surprisingly sexist and self-proclaimed "sensitive artist" clings to. For all of Marcus's chest beating and hilarious disappointment at being emasculated during an arm wrestling match, Gianna does bring out his sensitive side over the course of their collective sleuthing.

Marcus's interpersonal troubles don't rest solely with Gianna; he seems uncomfortable around every female or feminine figure he encounters. Carlo's mother, Marta, is a lovingly eccentric former actress (Clara Calamai in her last film role) who, with every encounter with Marcus,

makes him more and more uneasy. Her insistence that he is an "engineer/pianist" doesn't help matters. Looking back on these seemingly innocuous confrontations, it is a small clue to Marta's mental problems. In one of these scenes, Marta informs Marcus that Carlo is visiting a friend named "Ricci" and gives Marcus the address. When he arrives, the door is opened by a very androgynous-looking person we assume is a man, and this instantly makes Marcus skittish. Once it is revealed, with much drunken derision and self-hatred, that Carlo is "…not only a drunk, but a faggot as well," Marcus's friendly instincts kick back in and his prejudices fall away. His mass of character contradictions are what make him so interesting and real.

With a penchant for strong female characters, Argento, along with Bernardo Zapponi, have written a film that presents the male as emasculated and useless in a crisis. On the other hand, the women — and Gianna in particular — are presented as bright, articulate, full of self-worth, and able to prove their mettle at almost every turn. When the killer traps Marcus

David Hemmings searching for a clue in Antonioni's Blow Up. COURTESY THE DEL VALLE ARCHIVES/BRIDGE FILMS, MGM.

in his apartment, he doesn't call the police (men with guns), he calls Gianna for reassurance, knowing she will be there for him when nobody else will. In this scene, when Marcus feels threatened by the voice on the other side of the door, which threatens to kill him, in desperation, he grabs the nearest object that could be used as a weapon. As "coincidence" would have it, it is a small sculpture of a bird. Could this be an allusion to Argento's first film? After all, *Four Flies on Grey Velvet* has Michael Brandon driving right past a poster for the film, and in *Suspiria's* climax, Suzy Bannion grabs a feather out of an ultra modern glass sculpture of a peacock in order to stab Helena Markos in the neck.

The importance of Argento casting Daria Nicolodi in this film cannot be underplayed. Fortuitous is not sufficient enough a word to describe what this choice would lead to in Argento's life, personally and professionally. She became a muse of sorts, and together they collaborated on a string of films beginning with *Deep Red* and culminating with *Opera*. With Nicolodi, Argento seemed to have found some missing aspect of himself; their names are the male and female equivalent of each other, to put a finer point on it.

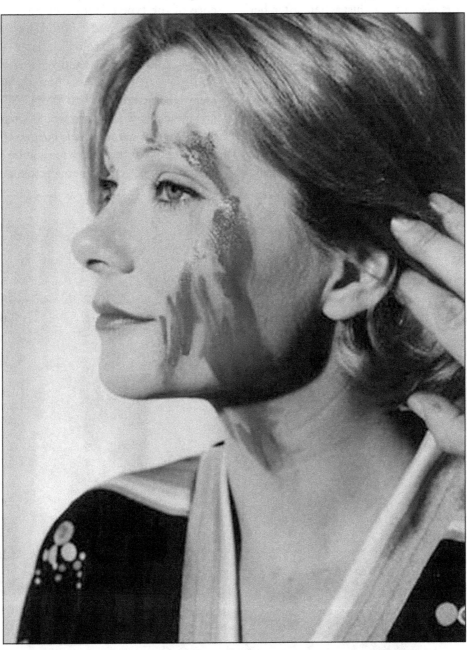

Macha Meril preps for her death in Deep Red. COURTESY THE DEL VALLE ARCHIVES/RIZOLLI FILM.

Having made such an impression in Bava's *Bay of Blood*, Nicoletta Elmi, who would later star in the Argento-produced *Demons*, became somewhat of a child horror star. Elmi's performance is one of the true highlights beyond the overall scenario presented. Elmi, whose red hair and freckles are the picture of innocence, becomes something altogether different once she sticks a pin in a lizard and grins with pleasure at the suffering she has caused. This small child is derided for being "disgusting," according to her father, for such sadistic behavior to an animal. As he points out, this isn't the first time she has done such a thing. It's made even clearer the child is also a masochist when, after her father slaps her in the face, she bites her lip a manner that is uncomfortably close to connoting a sexual pleasure. Once she is away from her stern and reasonably upset father, she manipulates Marcus's assessment of the situation when he asks what happened, with a snarky "Nothing, my father's a bit loony."

The character of Carlo is of significance not only for the film's plot but also for Argento's use of the outwardly non-stereotypical gay man, who is internally the epitome of the ultimate mama's boy eclipsed only, perhaps, by Norman Bates. The audience doesn't learn of Carlo's sexual predilections until Marcus discovers him at the home of a very stereotypical 1970s gay man replete with a silk robe. Casting a woman — Geraldine Hooper — in this role, further compounds the thematic presence of the uncertain nature of human perception. Carlo's introduction — although we don't know it's him yet — as a small child in the scene that interrupts the opening credits, is important on several levels in reading the film's psychology. Setting this scene during Christmas on a subconscious level informs the audience of the type of film they are in for: every usual bastion of safety and comfort has been done away with. This scenario also tells us later — when we learn of the child's identity and what occurred that fateful day — that Carlo was brought up in a less than ideal circumstance. With these childhood traumas, how much of what Carlo would later become can be chalked up to nature versus nurture?

Argento's influence, whether intentional or not, can be seen in genre cinema across the board: two of

Marc's emasculation courtesy of Gianna's Fiat. COURTESY MAITLAND MCDONAGH/RIZZOLI FILM.

my favorite instances being from David Cronenberg's *Scanners* and Rick Rosenthal's *Halloween 2*. The Halloween connection is especially interesting since Deborah Hill and John Carpenter have both, in the past, spoken of the film's influence in their work. Cronenberg's demonstration of the ability of "the other" to read people's minds, to an often deadly degree in *Scanners,* is an interesting variation on the opening of *Deep Red* and the parapsychology discussion. In both cases, someone ends up dead. Helga Ulmann sees a portent to her own death, which she cannot stop. The man who volunteers to be "scanned" in Cronenberg's film turns the tables on the man who is holding the lecture, when the two literally go head to head, leading to the lecturer's demise when his head explodes due to the warring brain waves the two share. Rosenthal's film, written by Carpenter and Hill, contains two scenes that seem to glean inspiration from *Deep Red*. In a sequence utilizing a hydrotherapy bath, a nurse is drowned in a very similar fashion to the drowning of Amanda Righetti. Later, in a school, Dr. Loomis finds a child's drawing of a violent act reminiscent of little

Carlo's dreaded doodling on the wall of his childhood home. A not surprising nod to *Deep Red* can be seen in Lamberto Bava's *You'll Die at Midnight*: Anna knows she saw the killer, Tribbo, in a mirror in her apartment, as in *Deep Red*. David Hemmings saw something in a mirror, but he isn't sure what.

Argento's wholly unique presentation of what could have been a rote thriller, ensures it has a place in film history. At face value, the story could have gone a hundred other ways, yet by placing the story in the context of this hyper-stylized Turin of the 1970s via the occasional Edward Hopper and 1940s influence, Argento has again skewed reality in the same fashion as the world of *Four Flies on Grey Velvet* — slightly too modern to seem real. *The Five Days*, the film prior to *Deep Red*, was a historical piece via the politics of Italy in the 1970s, which would inform this slant on current Italy in *Deep Red*. The more one digs into Argento's work, looking forward while keeping one's eyes in the rearview, is an all too common occurrence, culminating in a literal translation during a shot in *Non Ho Sonno*.

An Italian Fotobusta for Deep Red.

SUSPIRIA

Author and film historian David Del Valle told me an amusing story about a screening of *Suspiria*:

I was with Argento when he first met Barbara Steele. This was in the mid-eighties when Harmony Gold was courting Dario for a few projects. I remember she was wearing these stiletto heels. She said to me, "I need to wear these for Dario!" And she stopped dead in front of him and stomped her foot on the floor and said, "Why haven't you used me in one of your films?" And he was very effusive. But she got her comeuppance. He made her sit through Suspiria seated between himself and Jessica Harper. And in this manner, Barbara watched the movie for the first time. And when it was over, she said to me, "Do you know why I will never work with him because of what he did to Alida Valli? I would look exactly like her if I worked for him." And of course she had a point because Barbara doesn't look like she did in 8½. She said to me, "He'll light me from the floor; I'll look a hundred and ten! Forget it! Let him use Udo [Kier], put him in a black wig, he'll work out fine!"

My first viewing of the film wasn't as exciting, however. But it wasn't so terrible, either: a dark living room, a bowl of Halloween candy, some soda, and the Fox-Lorber VHS of *Suspiria* in widescreen. I remember this being a "big deal" at the time, as many people had told me I was lucky to be watching it in widescreen on video, as for years most presentations had been cropped down to 1.33:1 from its native 2.35:1 ratio. Initially, I was blown away by the film because of its amazing visual and aural assault, yet, at the same time, I was disappointed by the rickety plot and script. It took me

watching the fever dreams of *Inferno,* soon after, to really get into the mood and begin to appreciate just what these films were.

To return to François Truffaut's question to Alfred Hitchcock about the logic of his films being that of dreams, Argento's follow-up to *Deep Red,* 1977's *Suspiria,* would push the limits of this reasoning to new heights never before seen in a modern horror film. Part German Expressionism and Art House experimental shocker, *Suspiria* borrows from Mario Bava and Robert Weine in equal measure, while fusing Argento's vision into his influences to stunning effect. Argento's world here is conceived of pieces of other times and places. Intellectually, we know it is Germany, not too far in the past or in the future for there are still cars and airports that look like ours, but the film exists on a tangential plane of reality that is completely off base from anything we would call "reality." Argento's progressive-rock-laden opus meets the criteria for what Truffaut describes to Hitchcock as dream logic: "a succession of strange forms, one on top of the other overlapping almost like a nightmare." John Carpenter described it to me: "I think he wants to put you in this dream you can't wake up from."

While not on its face a giallo, there is a certain mystery and detective element to the film that reminds one of the previous gialli Argento had made. Argento also includes the ever-present visual reminder of the giallo, the black-gloved killer, most notably when Stefania Casini is done away with via straight razor to the neck while drowning in a room of razor wire. This time out, the beloved staple of the giallo is wearing a flowing cape while doing his deeds, making him or her even more gothic and mysterious in this strange nether world.

Like his fellow countryman Mario Bava with his films *Black Sunday/La Maschera del Demonio* and *Kill, Baby, Kill/Operazione Paura*, Argento wouldn't reach the pinnacle of his creative powers with a giallo but with something far more preternatural. Bava had pioneered the giallo with *The Girl Who Knew Too Much/La Ragazza Che Sapeva Troppo*, yet it was his first film, *Black Sunday*, that most profoundly changed the face of Italian horror cinema and became what he is most known for.

Italy had been rather late getting into the horror genre, and Bava was involved in the first horror film produced there, *I Vampiri*, which was directed by Riccardo Freda and Bava jointly. With *Suspiria*, Argento would take a cue from Bava — a longtime friend — and again change what the horror film could be, with something wholly unique to the genre and film at large. There isn't really another film like *Suspiria*, before or after, and it stands as a crowning achievement for Argento.

Suzy Bannion (Jessica Harper) is a young ballet student who has transferred her studies to the prestigious Tanz Akademie in Friebourg, Germany, from New York City. Upon arriving, a pair of students is brutally killed, yet our young heroine soldiers on with her studies. She meets a fellow student, Sarah (Stefania Casini), and the two become fast friends, while the mysteries of the school become more and more obtuse. Strange things pile up, one on top of the other, and it's up to Suzy to untangle the mystery of the school.

Beginning with *Suspiria*, Argento took a turn from using male protagonists to incorporate many more female characters into his films, outside of playing the victim roles. Perhaps this is due, in part, to having a daughter by this time and having Daria Nicolodi guiding so much of what he did. The force of the women in Argento's life cannot be understated. His mother, Elda Luxardo, a rather well-known photographer, taught him the beauty of the female form on film. His children are both female, and the most significant woman in his life — in a near thirteen-year relationship — was an actress who he had admired from the stage and then placed front and center in a film, which proved to be a watershed moment in his career.

Udo Kier, Barbara Steele, and Russ Lanier at Harmony Gold Studio. Note the copy of Maitland McDonagh's Broken Mirrors, Broken Minds *in Barbara's hands.* COURTESY RUSS LANIER.

Much can be said of Argento's use of the woman in *Suspiria*. In an interview from *Bizarre* magazine online, in November of 2009, Argento said, "Yes, take *Suspiria*. There are only three men in it: one is blind, one can't speak, and the other is gay. It's the women who have the power." Suzy Bannion's dilemma is rooted in that of a fairy tale, and she is the classic heroine who rises above her situation and refuses to become a victim of circumstance. It could be torn from any number of stories from *Cinderella* to *Rapunzel*; poor Suzy is at the mercy of a female figure who is charged with Suzy's welfare, yet has anything but her welfare at heart.

Joan Bennett's "Madame Blanc," the headmistress of the academy, is Argento's vision of Snow White's evil stepmother/queen. And, like every queen, she has minions. Miss Tanner (Alida Valli) is Blanc's head instructor who "cozies" up to Jessica Harper and has reign over the school's male lackey, Mark (Miguel Bosé). In fact, the entire staff is under Blanc's control, as are some of the students, it seems. Olga (Barbara Magnolfi) has only herself in mind when dealing with Suzy's dilemma. And, as usual, witchcraft and money are entwined in another of Argento's digs at the power of the wealthy and the lengths they will go to contain it.

This, however, isn't something new to the horror film and the type of mythos *Suspiria* is creating. Woman has been vital to all modes of storytelling throughout history. In Slavic myths, there is Morena/Morana, a woman who controlled all magical forces, the winter weather, and death. She has been described over the ages as "cold and beautiful," much like Mater Lachrymarum is ascribed as being "the most beautiful and cruel of the three" in *Mother of Tears*. Jessica Harper's heroine in *Suspiria*, who Argento said would "make a good Snow White," has much in common with several fairy tale heroines, but unlike those immortal stories for children as reminders of the terrors of the world, Suzy Bannion must save herself. She has no Prince Charming to

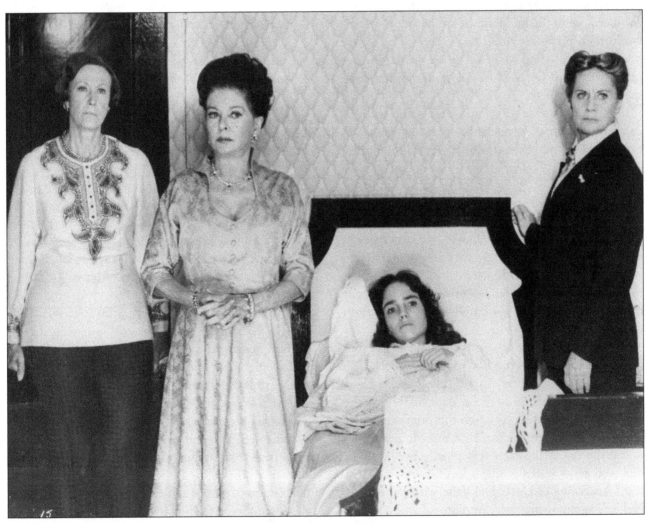

Susy, fallen ill, surrounded by the magically maternal staff at the Tanz Akademie. COURTESY THE DEL VALLE ARCHIVES/20TH CENTURY FOX.

swoop in and wake her from death with a kiss or a hunter to wander by and save her and her grandmother from the evil wolf in grandma's clothing.

Sexuality and even the act of sex are again strangely absent in this most modern of horror films. Our heroine is surrounded by women and has not the least interest in them. Every girl has a crush on the only male at the school, but of course he is gay. The teachers are possibly older lesbians, but nothing is made of this. However, there is a single moment of harmless flirting between Suzy and Mark, the "houseboy" of the Tanz Akademie, when everyone is sleeping in the common room, with sheets up to divide the room. Once the lights dramatically dim, drowning the space in red light, Mark pops up to give a very fey wave to Suzy, which makes her smile. She seems to be the only one in on the fact that this rather handsome boy all the girls seem to have some affection for has no interest in them. In fact, the boys, who typically would be kept away from the girls in separate dormitories at least, or perhaps another floor of the building, are so "harmless" in this world that Suzy only needs go across the hall from her own room to find Mark. Once she's with him, her phone call from Dr. Mandel is lost among a strange "storm" outside.

However, *Suspiria* exists on a level of the artificial, so even the human characters can be forgiven some rather ridiculous behavior. When Suzy falls ill during a dance exercise, Dr. Verdegast — a nod to Lugosi's "Werdegast" in *The Black Cat*, perhaps? — shoves a glass pitcher of what we assume to be water into her mouth, while she lays in bed. Meat and other food products are not kept refrigerated, but rather stored in the attic in wooden crates that are soon crawling with maggots. In a world where daily life takes on the tone of dream, the separation between day and night becomes blurred when one barely leaves the confines of the inside world.

The mystery in the magic is brought to the fore when Suzy goes to visit Dr. Frank Mandel (Udo Kier), who explains along with his colleague, Professor Milius (Rudolf Schündler) the dark history of the school she is attending. Through this brief expository scene, we are given the key that Suzy is needed to defeat the evil. Milius says very plainly, "…the coven deprived of its leader is like a headless cobra, harmless." According to David Del Valle, who was Reggie Nalder's agent at the time, Argento asked Nalder to play Frank Mandel, but Nalder wasn't available and so the role went to Kier.

The woman, again full of power, has now transmogrified into a serpent, and even verbally invokes the image of Echidna, the half-woman, half-snake creature of Greek mythology who was the "mother of all monsters." Helena Markos is, in this case, the mother of the witches of the world the film inhabits, and although it is never spoken, perhaps she was a maternal figure to "The Three Mothers," who we never hear spoken of until *Inferno*.

When asked about the "timeless" feel of the environment of the film and the techniques used to achieve this with his contribution to the project, Luciano Tovoli said,

> *All of the lighting effects and special effects were all done with the oldest film techniques. There is nothing modern, even for the time really, about the way that film was made. But this was a conscious choice that Dario made to give the film a timeless feel. It was very much homage to directors, cinematographers, and production designers that he loves. Beginning with Méliès, who chose to transform the reality with the specific medium of a simple single camera, and half transparent mirrors, backward camera movements and all these old techniques and very simple technology available at the time.*

Another Italian film director, Francis Ford Coppola, would also employ many of the same primitive and outdated techniques, on a much grander scale, when making *Bram Stoker's Dracula* (1992). Both films are created "out of time," since neither relied on the latest in film technology to make their visual statements.

A source close to the film who wished to remain anonymous confided to me that the film originally had another ending, which was not shot due to production cost. Instead of the students going away to watch the Bolshoi Ballet, the school was to be having its end of term performance. It was to be during this performance that Suzy would encounter Helena Markos below while the students would be driven mad upstairs, and while the school collapsed on fire.

Tovoli's sumptuously garish lighting and Guiseppe Bassan's neo-deco and semi-gothic production design are a perfect compliment to each other in Argento's visual playground, an illustration by Erté conceived in the nastiest of moods and executed in blood. However visually stunning the film may be, it is Goblin's groundbreaking musical score that sets the bar so high with its shrieks, howls, and moans — a few simple themes repeating themselves as if from a music box forged in hell. John Carpenter said to me, regarding the influence of the music in Suspiria, "Well, of course there is, but also the main theme from *The Exorcist*. One of the first rounds…I mean the repeating themes. That thing got in your head, too. And I think that the *Suspiria* theme resembles Tubular Bells. I love minimalism in music."

Suspiria has shown its influence in other work, some in unlikely places such as the Anthony Perkins vehicle from 1989, *Edge of Sanity*. The film visually resembles *Suspiria* quite a lot, from its pseudo-Victorian-era setting to women dressed as Madonna circa 1985. A prostitute in the film even wears Madonna's iconic "Boy Toy" belt. The film's lighting scheme seems inspired by Tovoli and Argento, as does the film's time shifting visual landscape. Perkins plays a Dr. Jekyll variant who becomes addicted to "crack cocaine" and becomes a murderous deviant who flirts with all manner of sexual delicacies.

Every artist eventually becomes associated with a single work or phase in their career, and Argento will forever be remembered most for *Suspiria*. Not because

it is his "best" film but merely because of its ground-breaking bravura, much in the way Hitchcock is linked to *Psycho* for creating the "slasher" film and turning the tide for horror movies. Likewise, Orson Welles is tied to *Citizen Kane* for its singular achievements in the language of cinema.

Suspiria, upon its release, was hailed by some and decried by many. Janet Maslin, in the *New York Times*, said of the film — in a rather fair assessment during the film's original U.S. run:

> …*Mr. Argento's methods make potentially stomach-turning material more interesting than it ought to be. Shooting on bold, very fake-looking sets, he uses bright primary colors and stark lines to create a campy, surreal atmosphere, and his distorted camera angles and crazy lighting turn out to be much more memorable than the carnage. Suspiria is really quite funny during those isolated interludes when nobody is bleeding.*

The residents of the Tanz Akademie. COURTESY THE DEL VALLE ARCHIVES/20TH CENTURY FOX.

INTERVIEW

LUCIANO TOVOLI

(Cinematographer, *Suspiria, Tenebrae, Dracula 3-D*)

A native of Italy, Luciano Tovoli has managed to work with directors from around the globe on a wide range of projects since 1968 from Antonioni on *The Passenger* (1975) to Julie Taymore's *Titus* (1999). Argento isn't the only director with whom he has worked with repeatedly. Tovoli has worked with Barbet Schroder on a number of films including the Academy Award Winning *Reversal of Fortune* (1990) and *Single White Female* (1992).

DB: What about cinematography drew you to the profession?

LT: I was first interested in still photography. I love the purity and simplicity of it, especially black and white. Professionally, I never did anything with still photography and jumped right into cinematography. It was my love of what you could do with the still image with such masters as Cartier Bresson, Ansel Adams, Edward Weston, Paul Strand, and Gene Smith, among many others, that led me to explore being a cinematographer. I was intrigued with how these principles would translate to film and the challenges each project would bring. Every film has a different mood and atmosphere and I love creating these worlds.

DB: Who were some of your influences in the field of cinematography?

LT: There are two Italian cinematographers specifically that I was always influenced by. Gianni di Venzano, who worked on several films for Michelangelo Antonioni. These black and white films he shot, I really admired and still do. G.R. Aldo was the other and he is most known for his work with Luchino Visconti on *Senso*.

DB: How important do you feel formal education is in your field? How can it help or hurt one's creativity and skill?

LT: Formal education is very important because it's highly technical. It's a great way to build your personal aesthetic and style. But the more you do it, the technical becomes less important and your own personality

as a cinematographer defines you. It is this personal eye, the way you interpret a screenplay and break down each scene visually, that is the greatest challenge.

DB: How did your early experiences form the cinematographer you are now?

LT: Of course, looking back with the experience I have now on such a varied number of films, I just keep growing as an artist. It doesn't matter if the budgets are large, as in Hollywood or France, or the smaller in Italy, the result should always be the same. You must come to each project with an innocence about your work and strive to prove yourself all over again. I still have the same aesthetic I have always had and directors must like it because I continue to work.

DB: How were you first introduced to Dario?

LT: Argento approached me because he liked some of my previous work and he asked me to make *Suspiria* with him. It really was that simple.

DB: Were you a fan of Dario's before you worked with him?

LT: At the time, I wasn't a fan of his work because I didn't really like genre films. But his reputation intrigued me. I knew he was capable of great things. I have to admit I was quite ignorant of his work and horror in general, but I don't consider *Suspiria* to be a horror movie in the strictest sense. When I met him and we started working on the project, I realized that my ego had deprived me of something so interesting and that would later become so important to my career.

DB: In working on *Suspiria*, how did the technology at the time affect the photography? Are there things you wish you could change or improve with modern technology?

LT: All of the lighting effects and special effects were all done with the oldest film techniques. There is nothing modern, even for the time, really, about the way that film was made. But this was a conscious choice that Dario made to give the film a timeless feel. It was very much homage to the directors, cinematographers, and production designers that he loves beginning with Méliès, who chose to transform the reality with the specific medium of a simple single camera and half transparent mirrors, backward camera movements, and all these old techniques and very simple technology available at the time. *Suspiria* was the last film to utilize the old Technicolor transfer dye system before the machines had all been sold off to China. I don't think that with today's technology that we could improve *Suspiria* with CGI effects and trickery. It has a very specific visual and physicality about it that corresponds exactly with what Dario and I dreamed of at the moment of creating the project. I don't think that we can improve a masterpiece through modern technology and I do consider *Suspiria* to be a true masterpiece in terms of its visual strength and also with all of these old techniques, considering it is a modern film.

DB: When Dario discussed the mood of his film with you, how does he explain what he wants? And how specifically do you usually achieve it? How close is the collaboration or are you left alone to work on this?

LT: As I said before, I wasn't really enthusiastic to participate in a horror movie at that stage in my career. I felt it was a bit below me, honestly. But after a few conversations with Dario and of course reading the script with him, he changed my mind and I accepted the project. So I asked to be left alone to prepare, again, my ego as a young professional. Our agreement was that if he liked what I did alone, I would work on the film. I just didn't like to be interfered with when I was younger. So I went off and did a lot of tests of different lights and color possibilities, building a visual scheme for the film. Luckily, Dario adored what I did and we then went on to a very happy collaboration. We didn't talk a lot about style and aesthetic, but we found ourselves absolutely in the same line, a very narrow and precise one.

I can't say that in the end I was really left alone to visualize the film as I would have liked initially, but I'm glad it didn't work out that way. He is such a great director that he has opinions and propositions on all possible things and usually he's right! So I felt completely free to propose what I wanted and know that he would usually agree with me and guide my ideas with me into something that I think is one of the best films I've worked on.

DB: I see *Suspiria* as a sort of fable or fairy tale and it's extreme artificiality helps immensely to convey this feeling. Since it is a fantasy, how did Dario approach you about the stylization of the film? What were his original intentions and do you think they were met?

LT: Our main preoccupation during the preparation of the film had been with Dario and the production designer, Guiseppe Bassan, to create a distinct world with a few similarities to our own world. By starting with the world we recognize and changing so many elements in it to create an abstraction on our past and the present, it also recollects cultural and individual destruction around the world in all forms of art. I see *Suspiria* as the representation of the eternal fight between art and the marketplace. Between artists and the people who make art available to the masses. For that reason, we had to be so precise, so inspired. And for that reason, we filled the frame with as many strange creations as we could. This had to be something that couldn't be changed by distributors or censors. It had to be a clear, artistic statement as undiluted as possible upon release.

It was a very specific moment in time for the creative team and it has created something that I think is very magical and unique in cinema. There was a confidence we all shared in making that film that I have never found in any other project I have worked on since.

DB: Dario has said Disney's *Snow White* was an influence on the look of the film; was this ever broached with you?

LT: I never discussed this use of *Snow White* with Dario. It may have been an influence to him, but he never expressed that to me at the time. I think it's dangerous to reference specific films when you are creating something because there is always the risk of imitation and with a classic like that, you are just setting your bar lower for the inevitable criticism. And how can you reach the same place as the original piece you are citing? Of course, you can reference different art, artists, in other artistic mediums, which Argento always has done when I have worked with him. He is less about specific films or artists than about culling several sources of inspiration and making these things his own.

DB: I see the horror sequences in *Suspiria* as very beautiful, almost poetic in the way they are lit, photographed, and enacted. The fact that they are unpleasant images does not matter. Do you believe the violence to be beautiful and artistic?

LT: The subject of each sequence is unique and solitary to itself, even though it must fit within the whole film. And yes, the violence is striking and poetic, but you see this so rarely, but I think we captured it nicely.

DB: Did the music of Goblin affect the mood of the film in terms of your work?

LT: In what I did, not at all. I think of film as a silent medium and I concentrate only on the visual. I cannot be polluted by anything else in my thinking.

DB: In making *Tenebrae*, Dario wanted to create a Rome of the future with no landmarks or things you would think of as typically Roman. How did this idea of a fantastic version of Rome affect your work in creating the mood and the photography?

LT: Rome is a very romantic city, where all the buildings are warm with magnificent sunsets to be seen. Of course, Dario's idea, which I was to translate to the screen, was to go in a more cold and modern direction. We searched the city to avoid anything colorful and I lit the night scenes very clear and bright in a way that neither the victim nor murderer could hide in shadow. I liked this style very much and for this reason, maybe this is why I haven't made a romantic film to date!

DB: The photography of *Tenebrae* highlights the clean lines and sharp angles of the environment in the film. Did you draw from anything to create this?

LT: I love the work of Mondrian and Bacon. They are my favorite modern painters and I didn't realize until after we had finished the film how much, visually, it brings their work to mind. I try to not search out specific visual references the way Dario does. I like to find the appropriate style for each film and then build it myself.

DB: Most of the characters in *Tenebrae* all seem to have relationship troubles in one way or another. Did the characters' inward coldness inform the outward appearance of the film for you?

LT: Not in any conscious way, no. Dario never told me that the look reflected the characters' interior state in any way.

DB: The title *Tenebrae* means "shadows," the inner darkness in people. It is in direct contrast to the physical brightness of the film itself. Did this juxtaposition of literal meaning and metaphor of the soul present any specific challenges?

LT: My problem was to be able to create a look that had to be as distant from *Suspiria* as possible and I chose for this story that clean, hyper-lit, Mondrianesque image. You have to know that to visualize a film and work in this capacity can sometimes become dull and repetitive. It is a challenge to stay inventive and you must work to surprise yourself. Any artist can easily become monotonous and fall into a creative coma for years and then realize later this is what they have done. And this happens more often than most people want to admit to.

DB: How has working with Dario affected the way you work with other directors and has he taught you anything in the way you think about your craft?

LT: Working with Dario has been one of the most important creative moments of my career. I learned the passion that I already had was more, the professionalism I was always building toward was greater. And my respect for film as culture grew immensely just being around him. Prior to working with him, I was very much of a naturalistic mode of thinking in terms of my craft. I learned that images could be completely abstract and at the same time, for the proper film you are working on, can be very realistic depending on the story. In making those two films with him, my vision of the filmmaking process changed and improved greatly. And I'm a better cinematographer for it.

INFERNO

A considerable percentage of the people we meet on the street are people who are empty inside, that is, they are actually already dead. It is fortunate for us that we do not see and do not know it. If we knew what a number of people are actually dead and what a number of these dead people govern our lives, we should go mad with horror.

GEORGE GURDJIEFF

Russian philosopher and esoteric professor George Gurdjieff creates an unsettling tone with the above quote, which is used in a bastardized form in Argento's script for *Inferno*, the 1980 follow-up to *Suspiria*. Shortly after Rose Elliot (Irene Miracle) is introduced in the film, she is investigating "The Three Mothers," a strange book she has discovered. While visiting the neighborhood's antiquarian-book dealer (Sacha Pitoëff, who conveniently lives right next door), she expresses her concern with the strangeness of her environs since moving into her apartment and in relation to something the strange book mentions: specifically that there is "a very strange, bittersweet smell." It is then when he tells her, "They say that comes from the cake factory. It's been here as long as I have. Does it bother you? You'll get used to it after a while. You'll stop noticing it."

"That's not the only weird coincidence." She continues, "If you read the book — " He cuts her off to interject that "There are mysterious parts of that book. But the only true mystery is that our very lives are governed by dead people." In reference to the influence of Gurdjieff and his philosophy informing the film, Leigh McCloskey told me in an interview: "That's part of, I think, the astral connectedness that happens in his work [Argento's]. These strange netherworlds

that are the realm of sleepwalk. Where you can't quite awaken, you're stuck in a horror. Something dreadful that is sweeping you along…"

Inferno, possibly Argento's most puzzling film on a narrative level, tells the tale of Rose (Irene Miracle), a poet living in New York City who buys an ancient book, which bears secrets pertaining to her current residence. Once she goes missing after discovering a little too much, her brother Mark (Leigh McCloskey), also falls prey to the curse and allure of the "dwelling of the damned," which she inhabits. Being "stuck in a horror," to borrow a phrase from the film's leading man, is as apt a way as any to describe the film's mise-en-scène. Our "hero" is able to do almost nothing to extricate himself from the situation he has found himself in, and so he tries in vain to find any avenue of assistance. His utter uselessness as a character only drives the audience deeper into his dilemma. However, the film kicks off with a very dour mood. From the credit sequence where Irene Miracle is seen cutting the leaves of a copy of "The Three Mothers" with a letter opener resembling a sacrificial dagger to Leigh McCloskey opening his hand to discover an army of ants in homage to Buñuel's surrealist masterpiece *Un Chien Andalou*, the film's pervasive sense of dread leaves the viewer nowhere to feel comfortable. While preparing to shoot this "homage" to *Andalou*, Leigh McCloskey told me, "The insect wrangler put these ants on me and asked me if they hurt. I said that no, they were fine. Then he looked a little puzzled and said, 'Well, they bite, like fire!'"

Of course, any "normal" person would leave their apartment — or their sibling's, in Mark's case — after the events that unfold for each character early on. However, Argento has never concerned himself with

Argento and Sacha Pitoëff in the Antiquarian's shop. COURTESY INDEPENDENT VISIONS.

Argento on the set of Inferno. COURTESY 20TH CENTURY FOX.

what's right or wrong, either morally or logically. The comfort of common sense or the innate instinct for human preservation are nowhere to be found in the film, and perhaps most horror films, for the simple reason that if these characters heeded to their inner monologue to flee, there would be no story to tell and no analogue for the audience to experience these strange set pieces through.

Another quote from Gurdjieff comes to mind that expands upon the philosophy of the work: "It is the greatest mistake to think that man is always one and the same. A man is never the same for long. He is continually changing. He seldom remains the same even for half an hour." A literal interpretation of this quote can be read into Argento's use of three protagonists for the film to build its narrative. Rose would seem to be the film's logical heroine until she is murdered, then Sarah takes over after reading Mark's letter from Rose, only to meet the wrong end of a knife. Ultimately, the story belongs to Mark once he arrives in New York City to find Rose, which he never does.

And in the film's fiery conclusion, which echoes its title and the end of *Suspiria*, Mark is left to stand and stare, bewildered at what has just happened to him and likely knowing that his sister will never be found.

The film's most famous scene, also serving as a thematic tie for the entire piece, occurs when Rose puts her hand into a puddle to retrieve her keys and discovers an underwater room. The complete submersion of the self into the unknown, which in the case of Rose being the puddle she swims into to fetch her house keys could be seen as a hallucination, or fever dream. There is also the age-old metaphor of water representing birth and renewal. Could Argento be hinting at a rebirth of sorts for the character of Rose, and she will be born again through the guise of Sarah, and then her own brother? *Inferno* feeds into this line of thinking and doesn't allow for any real plot or identifiable characters to get in the way of a pure nightmare. The fractured narrative, which is filtered through the three previously mentioned protagonists,

McCloskey, on set with the insect wrangler, prepares for the hand full of ants shot. COURTESY LEIGH MCCLOSKEY.

creates confusion as to whose story is actually being told.

McCloskey's recollections of the shooting reflect a less than ideal situation, as it was summer in Rome and the temperatures outside were uncomfortable as it was. Once the lights were turned on at De Paolis studios, the heat became unbearable. Photographs from the set clearly show Leigh's misery as he sweats his way through the shoot, looking worn out from the effects of the cruel heat. Outside of the "Inferno" on set, it seemed to be pleasant, and he and Dario got along. At one point, according to Leigh, Dario told him, "You are the only American actor I would ever care to work with again."

McCloskey was also surprised by the lunch provided by the Italian crew. "They gave me this boxed lunch. It was a little bit of food; I think a sandwich or something and a bottle of wine and some Sambuca. Now, I could have drank my lunch, but I would have returned to the set a bit altered and stumbling around, 'Hey, is it time to crawl on the floor again?'"

An actor and model since his teens, McCloskey has always been aware of his image, but his rather unflattering 1980s hairdo is another story altogether, as he told me standing in his dining room: "The hairdresser on the set gave me a terrible haircut, literally the bowl on the head cut. When she was done she said that I had bad hair! I had never been told that before. But it was her fault; she gave me this weird haircut. So that explains why my hair looks so strange in this movie. I never had my hair like that again."

McCloskey and the rest of the actors look incredible thanks to Romano Albani's photography in *Inferno*. It may be heresy to some, but I believe the film to be even more sumptuous in its design and photography than *Suspiria*. Replacing the primary color palette with one a bit more pastel and cool, Albani reinterprets Tovoli's visual design for *Suspiria* and creates a slightly cleaner space. As groundbreaking as Goblin's score for *Suspiria* was, Keith Emerson's music here is equally as impressive, just in a different mode. *Inferno's* score fuses rock music and classical pieces, coinciding with the film's intentionally hallucinatory anachronisms.

Argento's stylistic excesses are in hyper drive, with everything and nothing going on simultaneously. How a film with so confounding a narrative can be so compelling is testament to the director's control over the medium. Much like its predecessor, the film relies on visual cues to tell its story, and, again, you could probably turn the dialogue off and it wouldn't make it a bit of difference because all the narrative cohesion the film has. During Daria Nicolodi's cat attack, there is a moment when she is attempting to leave the basement and the door locks itself, preventing her from leaving. Argento shoots not the door locking itself from the outside, but the locking mechanism itself inside the door, almost to suggest the house has a mind of its own. Having been created to house one of the "Three Mothers," the house was, as Stephen King puts it, "born bad." Without telling us what is happening, the visual here is quite startling and quite surreal. A door lock is something we encounter every day, but not from the inside, thus making it foreign to the human experience for most. Making the mundane special or surreal is again something Argento does with all of his work to some extent or another. Whether it be *Tenebrae's* strangely cold vision of Rome or Suzy being hydrated via water pitcher, these things convey an otherworldliness that is off enough to be disconcerting.

When it is all said and done, *Inferno* closes much like the first film, with the protagonist outside of a building on fire with an odd expression on their face, be it the shock of survival or a bemusement of the strangeness of life — who knows? Some have faulted the ending of the film for hewing too closely to that of *Suspiria*, but I think it works as a sort of through line of the breaking point of the human soul. What does it take for someone to will himself or herself through an experience like this if it were to happen? How would that person then react to freedom once they have escaped the "horror" they were trapped in?

Irene Miracle doing an underwater handstand on the Fotobusta for Inferno. COURTESY THE DEL VALLE
ARCHIVES/20TH CENTURY FOX.

LEIGH McCLOSKEY
(Mark Elliot, *Inferno*)

A Julliard trained actor, McCloskey made his professional acting debut in an episode of *The Mary Tyler Moore Show* spin-off *Phyllis* in 1975. Over the years Leigh has developed into quite an accomplished artist, having his worked displayed in several galleries as well as illustrating spiritual texts and even a deck of tarot cards. In the late 1970's and into the 1980's Leigh made several appearances in such varied projects as the TV film *Alexander: The Other Side of Dawn* (1977), *Just One of the Guys* (1985), and the long running TV show *Dallas* in which he had a regular role as Mitch Cooper.

DB: Did you always want to study acting? How did you end up at Julliard?

LM: I always loved acting; it was my first love, really, even in school. I remember missing a cue in kindergarten in a PTA play and some bug bit me after that. After that, I always wanted to be in every play. I raised my hand and volunteered for everything. I always wanted to participate and I saw the humor involved in theater and drama. Then I became the head of the drama group in ninth grade. I graduated high school a year early and went to Cal State Northridge and I realized that I really wanted to understand the craft of acting rather than just why certain nights the performance was great or otherwise. And I figured out I really didn't have the tools of the craft of acting yet, so I auditioned for different schools and the one that I ended up with was Julliard, which was a fabulous choice to make. I was this Malibu kid who ended up being thrust into New York City and the shock there of gangs to living in the city and ultimately falling in love with it.

But it was quite a shift, but it also really broadened my creative horizons and so that's my journey there. There was a small group of actors who were chosen nationwide through auditions. And so we were very close knit. My old roommate was Kelsey Grammar, who has gone on to great fame and a number of my classmates have also done very well. It's interesting to see the journey of this core group that I traveled with at the time. It was really my period of studying acting, but also was the period where my artwork, which has become my other creative life, really started to emerge because in acting I found as in calligraphy this sense

of gesture, of breath of Chi. Using one creative form to really investigate into another and trying to find the tonal truth of the character, I started using paint, I started using my body. I was trying to find that central sense of a character. I came back from Julliard and moved to acting quite quickly. It was a very good foundation studying at Julliard; it really gave me the craft, so to speak.

DB: At Julliard, when you were studying at Julliard, were Patti LuPone, Kevin Kline, that first group of Houseman students still around?

LM: I was in group six and they were in two, I think. They had just graduated. They were doing the acting company at that time and we would go see them in *The Cherry Orchard* and other things. And of course these were under the direction of John Houseman. But William Hurt, Robin Williams, a number of other people that have gone on to really great careers, even Christopher Reeve was a part of this group. It was a great bunch of people to be learning with.

DB: How long did you study there?

LM: Well, the last two years of the program, you would tour with the company and do plays, but I left after two years. I met an agent in an elevator. I've always been raring to go. And I took that opportunity when it came to me.

DB: The first thing you did was an episode of *Phyllis*, the spinoff of *The Mary Tyler Moore Show*. I remember watching a VHS tape of some random episodes with a friend a few years ago and seeing your episode playing the boyfriend of Cloris Leachman's daughter.

LM: Yes, that was my first professional role; I'll never forget it.

DB: Well, if you want to relive it, I'm sure it can be found on YouTube.

LM: That's a great resource and your ghosts can haunt you forever!

DB: Speaking of YouTube, that is how I watched *Alexander: The Other Side of Dawn*. You said earlier that you've always had a love of art, of drawing. Interestingly, the first time your character is shown in the backstory, he's drawing. And your father is castigating you for "drawing a barn and not helping to build one." Could you relate to this as a creative person growing up?

LM: I actually had the inverse. My parents were very nurturing of my creative side. My mother was a teacher and my father was an artist as well. We would all go to the theater, the ballet together. My father was a marvelous artist, a sage, and a very wise soul. Creativity was really valued. But I knew from experience that people were used or beaten up because of their creativity. And they're given absolutely no quarter by family or friends and it's really unfortunate. In playing Alexander, I felt more of the angst I had heard about from friends of mine that grew up in almost hellish conditions in terms of believing in themselves.

DB: To have the film open and make that kind of statement with what the character was, what he lived in, it says a lot. And of course, in the '70s on TV, there was that spate of "teens in trouble" movies like *Sarah T Portrait of a Teenage Alcoholic* with Linda Blair.

LM: I hadn't consciously thought about anything like that. But I did design the mural in Alexander that the character paints on the wall of his apartment. Doug Cramer and Randall Kaiser knew I painted and drew and they asked me to design the mural. I do find it interesting that I hadn't actually thought about it in a larger context, but Alexander is a creative soul. There is a type of romantic figure there. He wants to transmute the sorrows of his life into something of lasting beauty. And that's pretty poetic, actually.

DB: The role and the film overall asks about a thousand questions and answers two, maybe.

LM: Exactly.

DB: And the way it's set up, once Alexander gets to L.A. and he's living with Buddy, whom he meets on the street his first day. And he asks Alexander, "You like girls, right?" And Alexander pauses and responds, very unsure of himself, "Sure, I'm just tired from the bus ride." After he has begged off of attending a party that was guaranteed to have a lot of girls. It's interesting that the character's sexuality is always in question.

LM: I think that's the key to Alexander. If I had to say anything, I would say it's that he sought affection. And that is why he was so hurt by the Juliet Mills character. He really was innocent. He just wanted to be with someone. I think that's why he's so noble with Eve Plumb's character; he's an idealist rather than identifying with any sexuality. I think that's why he becomes sexually objectified to a certain degree. It's a very interesting and complex character. I found exploring him quite layered because he wasn't really the announcement of a sexuality as much as looking ultimately for love and in Eve, he found, I think, the ideal of the feminine that he sought. He helps her out of the gutter, too, and he's saving himself at the same time. I think there's almost a sacred act in that. But in terms of his confusion with the football player…that really had to show the sense that he's receiving all of this kindness and attention in a world that told him to shut up, sit down, and get out of here, I hate you. And a lot of young people would relate to this. I would read letters; it wasn't so much that they felt fixed in who they were. They were really looking for someone to give them an affirmation that they existed.

DB: And with Alexander, a lot of gay teenagers are kicked out of their homes. And so to find somebody, when your parents don't validate you, somebody has to.

LM: I really think that's the whole point of gangs, of anything where people don't have any support system. My God, this is why people are so judgmental of each other. We have to start realizing how difficult it is to be human. We are asked to survive the insurmountable, you know, and this is why a little compassion would go a long way. And that's one of the things I felt ultimately I had to do with Alexander is create a portrait where there wasn't a judgment, but rather an invitation to say "this might be a made up story, but it's certain, not made up." And there was a whole subplot with more drug use that they couldn't get past the censors. These beautiful souls are often destroyed by the difficulty of it all. I hope someday we will recognize what's remarkable about being human is that so many individuals have taken on such a difficult journey of having to find themselves and ultimately having to be true to themselves and surviving themselves. And that it's not just the individual, but it's actually a human act. I think that all of that comes from these journeys I believe are part of making greater and greater sense of who and what we are as human beings and how we really need to ultimately be kinder and less judgmental with each other.

DB: Working with two gay directors on *Dawn Portrait of a Teenage Runaway* and then *Alexander the Other Side of Dawn*, do you think it made them something different than they would have been otherwise?

LM: Well, a lot of the production people were gay and I think that's why it was important to them in terms of the tone of theme. There was a lot of attention to making it a fair portrayal of people no matter their sexuality and they wanted to make something that would touch people and be relatable.

DB: *Alexander* and *Inferno* are only three years apart and you couldn't have two more opposing projects. So, first, had you seen any of Dario's work before taking on the part of Mark?

LM: I had seen *The Bird with the Crystal Plumage* and a few of the others. I remember Bill Murray came up

to me and said to me, and this is the first time I met Murray, he said, "You're doing a Dario Argento film? That's great, he's interesting." And that's when I felt I needed to check into this director I would be working with. I learned about him along the way.

DB: It's interesting that the films were made so close together, yet with bigger hair and a mustache, you look quite a bit older. In fact, you almost look like a different person from one film to the next.

LM: Well, at that age, I wanted to look older. But now you get to my age I am now and you think, God, what was your rush, kid?

DB: When you were first offered the part, was there an audition?

LM: It was an interesting connection with Alexander because Herb Wallerstein, who was the unit production manager on that, went over to 20th Century Fox as a producer and he suggested me for

Mark ponders his troubles. COURTESY LEIGH MCCLOSKEY.

the film. James Woods was originally going to do the part and he passed on it. So I went in and met Dario and talked.

DB: This was your first film in Europe, right?

LM: Yes and in terms of my sense as an artist, this had a profound effect on me. What began at Julliard grew a great deal there. Italy's effect on my artwork with the architecture and that sense of history was so great. I went back to make *Hearts of Armor* in 1982. But *Inferno* was the first foreign film of mine.

DB: How did you find working in Italy as opposed to the states?

LM: The film wasn't shot with sync sound. We just made a working track and at the end of shooting, we went into a looping stage and had to put down everything, not just the edited dialogue. I had to lay down tracks on every single shot, which was a bit arduous and one chides oneself when you sound like Bob Newhart

with the "um, ah, um." And during the shoot, it wasn't silent, things were being worked on. It was distracting in a way. But I've always found the differences in territorial places a creative challenge. But it was hotter than you can imagine. There was a heat wave and the natives all left Rome. And then in the stage with the lights, it was probably 125 degrees. It was an inferno! I wanted to write a book, "Only in Italy"...there were things that were so funny, I just thought, well, people live differently.

DB: Do you recall if Salvatore Argento was around much?

LM: If he was, it was only peripherally in my reality. I don't recall.

DB: But Claudio [Argento] was around and acted as translator?

LM: Yes, he was the one who spoke English. He would relate Dario's ideas and suggestions to me. With Dario, it was more gestures, miming.

McCloskey and Nicolodi on set. COURTESY LEIGH MCCLOSKEY.

DB: I've heard rumors that you didn't get on very well with Daria Nicolodi? Do you have any idea where this would come from?

LM: I didn't really know Daria, but certainly there was no bad blood between us. I usually am one of the easygoing team players on a set, so even if she didn't care for me (which is possible, but I had no idea), I had nothing against her and thought her very pleasant when we met. We just really didn't spend any time together, not even enough to not like one another.

DB: When you first read the script, could you imagine, looking at that on paper, what it would turn into? I wouldn't think it would make a whole lot of sense.

LM: I was told that he was a director whose work was more of a dreamscape.

(Leigh starts to cough.)

DB: Are you OK?

LM: Yes, but it's the Three Mothers, Lachrymarum, Suspiriorum, Tenebrarum; it's a curse! But back to your question. Dario and I had that bridge of the love of art; he would look at my drawings and we talked about different things we liked. I don't think he was comfortable with actors, but he was big on ideas. So we would talk in his realm of ideas and thoughts. He's deeply introspective and quiet. He's not a screamer. It's as if he's seeing it in his head. And there is a visionary aspect to what he's doing. You can see in the film there is this relationship to alchemy, to process. I think his context deals with this dreamlike, odd relationships…strange metaphoric relationships, symbols, and things of that nature. Characters are metaphors. People wonder why my character seems almost dazed. He wanted him to seem to be not quite there. As if there were something possessing him that kept him a bit vague.

DB: You mention your character being in a daze and possessed of something. In the film, when Mark goes into the building the first time, there is a plaque on the wall that says "Gurdjieff lived here." He was a Russian philosopher and teacher. It's interesting that he would have lived there. It seems to inform the philosophy of the movie. And as you said with the character being dazed, he had this idea that people are in a permanent state of sleep, in a way.

LM: That's a great point. I'd never thought of that. And also, he said that we are all automatons and we're all sleepwalking.

DB: And there there's the line that the Kazanian says to Rose about "Our lives are governed by dead people."

LM: That's part of, I think, the astral connectedness that happens in his work. These strange netherworlds that are the realm of sleepwalk. Where you can't quite awaken, you're stuck in a horror. Something dreadful that is sweeping you along, but that's a very good point.

DB: And it's interesting how this all ties into your artwork and what you do creatively. It all bleeds together in a fate-like manner.

LM: If we think of how there are formal relationships, patterns start to make more and more sense, this mosaic of our life emerges. I do see these threads. These fascinating synchronicities when I've played my opposites and even a character closer to me. There is a sense that we are all a well-written novel. One thinks life is just random, but in fact, that is a type of orchestration; I call it "The Divine Choreography." It's not that something is a fact or makes sense absolutely, but isn't it extraordinary that there are all these correspondences. And if you listen to that language, then everything takes on a deeper resonance and a greater relevancy.

DB: When the movie was released, the head of Fox didn't really respond well to it.

LM: No, she didn't get it. I was in a screening with her and that's the only time I saw it before video and she said something like "Just cut it to ninety minutes."

DB: Have you kept in touch with any of the cast members or Dario?

LM: I saw Dario about twelve years ago at a retrospective of his work, but not really, no.

DB: The painting of your studio is beautiful. It's insane in its ambition. I mean that in the most complimentary way, but I don't know how else to express that.

LM: Maybe there's some madness there? I always liked Dali's comment, "The only difference between myself and a madman is I'm not mad."

DB: You started painting the studio shortly after 9/11 and you've been working on it ever since in some way or another. This ongoing project must feed you creatively in a way that you never saw coming when you started.

LM: It does, yes. I can say that my artwork comes from knowing as an actor that you dive into the not knowing of something more than what you do know because the latter just isn't interesting theater. For me, there was this spontaneous eruption of this language called "the watcher language." It's this figure that repeats. It's like when a musician improvises or riffs. We're allowing something to flow through us and take us on an adventure. You're not trying to control it, just see where it takes us. What became profound is that it announced itself early on. It called itself "The Hieroglyph of the Human Soul." And as an actor, you learn to listen to the voices because nobody can tell you how to play any role, so you really have to listen to those inner conversations. And it took me deeper and deeper into this story that has revealed over the years

the story of creation and of the returning home. It's s bit like The Wizard of Oz and Dorothy.

Years ago, when I gave Dario a drawing I did based on the premise of the film [*Inferno*] and after that in 1986, I began work on the major arcane of the tarot, not because I had this ambition to do so. I was only going to do a few drawings. The ideas really fascinated me and like a good role as an actor, I became bitten by going deeper and deeper into the territory and so I spent seventeen years working on twenty-two black and white drawings. I wrote a book called "Tarot ReVISIONed." And that mythically, I say like a piano, because there are twenty-two keys and they are black and white, these create the mythic and archetypal framework, essentially the psychological framework. Then when the towers fell on 9/11, I just fell to my knees onto the earth thinking, "We've come so far and this is something from a bad Hollywood movie." Well, I'll start telling the story I feel is worthy of generations that I want to tell my daughters and my friends and those I love. And from that initial seed, then over the past eleven years, and I'm still working on it. This

One of McCloskey's headshots after Inferno. COURTESY LEIGH MCCLOSKEY.

painting, this entity has evolved to cover the floor, the walls, the ceiling, furniture, and the insides of cabinets, even behind paintings.

I find myself inside such a remarkable theater piece that I can't help but go deeper and deeper and as I do, interestingly enough, the metaphor becomes stronger and stronger that when we think of the creative act we're thinking of spontaneous creation, which is what we humans are born of. And in this environment, of which I understood as my library, my studio, my hieroglyph, it's my home, so it's domestic space, meaning it's where we love together and express ourselves nakedly with each other. It's a different truth. I like the story that we've come full circle; this is a cave painting and it has a library, so we've left the cave and there is this knowledge what is it to be human. What is our possibility, our purpose? And the library is that we've gathered this sense of really the remarkable diversity and capacity of what it means to be human. Rather than trying to go somewhere, I realize we are the outcome of a great journey. And therefore, returning home to understand, just as in the DNA, we share the same weave. And that each of us now are unique, a blossom of creation and just to finish this point, I did a talk that was ten minutes long and my painting "Phoenix Arise" I created in card form first for my book. When I dropped these cards and the paintings now create a double helix and mandalas, it reveals the creation blossoming. You can tell I'm just very excited about this because it's growing through me and I like this version of being human better.

DB: Well, looking at your career, it's been a really broad and winding path. You've been in every soap opera known to man. And done a really interesting variety of things. But *Inferno* stands apart in the film and TV work; you didn't attempt anything else like it again.

LM: Well, the soap opera fans are the most loyal and loving. They know more about you than you do. I've lived many lives and they all seem to have these invisible walls between them. But it's more fun that way, probably. I think it's because really looking back, Dario was the artist. The director with such a vision and he followed his own inner muse. And he really realized what he knew was true and told the story he wanted to tell. And again, the trouble with the American release isn't his doing. He told his story, but I think that's why when I look at my other films, there were many different reasons for doing them. You have to pay the bills, of course. But I think when you get at it, in a way he was the one director that I gave some of my artwork to because we really did share a level of vision. It's more interesting looking back now than even when I was going through it. All of these different experiences do have a strange choreography.

Leigh McCloskey's drawing inspired by his experience making **Inferno.** COURTESY LEIGH MCCLOSKEY.

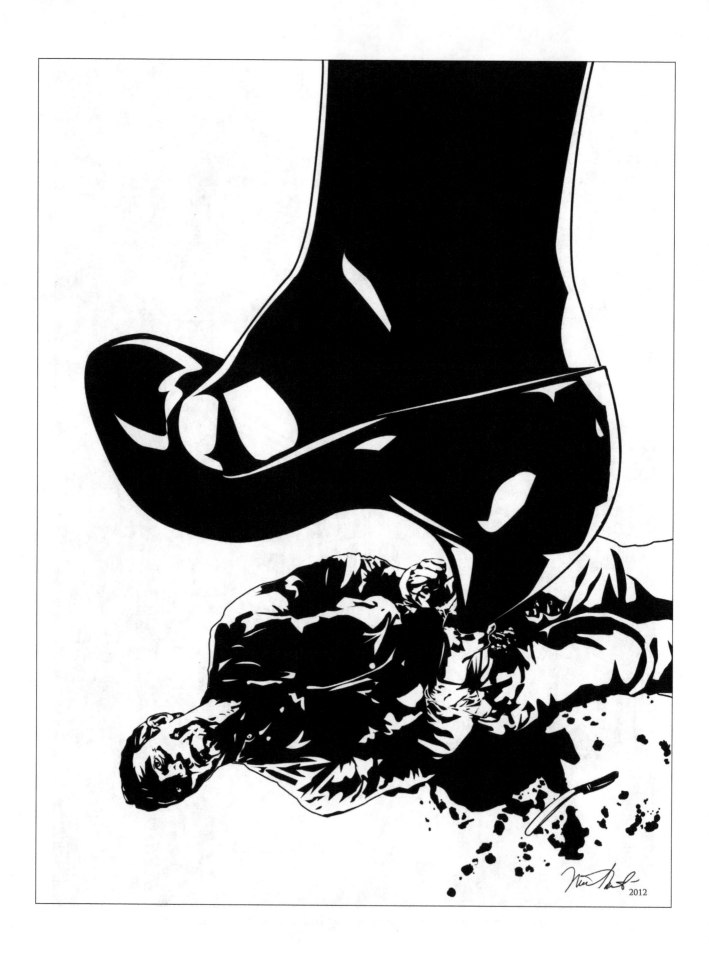

TENEBRAE
UNSANE

What I consider to be his finest giallo, *Tenebrae* takes all of the usual trappings of the genre and distills them into a beautiful concoction that is pure Argento. While most people seem to lay claim to *Suspiria* being their first, and favorite Argento film, *Tenebrae* was mine. I saw it in my early teens thanks to a neighbor having a copy of the U.S. prerecord under the title *Unsane*. I was attracted to it after seeing John Saxon's name on the video box, as I was a huge fan of *A Nightmare on Elm Street* and *My Mom's a Werewolf*…the things we watch as kids.

As expected of the genre, we have the black-gloved killer, an artist thrown into the midst of a murder mystery, and a super stylish bunch of people being killed with much flourish. After the box office and critical failure of *Inferno*, Dario took a page from his own life for inspiration to follow up the supernatural happenings in the second chapter in the tale of "The Three Mothers." The story has been told in much more detail elsewhere and many times, but here's the brief version of the genesis of *Tenebrae* that Dario gave me in 2000.

While staying in a hotel in Los Angeles to promote *Suspiria*, Argento began receiving phone calls from a fan, which at first seemed innocuous and flattering but soon became threatening. Argento told me this anonymous person said he was "the corruptor" and that Dario's films had "ruined his life." Dario let out a laugh at such a ridiculous accusation. "These people are crazy, yes?"

Tenebrae puts Dario back in giallo mode, crafting a murder mystery worthy of Agatha Christie with its intricate plot and collection of suspects and various motives. The film concerns Peter Neal (Anthony Franciosa), an American writer in Rome, doing publicity for his latest novel, titled, conveniently enough, *Tenebrae*. No sooner does Neal land in Rome than the bodies begin to pile up around him. Naturally, he becomes the first suspect in the killings, but as these things go, it cannot be that simple.

To silence the critics who proclaim loudly that Argento is incapable of putting together a coherent narrative, I would point them to *The Bird with the Crystal Plumage* and *Tenebrae* as examples of what Argento is capable of in terms of "traditional" storytelling. The plot is, on its face, the stuff of any B-movie thriller: A bestselling writer gets involved in a series of murders based on his latest novel and decides to track down the killer assisted by his secretary and personal assistant while abroad on a promotional tour for his latest work. Simple enough stuff, yes? On paper I would agree, but on film, no. From the opening credits, where a blinding hot fire provides the background for a reading of a passage from Peter Neal's novel *Tenebrae*, to the ending shot of Daria Nicolodi screaming bloody murder, the film unravels one plot twist after another, culminating in an astounding finale that is possibly the finest film of Argento's giallo output.

After making several highly influential gialli, it is interesting to see the mark of this film specifically, in other people's work outside of Italy. *Psycho 3*, directed by Anthony Perkins, looks very much like a giallo via Ken Russell. Perkins had worked with Russell on *Crimes of Passion*, and his influence can be seen throughout the film. There are several giallo-tinged pieces in it, most obviously the primary-colored lighting in certain scenes inside the Bates Motel, which resemble the "A Drop of Water" segment from *Black Sabbath*. Most

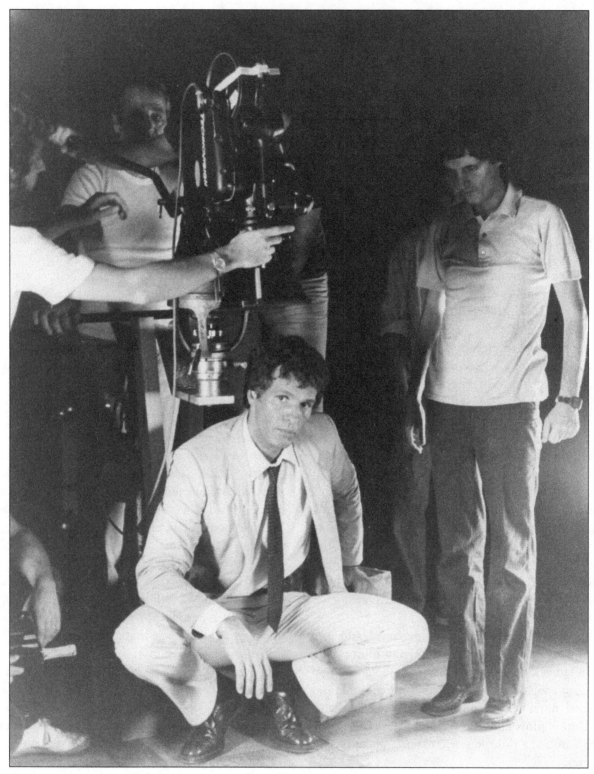

Giuliano Gemma and Dario Argento on the set of Tenebrae. COURTESY OF INDEPENDENT VISIONS.

notable is a scene in a phone booth that echoes Tilde's "fashion conscious" murder, as a still nude — presumed prostitute — is kicked out of a room at the Bates motel by Jeff Fahey's character, Duke. Seeking assistance, she finds a phone booth, and while she is pulling on a yellow (!) sweater, an unseen assailant with a blade slashes her to death. To cap it off, the murder ends on a shot of the phone dangling in the booth, much like the final shot of *Blood and Black Lace*.

Brian DePalma's *Raising Cain* famously cribs its final shot of John Lithgow from the revelation of Peter Neal standing behind Officer Giermani during the film's conclusion. Argento had done a similar reveal in *The Bird with the Crystal Plumage*, when Sam is in Needles's home: as Sam bends over, Reggie Nalder is seen dead behind him. Welsh director Julian Richards told me that he too recycled this shot for his 2003 film *The Last Horror Movie*, in the opening scene of a film within the film. Most recently, *Tenebrae* was paid tribute in Quentin Tarantino's *Kill Bill Volume 1*, in the House of Blue Leaves sequence when Uma Thurman chops off the Japanese schoolgirl's arm in a bloody nod to Veronica Lario's arm amputation.

Another accusation thrown at Argento is his alleged inability to get good performances from his actors. I would counter with Anthony Franciosa, who gives a great performance as Peter Neal. I would rank it with Karl Malden in *The Cat O' Nine Tails* and Max Von Sydow in *Non Ho Sonno* as the best performance Dario has gotten from one of his male leads. Franciosa gives Peter depth, where other actors in his shoes could have easily cashed the check without bothering to really do any work. But Franciosa really takes care to make him likeable and, more importantly, believable.

One of my favorite moments comes when Peter is with Gianni in the assistant's car, after escaping Christiano Berti's house after a night of detective work. Upon first viewing, the logical way to read it is that Peter is reacting to almost being murdered and surviving the ordeal, but once you watch the movie a second time, and know what has actually happened, you can see that he is acting the victim and relishing it because he knows he has given himself the perfect alibi. Franciosa is spot on in this scene. These small moments are what make this film shine.

Argento and Veronica Lario preparing for her amputation. COURTESY OF THE DEL VALLE ARCHIVES.

Franciosa is mostly known for appearing in the American TV show *The Name of the Game*, the play *A Hatful of Rain*, and alongside Paul Newman, Joanne Woodward, and Orson Welles in *The Long Hot Summer*, based on the William Faulkner novel *The Hamlet*. Later, however, he would appear in the 1980s versions of *Alfred Hitchcock Presents* and *The Twilight Zone*, two hugely influential shows, which he somehow missed out on being a part of during their original runs, considering how much television work he had done during the time these shows were on. While many actors put themselves to pasture abroad and take anything for a paycheck, it seems, Franciosa really took *Tenebrae* seriously and it shows. Although Argento claims he and Franciosa did not get along terribly well, due to Franciosa's showing up drunk or hung over to the set, you would never know there was any sort of rift between them behind the scenes to affect the outcome on screen.

Argento regular Daria Nicolodi plays Peter's secretary, Anne, with a quiet strength that has a hint of sad vulnerability, as she loves a man who can never love her back. Sadly, the role is underwritten, and she is given little more to do than act as a catalyst to get a few plot points moving. Nicolodi has stated that she was more interested in portraying Jane, Peter's fiancée; however, when the American actress who was supposed to play Anne dropped out of the film, Argento asked her to take over the part.

The all-important role of Cristiano Berti, the critic who accuses Peter of peddling degeneracy, is portrayed by John Steiner, Daria Nicolodi's costar in Mario Bava's *Shock*, in which he plays her husband. Berti is interesting due to the fact that he is a direct answer and attack on Argento's longtime critics, who insist that he is peddling immorality and "perversion." He also shares a common trait in Argento's films of having an unanswered or ambiguous sexuality, much like Roberto Zibetti in *Non Ho Sonno* and Asia Argento in *Phantom of the Opera*, to name a few. As he rails against homosexuals and other "immoral" people, while talking to Peter, he is rather effeminate and comes across as very gay. Could it be a case of repressed homosexuality manifesting itself in murder? Or is there more going on here? All we ever learn is that Berti is obsessed with Neal and is bent on bringing the murders in the novel to life — or death, as it were. Berti's mysterious sexuality also ties into the sexual themes in the film on a larger scale. Most obvious is the murder of the lesbian couple Tilde and Marion, who are killed because of their deviancy in the eyes of the killer.

Steiner told me that he took the job, in part, because of Argento's reputation and the fact that he had met him while making Bava's *Shock* alongside Nicolodi and found him to be pleasant.

Dario was very intense, but quite calm. Even when we shot my murder scene with this axe flying into my head, he would only really concern himself with the little details. He is so very focused and he was nice to everyone. And getting to work on the same film as Daria was great. She is so sweet and really a pleasure to be around. I'm sorry we didn't really have anything to do together in the movie.

Much like *The Bird with the Crystal Plumage*, Argento shows us a Rome without any of its famous landmarks — gone is all romanticism of his native city. In its place, we get a Rome unlike anything I have ever seen in a movie. It is sparsely populated, there are very few children, and people are often fighting with each other. In this new Rome, most of the inhabitants are fairly well to do; the film's first victim, portrayed by Veronica Lazar, lives seemingly alone in a nice apartment, even though she resorts to stealing books. Argento manages to build a slightly surreal and beautiful place for his characters to inhabit. The almost clinically cold environment this film inhabits lends an odd sense of unreality to the proceedings, while still keeping us grounded in a world that looks and feels familiar. The cold, white setting, punctuated by shocks of red, owes a debt to Godard's *Contempt* as well as Zulawski's *Possession*.

Gone are the baroque settings of *Suspiria* and *Inferno*, replaced by a Rome that is so frigid and uninviting, nobody would ever want to visit for fear of being murdered. Many are quick to claim *Suspiria* and *Inferno* to be the most visually beautiful in terms of their design and overall mise-en-scène. However, this short shrift given to *Tenebrae* and Argento's other gialli discounts the director's attention to detail when it's not given such an "exotic" setting as in the supernatural world of "The Three Mothers." Production designer Guiseppe Bassan and his team create a world dominated by only four colors: red, brown, white, and blue. Almost every costume and set are part of this color scheme, to give the world an almost "obedient" design, much as the supernatural films are dominated by primary colors.

Once again, Claudio Simonetti and company (well most of them), this time going by their last names of Simonetti, Pignatelli, and Morante, turn in a great

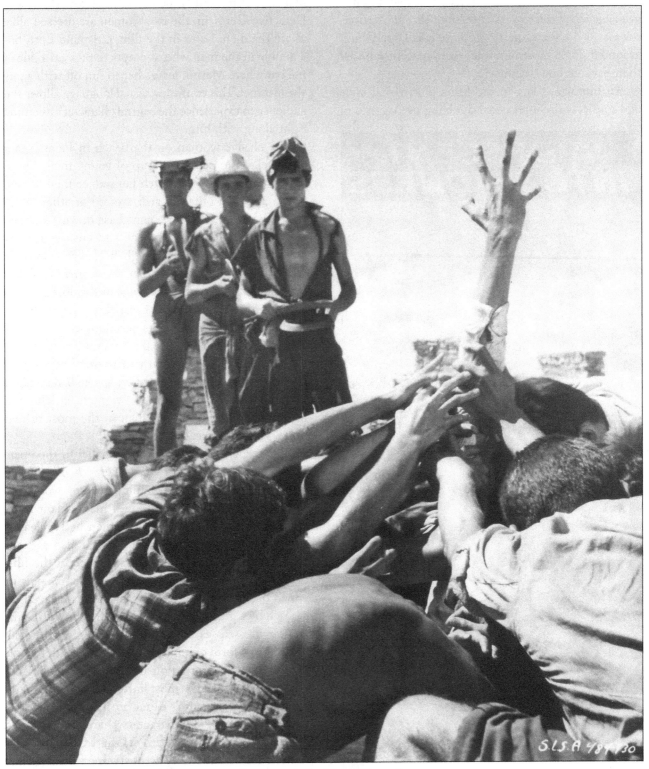

Young Sebastien is attacked during a pivotal moment in Suddenly, Last Summer. COURTESY OF THE DEL VALLE ARCHIVES/WARNER BROS. PICTURES.

disco-tinged score that enhances the film perfectly. The opening theme with Simonetti singing the word "paura" — meaning "fear" — alongside a great guitar and keyboard riff is actually pretty danceable, and it is available in several reworked versions through various releases. Like the score to *Suspiria*, it is largely built around a single piece of music with variations on that theme throughout the movie.

An important key to the film's plot, visual style, and music, is the intentional doubling by Argento of

Pulpy U.S. ad for Tenenbrae *under its American title,* Unsane. COURTESY BEDFORD ENTERTAINMENT/ MATILAND MCDONAGH.

the actors. Most notably, Anne and Inspector Altieri resemble each other, so much so that Peter confuses one for the other during the film's final scenes. The first time Peter and Anne meet Inspector Altieri and Detective Germani, the two women are dressed alike, as are the men. Later in the film, Cristiano Berti has a double in the man who attempts to pick up Tilde at the bar where Marion leaves her to run off with a guy she just met. This confusing visual language allows the audience to experience the central character's dilemma right along with him.

The elusive woman on the beach in Peter Neal's flashbacks commands a group of young men, whose faces we never see. We watch her seduce them at one point, and one puts his arm around another while they watch her. After the men chase down Peter, the woman spits blood in his face and ensures further humiliation by shoving her high-heeled shoe into his screaming mouth. The fact that this woman is played by a transsexual male, by the name of Eva Robins, only lends to the disorientation of sexuality inherent to the world of the film, and it begs questions of Peter's past and present personality. Are these men all homosexual? Was Peter involved with any of them? Did they all rape him while she watched? Perhaps he had an affair with the woman? This traumatic vignette enriches the mystery of Peter Neal as a man in the most primal sense. Who is he, really?

This scene has an interesting parallel to the opening of Curtis Harrington's *The Killing Kind* where a young man is "forced" into raping a young woman at the insistence of his friends, and this incident leads to his going on a murder spree when he is released from prison many years later. There's also a more than passing resemblance to a sequence in the film of Tennessee Williams' play *Suddenly, Last Summer* in which Sebastien, the sensitive poet son is ravaged on a beach by a group of men. As with most of Williams' work, repressed sex which can often be linked to violence in one form or another, often goes hand in hand in a sublimation of emotion and truth, which will only take bloom among the most horrendous and dramatic circumstance. Argento's often terribly confused and emotionally crippled characters share similar traits. Here, with the killers, both Peter and Cristiano take their issues with morality and sex out on their victims.

Bedford Entertainment handled *Tenebrae*'s release in the Unites States, under the title *Unsane*. The film was released on a very small scale before being issued on VHS by Fox Hills Video. In the August 1987 issue of *Video Watchdog*, Bedford's Steve Macklin says: "We had to get away from the Italian title and *Unsane* was sort of on the table until someone came up with something better. No one ever did. Argento came to New York and we unfurled the poster for him with the new title and he *loved* it! The picture had a brief release in Texas and Florida and didn't do any business, even with two campaigns."

Macklin goes on about the truncation of the film:

Argento's 101m thriller played on pay-per-view cable systems in 1985 in an atrocious, splicy, butchered, 89m edition that eliminated most of its violence and atmospheric transition shots, including a celebrated Louma crane shot that prowled the exterior of a Roman apartment house. The original closing theme music by Goblin veterans Simonetti, Pignatelli, and Morante was replaced with an unrelated and inappropriate dance track [by Kim Wilde] called "I Want You.

I'm surprised that I'm hearing this…" Macklin stated upon hearing of the changes. *"I can't remember having made such edits, but it would be my position to keep [the nonviolent material] in. And I can't think of a bloody reason why I'd spend money to change the music on the final credits! I have a partner on this film who handled the ancillaries while I handled the theatrical market and whether he had to do some extra tap-dancing to please pay-per-view, I don't know, but I'm surprised to hear there's eleven minutes off.*

The film itself wasn't the only thing to be altered; in France, the simple graphic of a woman from the chest up, in the last throes of death from a slashed throat, was victim of the censor's eye. To correct this "problem," a red ribbon was placed around the victim's neck in a ridiculous bit of unintended irony to make the film appear to be less graphic than it is, so as to not offend anyone, one assumes. When I first met Argento, he told me of the censorship issues the film had endured, and he mentioned the French poster. "It's a horror movie, what do people expect? Now she's wrapped up like a Christmas present; it's ridiculous!"

In its complete Italian cut or the butchered U.S. version, *Tenebrae* is a deft expansion upon themes laid down in *The Bird with the Crystal Plumage* and its roots in American pulp fiction. Peter Neal is the transplanted writer (another variation on William Sweeney in *The Screaming Mimi*) who becomes involved in something far more bizarre than anything he could ever write. Argento's next film would turn out as the strangest for him to date, leaving the "filthy slimy perverts" of Rome behind to play with the filthy, slimy insects of Switzerland in *Phenomena*.

PHENOMENA
CREEPERS

Swapping Italy for "The Swiss Transylvania," Argento's *Phenomena* stands as a singularly bizarre film in an increasingly strange filmography. As much as *Suspiria* and *Inferno* were a complete stylistic departure from the previous gialli, *Phenomena* attempts to join the two worlds with varying degrees of success. Its scientific concerns regarding entomology and Jennifer's psychic connection to the insect world, pulls on the thread of the post mortem retinal image experiment in *Four Flies on Grey Velvet* and the XYY chromosome theory from *The Cat O' Nine Tails*.

Jennifer Corvino (Jennifer Connelly) is a young American girl who is sent to a boarding school in Switzerland by her famous actor father, only to discover there is a killer loose on the grounds. Being the new kid in school isn't easy when you have a famous father, you sleepwalk, and you can telepathically talk to and control insects, but somehow Jennifer makes it work. Throw a chimpanzee, an entomologist (Donald Pleasance), and a murderous mutated child into things and it's obvious why the film played in very few theaters when released by New Line Cinema here in the United States under the title *Creepers* — missing some eleven minutes of footage. It is perhaps the most unhinged and maddening film in Argento's canon.

Jennifer Connelly has always seemed to shy away from the film, and it's a shame, as her performance isn't nearly the disaster she claims it to be. How often are child actors asked to do things of this nature? She acquits herself rather nicely, I would argue. Daria Nicolodi steals every scene she's in as the manic Frau Brückner. Carolyn De Fonseca provided her voice for the English language track and does an acceptable job of things. It works much better as her voice is closer to Daria's in tone than, say, Theresa Russell in *Tenebrae*. Nicolodi is playing to the balcony through the film, and it's a crazy-making performance that works with the tone and scope of the film.

Screen legend Donald Pleasance doesn't fare as well, unfortunately. Starting off with a completely unconvincing Scottish accent, Pleasance isn't helped by the fact that his character is largely there to give us some exposition and explain some scientific things to Jennifer. However, there are a few scenes between the two that are somewhat sweet, but again, that accent really crippled Pleasance's work.

The pastoral landscape of the film is a far cry from the mostly city-bound settings of films past. For a filmmaker with a decidedly "urban" eye, Argento showcases the mountainous landscape beautifully, allowing nature and even weather to play an integral role. In 1965, author Joan Didion wrote, in the *Saturday Evening Post*, an article titled "The Santa Ana," in which she describes the foehn winds that Dr. McGregor warns Inspector Geiger of. She writes:

> *There are a number of persistent malevolent winds, perhaps the best known of which are the mistral of France and the Mediterranean sirocco, but a foehn wind has distinct characteristics: it occurs on the leeward slope of a mountain range and, although the air begins as a cold mass, it is warmed as it comes down the mountain and appears finally as a hot, dry wind. Whenever and wherever foehn blows, doctors hear about headaches and nausea and allergies, about "nervousness," about "depression."*

For hundreds of years, people have speculated that these types of weather conditions induce mania in many forms and in many countries. In Israel, their version of a foehn wind, called the khamsin, when studied by Israeli officials, caused a spike in serotonin levels and an array of symptoms from migraines, nausea, and violence in younger people. Older people became generally fatigued, apathetic, and depressed, as their production of adrenaline fell.

Furthering the argument that McGregor makes of the winds making people insane, Didion writes of an occurrence in Los Angeles where:

> *On November 24, six people were killed in automobile accidents and by the end of the week, the Los Angeles Times was keeping a box score of traffic deaths. On November 26, a prominent Pasadena attorney, depressed about money, shot and killed his wife, their two sons, and himself. On November 27, a South Gate divorcée, twenty-two, was murdered and thrown from a moving car. On November 30, the San Gabriel fire was still out of control and the wind in town was blowing eighty miles an hour. On the first day of December, four people died violently*

and on the third, the wind began to break." Some scientists have theorized the mental anguish some people experience during this weather phenomenon is due to the "unusually high ratio of positive to negative ions…that makes people unhappy.

The winds never seem to stop during the entire film; at night, the wind is constantly running through the mountains and whipping through the trees. When it is revealed that Brückner's child has been murdering the students, in a scene that mirrors the end of *Don't Look Now*, are we to believe the foehn is responsible? Or is it due to his genetic mutation? Is he a product of simply bad parenting?

Bad parenting permeates many of Argento's films, and *Phenomena* is no exception. Jennifer's father dumping her in a boarding school while he can go make a film in the Philippines could be said to make him unfit or at the very least lax. When Jennifer voices her concerns with the situation she has been placed in and can only reach the office of his lawyer, she realizes she is stuck there, and so the bad parenting accusation moves into a confirmation of neglect. Something Argento never addresses is why the school would remain in

Pleasance dies while his primate companion is helpless to assist him. COURTESY THE DEL VALLE ARCHIVES/DAC.

session in the same location when several students are found dead. Where are the police? Why would the staff put the students in such danger? But when you have a teenage girl talking to insects, traditional logic is not in the driver's seat.

The nascent sexuality of *Phenomena* takes hormonal frustration further than *Suspiria*, which is an almost sex free environment with older girls in a similar environment. The captive teenage girls at the Wagner School: gossip about boys; are prone to comical crushes on Barry Gibb and Richard Gere; and have middle of the night liaisons with soldiers. Ultimately, a few are granted a penetrative release when Brückner's monster child impales them. The phrase "The Little Death" comes to mind in more ways than one. After Jennifer meets McGregor, her roommate Sophie says of him, "He's not a man; he's got more hands than the entire basketball team."

As with *Suspiria*, there are links to fairy tales in the film, and the roots of this can be traced back to the common archetypes all children are raised with: the stepmother, the evil queen, and the prince or hero figure. Argento uses the archetypal figures carried over from *Suspiria* here as well. Jennifer's new "stepmother"

can be found in Frau Brückner, who then becomes the "evil stepmother/queen" figure from *Snow White* or the wicked new parent of *Cinderella*. Strangely, the "heroes" of the film aren't a dashing prince or any man at all, but a monkey and a swarm of insects Jennifer calls to protect her from her rather harsh fellow students. Instead of using insects as something to terrorize our main character, as would usually be done in a horror or science fiction film, she is able to use them as a key to her own salvation and does so with pride. Jennifer has a special gift none of the other girls can claim, and they are jealous and act accordingly childish as Argento also has several characters in *Suspiria* behaving the same. In one instance early on of Jennifer using her gift, she follows a firefly through the night as it leads her to a clue to the mystery. This is reminiscent of a scene early on in *The Curse of the Cat People* where young Ann Carter is bewitched by a butterfly while on a school outing, and she runs away from the group to follow the creature only to have it crushed by a fellow student, who catches it in mid-air when he attempts to catch it for her.

The uneasy mix of giallo and pseudo scientific/fantasy horror lends the film an unevenness bordering on "bad" filmmaking as it seems to not have a singular

The foehn even blows indoors as Jennifer professes her love to a horde of insect admirers. COURTESY MAITLAND MCDONAGH/DAC.

voice. And yet, at the same time, that voice could *only* belong to Dario Argento if you are familiar with what has come before it. *Phenomena* stands as the first time Argento began to cannibalize his own oeuvre by using elements from many of his previous films. Yes, there were references to a few things here and there, but, it seems with *Phenomena*, it really is Argento's every-thing-*and*-the-kitchen-sink filmmaking.

The shattering glass head traumas from *Four Flies on Grey Velvet* and *Tenebrae* are part of Fiore Argento's murder, which opens the film. The Tanz Akademie from *Suspiria* has its mate with the Wagner School for girls along with a narration similar to *Suspiria*'s opening. *Tenebrae*'s harsh lighting scheme is also brought back in many shots, infused with a blue tinge at times, which again recalls *Suspiria* and *Inferno* as it seems the film wants to be perpetually in an azure darkness that doesn't exist, much like *Tenebrae*'s overly lit night-scapes. Frau Brückner's institutional rape has shades of what we learn in *Four Flies on Grey Velvet* about sNina's repressed childhood spent in a hospital. *Phenoma* adds to the list of parental figures that harbor murderous children or are murderous themselves. Later, Mr. Betti in *Sleepless* would prove to be both as well.

Continuing with the stark visual style laid down in *Tenebrae*, Argento continues on with *Phenomena*, creating a similar stark style of bright, over lit interiors, and night that is bright, only blue instead of white. Romano Albani returns to work with Argento after previously photographing *Inferno*.

Aggressively and beautifully scored in equal measure by Claudio Simonetti, Fabio Pignatelli, and Bill Wyman of The Rolling Stones, *Phenomena* is the first instance of Argento using heavy metal songs to accompany the composed score. "Flash of the Blade" from Iron Maiden is used a few times and is the only outside track that "works," and that assertion is flimsy at times. The main theme in the film, with vocals by Pina Magri, is a truly haunting piece of work that stands as one of the strongest songs Simonetti has written to date.

Argento has drawn a direct line from this film to his next, *Opera*, with the implementation of heavy metal music. Yet in its next exercise, the music would stand in very stark contrast to the classical strains of some of the most beloved operatic compositions in the history of the form. And again, Simonetti would be back to fill in the spaces between the two forms with his unique musical vision.

Shattered Flower. COURTESY MAITLAND MCDONAGH/D.A.C.

OPERA
TERROR AT THE OPERA

When the word "opera" is mentioned, most people envision that stereotypical Wagnerian performer dramatizing the character "Brünnehilde" in Wagner's opera *The Ring of the Nebulung*, with the metal bra and Viking hat replete with horns. This trope has become legion because of the endless performances of Wagner's "Ring Cycle" and the legend that has been cast around it. Opera is at once a "classy" and "low brow" art form, which often revels in the most base of stories, whether it is murder or violent death, destruction of the family and society as whole, or sexual dalliances and, in the best scenarios, a combination of all three. Verdi's adaptation of Shakespeare's play *Macbeth* is the centerpiece of Argento's film, which was made in response to Argento being asked to mount a production of *Rigoletto*.

Betty (Christina Marsillach) is a young opera singer who is thrust into the lead of Verdi's *Macbeth* when the current diva of the company, Mara Czekova, is run down by a car in front of the theater. Her good omen quickly turns bad. On the night of her debut, there is an "accident" in one of the boxes and a stagehand is killed - one of the lights falls into the audience (in a nod to *The Phantom of the Opera's* famous chandelier drop scene) and the man is then impaled on a coat hook. It isn't long before a stranger begins stalking Betty, tying her up, and forcing her to watch her friends get murdered.

The high art of the opera and the genre gutter of the horror film are addressed in equal measure in several ways through the film, to the point of mockery in some instances. The company's diva, Mara Czekova, is all fits of unpleasantness and rage, although she is never seen in more than a long shot and a brief glimpse of a broken leg. Even then, she throws a glass at Betty while watching her debut on TV. Argento's use of extreme violence in some of the scenes accentuates the suggested operatic nature of the material due to the film's title and subject. The iconic image of Betty with the pins under her eyelids is a wry comment on the nature of the theatrical experience, whether it is a film or a live performance, and a bit of a challenge as well: You must keep your eyes open to watch and experience everything that is to come. Although what you are looking at may be unpleasant, that is part of the enjoyment.

Naturally, any film called *Opera* cannot escape comparisons with the Gaston Leroux novel *The Phantom of the Opera*, prior films, and, of course, Andrew Lloyd Webber's juggernaut musical, which premiered in the West End of London the year before Argento's film opened in Italy. Beyond the film's title and theatrical setting, there are several allusions to *The Phantom of the Opera*, most specifically with certain actions of the mysterious killer, who also wears a mask.

Early in the film, the killer watches Betty sing from an empty box in the theater, a point of view shot that continues with the murder of the stagehand. In contrast, Leroux's "Phantom" has box five reserved for him in the theater, as part of his blackmail, so he can watch Christine perform and keep a watchful eye on every aspect of the opera. At the end of Argento's film, Santini (Urbano Barberini) asks Betty, while she is tied to a chair, "How can you love a monster?" as if his physical appearance would be the reason she wouldn't want to be with such a horrible person. This idea also comes from Leroux's novel, as the phantom rationalizes that Christine cannot love him because of his physical appearance, rather than it being due to the

Betty is held captive for the first time while her boyfriend is murdered. COURTESY MAITLAND
MCDONAGH/CECCHI GORI.

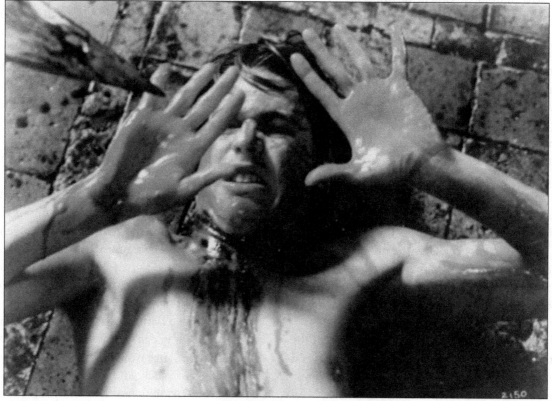

Poor Stefano is butchered while Betty looks on in terror. COURTESY MAITLAND MCDONAGH/CECCHI
GORI.

horrific things he has done for the sake of "love." Yet unlike Leroux's character, Inspector Santini is a very attractive man who most women would be drawn to.

The 1943 version of *The Phantom of the Opera,* starring Claude Rains, had it written in the script, at one point, that the phantom was Christine's father, much as Betty's "Phantom" is her mother's ex-lover, making him a stepfather figure of sorts. The familial tie to the murderer is yet another instance of the poor parenting and childhood traumas theme that Argento has mined so often in his films. However, this time around, there is a sadomasochistic and sexual component to the trauma that is missing in the others. Young Betty is shown in flashback to have watched her mother tied up by her lover, while he then proceeds to murder women they would kidnap, all in the sake of sexual thrills. This activity has obviously boiled over into Santini's obsession with his ex-lover's daughter, when he restrains Betty and tapes needles to her lower eyelids so she is forced to watch his brutality, all the while assuming she is receiving the same sexual gratification he is experiencing.

Claude Rains in Phantom of the Opera. COURTESY THE DEL VALLE ARCHIVES/UNIVERSAL PICTURES.

Continuing a run of sexually troubled films, beginning with *Tenebrae,* issues of sex and sexuality are rampant. Betty is given over to performance issues in bed and doesn't adhere to the apparent adage that, according to her boyfriend, opera singers are "incredibly horny" and they make love right before they go onstage to improve their vocal prowess. Later, after the same boyfriend is brutally murdered, Mark (Ian Charleston) picks Betty up in his car — an obvious red herring to tag him as the killer — and in discussing love and sex, Betty points out, "Of course I've made love. It's never worked." As we have just witnessed. And in addition to what we will witness and learn about Betty, she hasn't had the best examples of a loving, sexual relationship.

Sex has never been the most balanced of topics in any of Argento's films: witness *Tenebrae*'s lack of anything resembling romantic love — outside of Ann and Peter's single kiss, everyone is cheating or conniving against someone. *The Bird with the Crystal Plumage* is an orgy of unfulfilled sexual promise, and *Deep Red* has at its heart a budding romance between Marc and Gianna, yet gives much more explicit attention to the sexually suppressed and self-hating Carlo and his long-suffering boyfriend. *Opera* deals with an entirely different type of sex and sexual metaphor, most notably in the imagery of the killer's black gloves with latex gloves covering them. Argento has stated this was meant to suggest the dangers of sex with the HIV/AIDS epidemic. With the "sex kills" message in society throughout the 1980s, most notably in gay communities worldwide, this imagery carries the implication that there is never enough protection from others, and there is the potential of our own desires doing us in, depending on the activity we choose to participate in.

Santini's sex-fetish-obsessed maniac is a giallo staple that Argento had never really examined before. Yes, the previous films all had a villain with some form of sexually related trauma in their past, but nothing overtly sexual in their M.O. Other filmmakers in Italy had killers that embraced their sick, sexual urges and used them to commit their atrocities: William Rose's *The Girl in Room 2A* revolved around a sex and murder cult; and Sergio Martino's *All the Colors of the Dark* had its *Rosemary's Baby* inspired satanic orgies. Obviously, Norman Bates in *Psycho* is the prototype for all of these sex maniacs to come, his most obvious analogue being Michael Caine in Brian De Palma's *Dressed to Kill,* arguably an American giallo.

"All the terrible things I saw are from a nightmare I used to have as a child. I used to dream about a man wearing a black hood. Tonight, I saw that same hood." Betty admits to Marco after he takes her home on the night of Stefano's murder. In mistaking these memories for merely dreams, she refuses to allow the reality of her fantasy she has built up about her mother to shatter. When it comes to light that her dreams are actually memories and she connects what had happened to her mother in the past and how it ties in with her experiences in the present, she is able to put away childish things, become an adult, and become the master of her own destiny. She was unable to save everyone around her who died at Santini's hands, but she is quite capable of saving herself, now armed with some critical information she wouldn't allow herself access to previously.

The "operatic" violence in the film showcases some of Argento's most brutal and inventive murders to date. Coralina Cataldi-Tassoni's death in the wardrobe room is reminiscent of a victim of a string of unsolved crimes that swept through the area surrounding Florence, Italy from 1968 to 1985. The murderer — or murderers — was dubbed "The Monster of Florence" by authorities. In one instance, a woman had her necklace placed into her mouth and her reproductive organs removed. Tassoni's death also has another reference to *The Phantom of the Opera* when Giulia unmasks the killer, ironically something Argento would not stage in his film version of Leroux's novel.

Tassoni's death scene as Giulia is an especially nasty creation of Argento's. It is grand and surreal, such as

opera itself, and is at once restrained in its violence, yet brimming over with suggestion. As the killer cuts into her chest to retrieve the gold bracelet she dubiously swallowed, the close-up of the shears and the sound of crunching bone is far more effective than seeing a special effects bust being cut open. There had been a chest created for this scene that was to be cut open on camera; however, Argento wasn't happy with the results and wisely chose to shoot around it.

As fantastic and strange as Tassoni's death is, the most elaborate set piece of death in the film is the murder of Daria Nicolodi's character, Mira. The word "mira" means "look" in Spanish, and it can't be a coincidence that Daria is shot in the eye while looking through a keyhole and trying to ascertain the identity of the man on the other side. It's a deliciously evil pun. Mira's demise puts the identity of the killer right up on the screen, yet the audience, along with Mira, doesn't want to believe the obvious: that the man with the gun and the badge is exactly who he says he is, the police. And with the confusion and assumption that there can only be one cop on the scene, Daniele Soavi (played by Michele Soavi), Argento plays everyone for a fool quite successfully.

Though the film has an almost constantly crawling camera and the photography is impressive throughout, the bravura set piece is arguably the raven point-of-view shot, circling through the theater auditorium. In a way, the scene can be seen as a another riff on the chandelier drop in *The Phantom of the Opera*, only

Tassoni and Argento rehearse her death scene. AUTHOR'S COLLECTION.

transformed into the ravens flying down and circling above the audience. And once the ravens hone in on their target, Santini's eye is removed, the ravens exacting their revenge in Mira's stead.

This scene takes place against the backdrop of Betty and her costar singing "Fatal mia donna!" where Macbeth tells Lady Macbeth that he is horrified he has just killed the king, Duncan, in order to make Macbeth the new king of Scotland according to the prophecy relayed by the three witches earlier. She then proceeds to tell him he needs to be strong, that he has done the right thing. The juxtaposition of the onstage drama with the mayhem in the theater with the ravens is a thematically rich concoction. By selecting that precise piece of the opera, which happens in the first act at a dramatic turn in the plot when Macbeth has gone out to assure the prophecy of the witches, Argento suggests Betty is also assuring her own path and future by colluding to possibly murder a man to "make things right." Is murder ever justified?

Aside from the operatic pieces performed in the film, Argento's use of the distinct heavy metal music stands as a strange inspiration on paper, but works thematically — yet the implementation itself is questionable. Taking the example of the plot of *Macbeth*, the opera itself centers around an act of violence that is used to further one man's political future. A horrendous action, although wrapped in a gauze of beautiful music, is still a horror to behold. Musically, heavy metal music sounds angry and violent. Although it may not call for such things, that is the image it provokes due to the reputation foisted upon it. One is just a "respected" form of horror show, while society has put the other one into the cultural gutter. Running through the middle ground is a score with contributions by Claudio Simonetti, Brian Eno, Terry Tyler, and Bill Wyman. Their collected contribution creates, much like the score from *Phenomena*, a surprisingly cohesive whole composed mostly of haunting themes with occasional vocals.

The coda of the film, which takes place in Switzerland, has become something of a controversy among fans, and Daria Nicolodi has referred to it as "That Swiss nonsense." I would politely disagree with Ms. Nicolodi, as I find the finale to be a fantastic way of relating just how broken Betty is after this entire experience. While she may be living "happily" with Marco now, seeing Santini again unravels whatever shred of sanity was left. And, in the end, it seems the evil in Santini has won her over, despite her best efforts to resist. The evil has won out, and now she is left to pick up the pieces of

her broken mind, whatever and wherever they may be. In the end, there may be something liberating in this letting go of "sanity." Betty has been through a great ordeal and has had to face many things about herself and her family she never reckoned; this is merely her way of coping.

Many would argue *Opera* to be Argento's last "great" film. After its failure to garner a theatrical release in the U.S. — as Orion was in the midst of bankruptcy when it was to be shown stateside — it was released on video in the early 1990s as *Terror at the Opera*. The film did manage to get a nod of sorts by a character in the Anthony Hickox directed horror film *Waxwork*, and Argento is even listed in the "Thank you" credits.

After the disappointing box office, the personal loss with the death of his father during production, and the failure of such a daunting project that was so close to his heart, Argento didn't direct another film until his segment of *Two Evil Eyes* in 1990. In the meantime, he kept busy writing and producing films for Michele Soavi, *La Chiesa/The Church* and *La Setta/The Sect*.

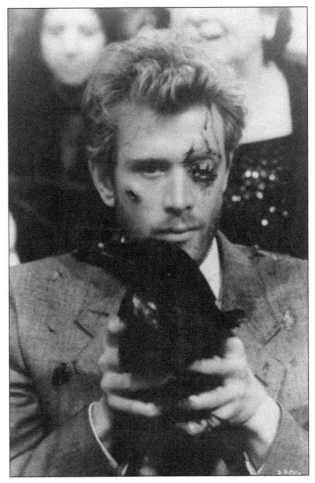

Inspector Santini clutches a winged assailant. COURTESY MAITLAND MCDONAGH/CECCHI GORI.

INTERVIEW

WILLIAM McNAMARA

(Stefano, *Opera)*

A student of the Lee Strasberg Theater and Film Institute, William McNamara made his feature debut in *Opera*. Although he's not a fan of horror films and the like, McNamara is probably best known for his turn as the psychotic killer in *Copycat* (1995) also starring Sigourney Weaver and Holly Hunter. He's also done memorable work in *Wildflower* (1991), directed by Diane Keaton and co-starring Reese Witherspoon and Patricia Arquette and *Stella* (1990), alongside Bette Midler and Trini Alvarado.

DB: Can you tell me a bit about how you got this part? This was your first project in Europe, yes?

WM: Actually I was in Italy shooting the mini series, *The Secret of the Sahara* for RAI TV and I think it was one of the producers Dario works with told me about *Opera* and insisted I consider the project. He explained who Dario was, how big his following was, etc…At the time I said OK because there was nothing else going on in the states for me. So I went and met Dario…I was taken to De Paolis studio during a break. I was working at Cinecittà on the mini series, and it was nice to see both facilities. Anyway, Dario didn't want to audition me, he just wanted to look at me in the light, and in the shadows. I just stood there, and he held me by the shoulders, and turned me around, looking at me at different angles. So, at the end of this "audition" I got the job and was being shuttled between the two studios at different times in the week, since they were being shot at the same time.

DB: So you had not seen any of Dario's films and knew nothing about him when you were offered the part?

No, nothing, but peaking of Dario's reputation…I auditioned for *Reservoir Dogs*, for Tarantino, and my script fell apart right in the middle of my reading! Quentin came over to me and told me I was fine, told me to relax and said, "By the way, I loved *Opera*. Man, it's Dario Argento!" I was surprised anyone had seen it. I didn't even know the movie had been released in the states. Or anywhere for that matter.

DB: What were your first impressions of the script once you read it?

WM: Well, I was given the English translation, and I don't really remember my thoughts on it, but I do recall that Vanessa Redgrave was cast so that alone was enough. Also, Ian Charleston from *Chariots of Fire* was in it. So I thought: Hey, this is a good crowd to be involved with. The problem was, and I almost left the production half way through, that I was offered the younger brother role in *Bright Lights, Big City* and I couldn't do it because of the Argento film. After that, Vanessa Redgrave dropped out. It was a lot of fun still. One thing though, I didn't know at the time is that they weren't recording sound. I haven't seen the movie, but I've seen clips and I was looped by a British actor.

DB: Who for some reason sounds a bit older than he should.

WM: Yea, it's crazy. I should have left them and done *Bright Lights, Big City*. But these things happen. Plus, Ian was a lot of fun and a great guy, so I'm glad I got to work with him and get to know him before he passed away.

DB: Do you know anything about the Redgrave situation?

WM: With Redgrave, they hired her for a week and they flew her to Rome and I guess she had been sitting around for the entire week at the hotel. So what happened was she flew back when the week was up! The producers were furious, because they had paid her for a week's work, but you can't keep someone sitting around week after week and decide when they can work. They didn't seem to understand that you hire from date to date and schedule the shoot accordingly. I think her agent wanted more money to keep her after the week, so that's how they lost her. So to replace her, the big star, with a steadicam after that…that's ballsy. But, that's Dario.

DB: How did you get along with Cristina Marsillach? Reports were she didn't get on with Dario very well.

WM: The Spanish actress? Yes she was a real sweetheart. She had a really rough role and Dario really pushes his actors, especially the actresses. I don't remember anything specific, but it's probably something like what Hitchcock famously did to Tippi Hedren in *The Birds*. It was all to get a specific reaction or emotion.

DB: You mention Dario was hard on the actors, did he give you a hard time?

WM: Not really, I do remember one funny thing though where Dario was not happy with Ian's performance and he was trying to give Ian some direction. And Ian asked Dario what he wanted him to do because he was apparently giving him some crazy directions. Dario said to Ian, "Think of yourself as being from another planet, you've just dropped down to Earth. You're an alien, and don't know anything about Earth. So I want you to be an alien in this situation. That's your motivation. That's your character, you're from another planet." Keep in mind, Ian is a very well trained English actor, but he took it all in stride and with great humor and had a good time. And you mention birds, there were fake birds on strings, real birds…

DB: Cristina was very new to acting at the time, did you find any trouble since she so green?

WM: Not at all, but remember I was new as well. It was my second or third gig.

DB: And your first onscreen death! Do you recall anything about that big scene?

WM: Well, I was covered in blood and there was a retractable knife. It was actually a bit scary. Oh, one thing and I thought it was ridiculous at the time, there were these mannequin hands that I had to hold up to the camera. There are some shots where it's a plastic mannequin hand.

DB: Since you've worked with so many people over the years like Diane Keaton in *Wildflower*, Peter Bogdanovich on *Texasville*, to name a few, how does Argento differ?

WM: He's very visually minded. Ronnie Taylor, the DP, is one of the best in the business, and Argento's films are very visual, and that's why I think my audition was him just looking me over. The actors are more like props, or mannequins. But he's also very quiet, and kind, and everyone seemed to get along and have a good time.

DUE OCCHI DIABOLICI
TWO EVIL EYES

A decade after working with George Romero on his now classic *Dawn of the Dead,* Argento would reunite with him to tell two distinctly different tales of Edgar Allan Poe. Originally, Argento wanted to do a version of *The Pit and the Pendulum* set in South America, and Romero was to do *The Masque of the Red Death* as an AIDS parable. Both were scrapped in favor of *The Facts in the Case of Mr. Valdemar* and *The Black Cat,* which ultimately made up the dual-story anthology film.

After a deflating realization by Romero that he wouldn't be traveling to Italy, but that Argento would come to the U.S. to shoot, it was down to business. One of the main reasons for shooting in Pittsburgh was to stay closer to the spirit of Poe, as Argento felt Europe couldn't work the way filming in Poe's homeland would. In the short opening credits montage of the Edgar Allan Poe house and his gravesite that Argento had shot, Poe's spirit is beckoned, but it never fully materializes. It's a shame this couldn't have been explored more, if nothing else than to provide some kind of wraparound to the two stories, because the abrupt stop and start between them is quite clumsy.

Romero's segment is up first and tells the story of Jessica (Adrienne Barbeau), the wife of a very wealthy and very sick Ernest Valdemar (Bingo O'Malley). With the help of his doctor and her boyfriend, Robert (Ramy Zada), the two plot, through hypnosis, to have the old man agree to disperse his assets to her. Naturally, all does not go as planned, as Valdemar dies much sooner than anticipated and Romero trots out his "Living Dead" theme to bring about the inevitable conclusion with a *Tales from the Crypt,* "Just Desserts" style

of ending. At one point, Valdemar even tells Jessica, "They're coming for you, Jessica" in an obvious wink to *Night of the Living Dead.*

Romero had made *Creepshow,* and in the segment called 'The Crate', Adrienne Barbeau gave a bravura performance that is unforgettable as Wilma "Billie" Northrup. Romero has her back, along with Bingo O' Malley and E.G. Marshall from that film, for a little reunion of sorts. Unfortunately, the film feels bloated and overlong as the story doesn't have enough to justify the hour run time. However, the script is well-written, the performances are all good, and there is the usual social commentary that Romero is known for: in this case, greed and its consequences. Romero also seems to be making a statement about the wealthy, as Argento does often in his work, with the entire situation of the film, culminating when Tom Atkins (as a police detective) says, upon entering the crime scene: "The sick stuff always turns out to be rich people." The final shots of the pyramid on the blood-spattered dollar bill echoes the shape of the obelisk pendulum used for hypnosis, which in turn recalls a grave marker. The red light on the pendulum flashes like a warning sign, a beacon of death in the night.

With the end of Romero's segment, the film jumps into Argento's. A book of crime scene photographs is shown to the audience while a yet unknown voice intones about the evil in humanity. Rod Usher (Harvey Keitel) is a crime scene photographer with a penchant for drink, trying to get some "contrast" into his work. One day, his live-in girlfriend Annabel (Madeleine Potter), takes in a cat, and Usher immediately takes a jealous disliking to the animal, and the feeling is mutual. Soon, their lives spin out of control in ways they could never imagine. Who knew a little furry creature could cause so much trouble?

Following a long line of Argento's leading characters being artists of some bent, Rod is a photographer and his wife is a violinist and teacher. Tom Savini, the effects artist on the film, had himself been a photographer during the Vietnam War, recording the various atrocities he came across during battle. It's interesting that Keitel would have someone who had photographed actual corpses so close at hand while playing at the same. Savini has said that shooting the maimed and dead through the camera lens gave him some distance from the gruesome subjects and somehow made it a little easier to deal with. The same can be said of Keitel, taking the photographs of death on the job and beyond, when he is murdering his wife. He then creates a tableau out of her death, laying her in the bathtub, filling it up, and creating a still life. The scene interestingly reaches back to *Diabolique* and, to some degree, *Psycho* with the corpse in the bathtub and the shots of the blood swirling down into the drain. In another nod to *Psycho*, Martin Balsam stands at the bottom of the stairs in the *House of Usher* looking up, ready to ascend much like he does in Hitchcock's immortal classic.

Keitel gives an interesting performance as Rod. He is a completely self-absorbed and obsessive man. He is equally comfortable killing a cat to take a few photos for his book as he is hacking his wife to death with a cleaver and putting her in the bathtub to hide her body from Martin Balsam until he can wall her up behind some shelves he apparently so badly needs. Madeline Potter as Annabel is all pale skin and pouty lips, looking like a Victorian-era porcelain doll. There's no question why she has had such a varied career onstage and in film, and why Argento cast her; she appears to be from another time. It seems Merchant and Ivory agree as she has graced several of their productions such as *The Golden Bowl* and *The Bostonians*. Also of note in the cast are television regular John Amos, Kim Hunter (the original Stella in Tennessee Williams' *A Streetcar Named Desire),* and Julie Benz in her first film, who would later go on to find success on the small screen in *Buffy the Vampire Slayer* and the Showtime series *Dexter.*

The film also has a potentially interesting and fun role for Sally Kirkland as a bartender at a bar called "South of Heaven" (the name which has religious and possibly sexual connotations) that was cut short by the producers according to editor Pab Buba. Kirkland confirmed that there was indeed more, but neither could tell me exactly what the more was. An Oscar nominated actress for the 1987 film *Anna,* Kirkland does her best to seduce Rod back into the grasp of the animal he so fears. If anyone were faced with this dilemma, they would have left well alone. When asked about working with Argento on the project, Kirkland had nothing but positive things to say about Dario:

"I was honored to work with Dario because he is who he is. I consider him to be the top of the horror craft. I was just like a groupie. He's very much an actor's director, and he was very patient. Harvey I'd known since the early sixties…we were in acting classes together and it was great to have an excuse to finally work together. But Dario was great and so careful with the way he insisted I be lit that I just felt beautiful. He made me feel glamorous and treated me like a queen. In fact, I remember I had a particular leotard with black stripes on it. It made me feel very beautiful and I asked him if I could wear it and he said 'Yes'. I had my own hairdresser do my hair. The jewelry was also mine. I was born on Halloween when the witches come out! So it was fun to sort of play that…"

Sally Kirkland and her feline pal meeting Harvey Keitel.
COURTESY MAITLAND MCDONAGH/ADC FILMS.

With the physical effects demands of the project so varied, Tom Savini's work in the film is quite good and far eclipses the rather dull work he would turn in for *Trauma*. When Rod slams that cleaver into Annabel's hand, it's completely believable, and I still cringe. I especially love the mechanical cats used for the strangulation and later the litter of demonic offspring are great fun to watch.

In contrast to the outlandish effects work, the film is shot in a very naturalistic way, highlighting the bizarre and supernatural proceedings. Predicting the look of *Trauma*, while still retaining Argento's lavish camera movement and fluid tracking shots. Even the dream sequence where Rod is ultimately speared to death looks as drab as the rest of the film. From Argento, one would expect a hyper stylized landscape, instead of the medieval British village square (a park of sorts, outside Pittsburgh) we are treated to.

In their first collaboration, Pino Donaggio — longtime composer for Brian De Palma — delivers a frantic and appropriately dizzying score that embraces the schizophrenic mania of Rod Usher and his dwindling mental state. On the opposite side of that, his music for Romero's segment is much more subdued, amping up when the creepers start creeping. After such a successful outing, I can see why Argento asked him back for the next film.

Through his career and life, Argento has always been vocal about his affinity for Poe, and he wasn't the first of his countrymen to release a film based on *The Black Cat*.

Argento's cowriter and AD on several projects, Luigi Cozzi, made his own film of *The Black Cat* — in title only — that has absolutely nothing to do with Edgar Allan Poe or his story of the same name, but was meant to be a an unofficial sequel to *Inferno*. The film was also released in some territories as a sequel to Lamberto Bava's *Demons*. Cozzi's movie revolves around a filmmaker and his writer friend attempting to make a film of the story of The Third Mother, whom they call Levana. Too bad Levana doesn't want her story to be told and really doesn't like the actress hired to play her. Long story short, Levana makes her way into the real world to make sure this film doesn't happen! Any connection this clunker has with either of Argento's films is summed up at a dinner party when the writer of the duo throws Dario's name out just so the audience knows that the filmmaking team in the

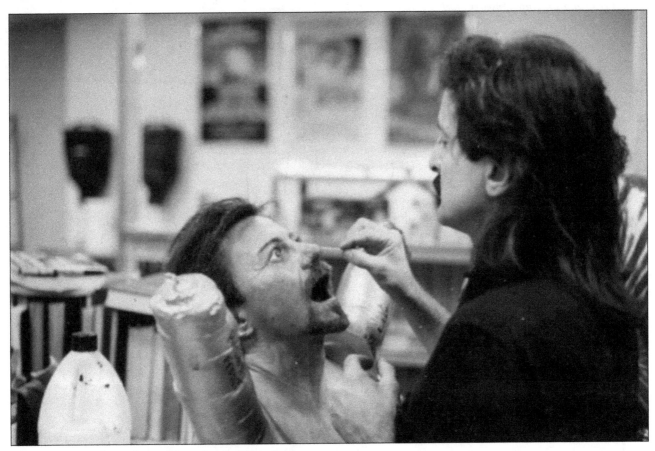

Tom Savini works on the prosthetic head of Keitel. COURTESY MAITLAND MCDONAGH/ADC FILMS.

movie are making a sequel to *Suspiria/Inferno*. That really is all there is plot-wise and it's terrible. There are some random shots of outer space — Cozzi must have had some footage from *Contamination* or *Star Crash* lying around — we have our leading lady seeing an apparition of a little girl in a dress carrying a ball — much like Melissa Graps in Mario Bava's *Kill Baby, Kill*) — who espouses strange "advice" to the leading lady, even from the television at one point.

According to Cozzi:

> *The distributor (Golan, formerly from Cannon) had made a deal to deliver to his clients a horror movie titled The Black Cat, but its producer, Harry Alan Towers, refused to deliver it and broke all deals with the distributor. So the distributor phoned me and said he was going to change the title of my movie in order to use it as a substitute for the missing Black Cat which he had to deliver to his clients who had already paid the advances for it. I had to accept this or I would have been in breach of contract. So I just shot some black cats walking here and there and changed the title… keeping my movie exactly as I had planned it originally aside from the meaningless title and the stupid, useless black cat shots.*

And when I inquired about the fairy/ghost girl who is a guide for the heroine, he said, "It's some sort of voice of conscience or double/split personality of the leading female character as a child."

Needless to say, it is almost guaranteed there will be more adaptations of both of these Poe tales on film in the years to come, and they will invariably be of wildly differing quality. At the opening of Argento's *The Black Cat*, Harvey Keitel says in voiceover, "It's the depravity that's in all of us. Perversity is one of the prime impulses of the heart. Who's never done something just because it was forbidden? To be evil only for the love of being evil?" Both directors have had long careers of making cinematic nightmares for people all across the globe. Is it an evil inclination for them? Surely a fun one if that is so, and it's their "depravity and perversity" that keeps audiences coming back for more, year after year.

INTERVIEW

PAT BUBA

(Editor, 'The Black Cat' — *Two Evil Eyes*)

Buba has a long association with George Romero, having worked on many of his films as editor. Pasquale has become a member of A.C.E. (American Cinema Editors) as he has worked on such films as *Creepshow* (1982), *Day of the Dead* (1985), *Stepfather 2* (1989), *Casino* (1995), *Heat* (1995) and most recently *Salomé* (2013) directed by Al Pacino.

DB: Can you talk a bit about how you got involved with *Two Evil Eyes*?

PB: When I was working on *The Stepfather 2*, I flew to Pittsburgh for a long weekend for a production meeting. Dario and George were there. Originally, George was thinking of doing "The Masque of the Red Death" about the plague. But someone else had just done that story somewhere else, so he showed up with "Valdemar."

DB: Do you remember much about these meetings? Does anything stand out to you?

PB: The first meeting was just a get together, really. And one of the reasons I went back was because Dario was producing the film with [his brother] Claudio. It was mainly an opportunity to meet them in Pittsburgh and I hadn't seen Dario since *Dawn of the Dead*. And luckily, the Italian producers were OK with George working with people he was comfortable with. At that point, I had cut a few of his movies. I was only hired to do George's segment, but ended up doing both. If I recall, when "Valdemar" starts, the credit states that I edited that segment and then later I have a credit as "Executive Editor," whatever that means. But I was hired on to Dario's segment because Claudio [Argento] had attended a screening with Dario of George's part of the film and then asked me to edit "The Black Cat." So I stayed and worked on them both. I was going to fly to Rome to finish the post on it. The final score, sound effects mix. I really wanted to do that. What could be better than hanging out in Rome with Dario? But as it turned out, they ended up finishing it themselves in Rome. So I didn't get to see it until it came back.

DB: Speaking of the post production, Romero has said that he wishes he could have gone back and done some work on the sound, especially on this film.

PB: We weren't involved in it at all. It's nearly wall-to-wall music and that's just not George's style at all. We had it down to a science, how to get a jump out of an audience. We'd always put a sound effect eight sprockets after you saw the first visual. We found that to be the best timing and then we would lower the dialogue slightly before a jump so people would lean in a little bit more. And it worked every time. And back then, effects were all photochemical and there were limitations on audio as well with how much space things took up on the optical track. Now everything is digital, so there isn't that problem. Mixing with George was always fun because we spent a lot of time doing it and he's very selective about sound effects. If I can say this, if there is one film I wish I could go and take a few passes on, I would say it's "The Black Cat." I think in terms of the mix and color timing, "Valdemar" has integrity to it. I would like to take another pass at that dream sequence. There was a lot of footage and what happened was that it was long. At one point, almost twenty minutes long. I cut it down due to run time and when you do that and you don't have the time to redo it, it comes down awkwardly; it's not as rhythmic. I cut out sections as opposed to pulling specific things. It was choppy, as I recall. Sometimes, and hopefully it doesn't happen often, you look at a movie you've done and it looks like a cut instead of a finished film.

DB: Speaking of that sequence, did Dario ever mention why he wanted that sequence to be set in a faux English village or whatever it's supposed to be?

PB: It was just because they had access to that location, Hartwood Acres Park, with that English mansion. My house in *Martin* was not because George was looking for that thing that was written into the script or anything. He took a train ride with my brother from Pittsburgh and saw the house. He never saw the interior until they started shooting. But George gets inspired and spins off from things around him. I'm sure the same is true with Dario: they took him to the location and he was probably just inspired by what was there. That sequence was never fully what it should have been because of the budget. They were wanting more fog, but couldn't afford more gear and the weather wasn't cooperating, so the rain kept interfering and making the fog dissipate. There wasn't a lot of coverage and the makeup was a little cheesy. It looked like makeup as opposed to reality.

DB: Were you around for the shoot of both segments then?

PB: Oh yeah, I was there from the beginning. Two weeks prior to the shoot to set up the cutting room and I was around for the entire shoot of "Valdemar" and then we edited that and then stayed around for Dario's shoot.

DB: Since you were around for the entire shoot, can you tell me what Dario was like dealing with that cast? He's not very well-known to most Americans; did this unfamiliarity work against him, perhaps?

PB: Well, in one sense you're right, but in the film industry, I wouldn't say most actors know who he is, but most behind-the-scenes people are aware of him. I remember when I first became a member of A.C.E. I had a pretty big-name editor of action films at the time tell me how impressed he was that I had worked with Dario. That cast…poor Marty Balsam was pretty old by then. Everyone talks about the references to Poe in the segment, but there's that shot that is a reference to *Psycho* of Marty at the bottom of the stairs and I remember that Marty didn't remember shooting that in *Psycho*. He didn't see the reference.
In fact, there was a section of the movie that was another reference to Poe that was taken out of the film. They had built a set with people buried behind walls and Harvey Keitel was shooting more crime scene photographs with John Amos. Due to time, I think it was removed. I think it was also removed because it was a little too close to the end scene with the girlfriend behind the wall.

DB: I'm assuming you cut as you went along to keep up with the schedule?

PB: Yes, and George shoots a lot of coverage, a lot of interesting little pieces for inserts. It's impossible to keep up day to day with camera, of course, that's a bunch of malarkey. He does give you a lot of alternatives. They were shooting six-day weeks, but George and I would get together and we would talk about it. Then he would go back and do pickup shots for certain things.

DB: You say that George shoots a lot of options for you as an editor. From what I've seen of Dario's work, he's the complete opposite.

PB: "The Black Cat" was one of the first films of Dario's that was going for an American feel and Dario's rhythmic sense is very different from what we're used to. And it was his first film using direct sound. But this was a little different for him and they shot multiple cameras. Harvey got angry once because someone reacted differently than he expected. They shot him first and then once they did the other side, it altered his reaction. "Valdemar" wasn't shot by Michael Gornick, so there was a lot more moving camera and action happening in front of the frame as opposed to action being developed with the editing like *Dawn*, *Knight Riders*, where the action comes out of the edit. "Valdemar" has a more proscenium feel to it.

DB: Let me ask about the lack of a wraparound segment. The film isn't so much an anthology film as it's two shorts films stuck together. Can you discuss this at all in terms of how the film was put together?

PB: They ran out to Baltimore and shot the prologue in the rain at his gravesite and his Baltimore home. Speaking of that footage, I didn't edit that intro section, only the films themselves. Unlike *Creepshow*, where we spent a lot of time weaving the stories together through the guise of the comic book, *Two Evil Eyes* was just kind of "this guy comes back to life, the cop gets shot, there's some blood on some money and then you cut to the second story." There's nothing to lead you from one story to the other.
　　Again, the movie was finished in Italy. If I were there, I would have insisted on *something*. Then again, rhythmically, there is a huge difference between the two guys. George's stories have thought and integrity and make more logical sense even if they're dealing with a subject matter that is impossible. The stories must make sense for him. He's very possessed by that. With Dario, it seems like he's more concerned with birds in the background of a shot. They're two different approaches. One of the highlights for me: Dario brought me an uncut copy of *Opera*, which I watched and it's just an incredible movie.

DB: So back to the lack of a wraparound; I wanted to ask you about Tom Savini's suggestion to have Keitel's character coming into the end of Romero's segment as the photographer of the crime scene and then he "walks into" Argento's. Do you know anything about this?

PB: I'm sure there were a few ideas floated around, but it wouldn't have been possible because Keitel didn't show up until Dario's segment. But that would have been great. The films were made completely independent of each other, though. There was no overlap. But to answer your question more directly, I don't remember anything like that ever being discussed. There was a big concern about the running times. They wanted to keep it under a certain minute count and both films were long. I think George's cut was around 58 minutes, I think, and Dario's was slightly longer.

DB: Can you tell me a little about what it's like to work with both directors as an editor?

PB: Well, George is a great editor in his own right. And I learned a lot about editing by working on his films. He doesn't like to sit in the cutting room and watch what you're doing. George would take a lot of the footage and put it to temp music. I would cut and he would take the reels into another room and put it to the temp score. While doing this, he would come in and say, "Hey man, we should change this or try that." But he's not one who sits by your side while you're making changes. I know his style and his humor to get what he's going for. There was a lot of trust there, so I had a lot of freedom. There was a translator there for Dario, but when Dario would come into the editing room, the translator wasn't around. My Italian was terrible at the time and I had learned as much Italian film terminology as I could. A lot of editing with Dario was that looking at dailies and he would express what he liked in terms of things that interested him. He totally trusted me to do any of the dialogue cuttings and he trusted that it would make sense. There was a shot of Harvey where he was hiding out at the lake and there were these birds in the frame with his head and Dario got really excited. Like I said before, he's much more interested in the rhythm of things and how things happened. The story and the dialogue didn't really matter. We were using Philip Glass to temp score and cutting a film on these old machines. Dario's sitting there pointing out sixteen measures of what he likes and wanting to throw the rest out. They were some long days putting that together. Dario and I would sit and have these great long talks and he's a man of extremes. Everything was "So great or oh so sad. Why is this so sad, Pat?" We always had a good

time and we got along great. Shooting under SAG and DGA regulations was hard on him; he's just not used to it. It pushed him a little in terms of the rigidity. The DP and steadicam operator Nicola Pecorini, who used to work with Bertolucci and who worked on *Opera* and is one of the greatest operators in the world, shot a lot of the movie, although there is another DP credited.

DB: I wanted to ask about meeting Dario on the set of *Dawn of the Dead*?

PB: Well, I wasn't working on that one; I was just a zombie. I threw the first pie and I got eaten. But George was his usual scarf-wearing, happy self and then Dario, if he stood sideways, would just disappear, he was so tiny. But he was very wide-eyed and excited to be there.

DB: Did you ever take Dario to Primanti Bros?

PB: Yes, we did, and we took him to this big Italian restaurant, too, that I don't recall the name of. George, Dario, and I went to this restaurant and I don't think Dario was impressed.

DB: So do you have any really strong memories from the shoot? Anything bizarre that happened? I mean, bizarre outside of it being a Romero/Argento film?

PB: Yes, I remember Asia was, I think, thirteen years old at the time and she would come to watch dailies. She was always very excited watching her father's work. And the producers, who weren't used to shooting direct sound…When you shoot direct sound, you roll sound first, then picture. So you always have more mag audio track to remove. So the assistants have to cut it all out where the cameras are rolling up and slates are called. So working in a hotel, they would brings us these big garbage cans to use as trim bins. I remember the Italian producers coming in the first time to watch dailies and they saw this big bin full of mag and they were grabbing it all by the handfuls, running into the editing room and asking, "Cosa hai fatto?" They wanted me to reuse it! Dario and his company were the producers, but there was no "parent." The situation with Jeff Burr and ITC working on *Stepfather 2* previously, that was rough. They were there every day over our shoulder. This was more like a family making a movie. And Dario was extremely supportive of Romero and his work. And the Argentos were producing the thing and they left him completely alone. The only thing they were concerned with was the running time because they didn't want to end up with a two and a half hour film. They were never critical; they just wanted to see the way he worked and get a feel for his process. They wanted to get a feel of the American crew, too. Dario would see an image from "Valdemar" that he liked during dailies, jump up in front of the screen, kiss it, and then grab his heart.

I have another great memory of going to this bar with the crew on the shoot and Dario would always join us. It was a Monday night. Frank Pearl was the camera operator, Pecorini's assistant. There was a Buffalo game on and Frank was bummed because his team lost. Again, Dario thought this was so sad. "Why is it so sad, Pat?" You could be working on cutting Phillip Glass into strangling a cat and a butterfly would fly past a window and Dario would stop and say, "Look, look, how beautiful." Randomly, the William Penn Hotel that we were all set up at, the Italian producers would go to the Sharper Image store next to door and buy the place out.

TRAUMA

"Do you have a favorite film of yours and why?" I asked Dario on March 4, 2000, while sitting at a small, crowded table in the restaurant of the Fairmont Hotel in San Jose, California. "Yes, I think right now it is *Trauma*. It is good, I am proud of Asia, and the story is close to me. Enough time has passed that I can appreciate it more. But this changes all the time; next year it will be different." I cannot say that I was expecting this answer when I posed this question. For many Argento fans, *Trauma*, and his American output at large, mark the beginning of a decided decline in his career.

I first came upon *Trauma* at a dump bin at a big box electronics store when VHS tapes were being phased out. For a few years, I had been looking for a copy of the film to watch, since a friend in the Midwest had been providing me with bootlegs of many of Argento's films. After some research, I discovered the film was out of print on video tape here in the U.S., and my source was unable to find a copy of this in any form. Imagine my surprise when I ran across a copy for two dollars, brand new, with that hideous artwork of Asia Argento screaming alongside the drawing of the "headhunter." I recall watching the film that very night, and while I enjoyed it, I remember being very underwhelmed by it. Over the years, however, the film has grown in my estimation, and it stands as a good — not great — film that is sadly overlooked in Argento's canon.

Moving across the U.S. from Pittsburgh, Argento and Company settled next in Minneapolis to make *Trauma* with his daughter, Asia, in the lead for the first time. Asia commented that she was quite nervous in taking this role as she didn't want to let her father down their first time working together. She also imparted that working alongside Piper Laurie was a bit nerve-wracking, but that Laurie took a liking to her quickly.

Reportedly inspired by Asia's half-sister Anna's struggles with anorexia, Argento claims it is a niece. In any case, it is a deeply personal project for both Dario and Asia. The film features Piper Laurie playing another madcap mother, after her now legendary performance as Margaret White in Brian De Palma's *Carrie*, Frederic Forrest as a psychiatrist of questionable reputation, and Christopher Rydell as an artist working for the local news who becomes wrapped up in the Petrescu family's latest drama.

A beautiful French Revolution diorama on a black background opens the film. As the camera glides around the little white and grey figures of men and women, a celebratory tune is heard as the crowd cheers excitedly. The camera continues to move until we see a red guillotine, its blade being raised, and slam: down it comes! The crowd raises their arms in a collective roar of approval. British film journalist Alan Jones has said one of the alternate titles of the film was to be *Moving Guillotine*, appropriate given this initial image in front of the main titles, a standout in this film visually and thematically. It's strangely high concept, and theatrical for a film that is so mellow in its tone in every other manner.

In several vital ways, Argento's first American solo film harkens back to his first Italian film, *The Bird with the Crystal Plumage*. They both begin with scenes that introduce us to the antagonist before the protagonist(s). Adriana Petrescu and Monica Ranieri, the female antagonists, use the men in their lives to cover their tracks: Adriana using Dr. Judd and Monica using her husband. And the men do what they do for these manipulative women out of "love", however twisted and confused it may be. Furthermore, both films feature scenes in which the antagonists trap innocents — a young boy in *Trauma* and Julia in *Bird* — and peer at their prey through holes carved into wooden doors. Stuffed with the usual Argento psychology of childhood tragedy, overbearing mothers, and disillusionment with authority, *Trauma* earns its title, and every character has something dark and scary hiding in the back cupboard of his or her mind.

Early on, an alternate title for the film was *A Deeper Red,* and the film also uses many references from that film as well. The murderer's M.O. recalls Martha's in *Deep Red.* Her murderous mother creation needed to hear the lullaby that was playing while she killed her husband, so she carries a tape recorder around to recreate the aural environment of the initial crime.

In *Trauma*, Adriana's child was killed when a storm knocked out the power in the hospital during delivery, so she must kill when it's raining, and in one instance she sets off a fire sprinkler in a hotel room. The murder of Brad Dourif's Dr. Lloyd in an elevator shaft is a call back to the finale of *Deep Red*, as in both instances the machine decapitates the victims. In another set of self-referential moves, Argento has a nosy young boy, who lives across the way from the Petrescu home, save the day, much like the little girl in *Opera*, who saves Betty by guiding her through the air ducts of the apartment building. Predicting *Non Ho Sonno*, the faceless doll in the warehouse of Brad Dourif's death, hints at the

Aura and David; mad love. COURTESY THE DEL VALLE ARCHIVES/OVERSEAS FILM GROUP.

dwarf puppet that is used to confound the police as to the real killer in that later film.

In an unexpected dash of depth and humanity, Argento attempts to give every character some kind of tragedy in their past as a motivator and to make them a bit more relatable than his usual assortment of cold, creative types. Adriana and Stefan have the struggle of being immigrants from another country, but seem to be making a go of it with their business of psychic divination. Although what Stefan does for a living, if anything outside of this, is a mystery. What is his role here? Aura is a young girl who is severely damaged by her own inner demons from the outset, only to be torn down even more by the death of both her parents. David obviously has very little self-worth as he is in a "relationship" with a domineering woman who treats him as a diversion. His drug problems are brought up almost immediately upon meeting Aura, when she insists she is fine and then throws up what she has eaten, before walking out on him after stealing his wallet. She may not be a drug addict but she does have an eating disorder, and she is a thief; she's far from "fine." In the work print version of this scene, it is the same up until the point where Aura leaves for the bathroom and David discovers she has stolen his wallet, but differs as he calls her a bitch. The line is taken out in the current version, perhaps to make David a bit more sympathetic.

Aura and David's relationship contributes an element of almost pedophilic lust and love, something Argento has never explored previously, but would later in *Phantom of the Opera*. While it is never expressly stated what David's age is, he must be somewhere around thirty and Aura, we know, is sixteen. Although age of consent in many states in the U.S. is fifteen and sixteen, there is something uncomfortable about their budding romance. Given that societal discomfort, it is probably one of the sweetest and most nurturing relationships in any of Argento's films. In addition to the romance between the two leads, there is the lesbian relationship between Hope Alexander-Willis' Linda Quirk and her girlfriend Alice played by Jacqui Kim. Their love life is merely alluded to and it's not terribly obvious it's there unless you look for it. With typical Argento style nothing is made of the lesbian couple it is so mild. He wouldn't go full on girl on girl "action" until *Do You Like Hitchcock?*

The character of Dr. Judd, with his own brand of junk psychology, brings to mind psychiatrists in films past, from Simon Oakland in *Psycho* delivering that classically dreadful monologue to wrap everything up, to another Dr. Judd played by Tom Conway, who does little to help Simone Simon with her fears of homeland folk tales she fears will come to pass if she is intimate with her husband in *The Cat People*. In an interview on the set of the film, Forrest said of Dr. Judd, "Dr. Tom is a little off the wall; he's had his license revoked a few times…he's having an affair with Adriana, Piper Laurie's character." Could this less than flattering portrayal of psychiatry tell us something of Argento's disdain for the profession? After all, everyone at the Farraday Clinic seems to be a bit shady and have as many skeletons in their closets as any other character in this world the film portrays. The doctors are just as damaged as their patients, so ultimately, who is really helping who?

Trauma's decided lack of blood and violence was an attempt at tapping into the American market, and Tom Savini took the job hoping for a repeat of the extensive work he had done on *Two Evil Eyes*. There are a few set pieces in the film that do retain some of the trademark Argento vision and oddity. Three of the murder victims express vocally, after being killed, while a man witnessing a murder of a nurse is shocked into further silence as he is in a state of catatonia.

In one of the film's standout set pieces, Linda Quirk (Hope Alexander-Willis) is decapitated in her hotel room after fleeing David and Aura, and she has a line after her head is cut off. Willis has a very impressive resumé having worked with Tennessee Williams, creating a role in his later career play *This is (an Entertainment)*. She told me of making *Trauma* and working with Dario:

I'm beyond claustrophobic. And I get on set; they had built this prosthesis for my neck…so the assistant director says to me, "You need to crawl on your stomach under this platform and put your head through this hole in the floor." So they put me in a situation where I can't move my arms and legs; I was panicking. I asked if they could lower the floor onto me instead of having to crawl into place. Well, Dario fucking flips out! Finally, he convinces me to do it. And he says that if something goes wrong or I get really uncomfortable, they would lift the floor off of me so I wouldn't have to crawl back out…So then we get into position and Dario puts all this blood on me. Then they start the water. The water is hitting my face and my eyes and it's making me blink. And Dario screams, "Cut, no, no, no, you can't blink!" But

A collage of photos from the U.S. presskit. COURTESY JOE ZASO/OVERSEAS FILM GROUP.

the water is hitting my eyes and I can't help it but to blink. And Dario is screaming, "She needs more blood on her! Give me the blood!"

Rafaelle Mertes's cinematography along with Billy Jett's production design create a smoky, film noir look in color. But even the color that is there appears toned down to the point of an almost sepia tone. The interior and exterior locations and sets are all full of wood, giving the film a very American, and in turn suburban, look, unique to the Midwest. Instead of trying to make the film look like anything he had made before, Argento embraced the warmth of the environment in which he was filming. The surrounding natural environments, the forested area outside Linda Quirk's home as well as David's with the lake provide a contrast to the flat and ugly sprawl of America. There are no picket fences with nicely manicured lawns where happy families have barbeques; merely familial nightmares. Jett's sets, specifically Dr. Judd's office create a strange atmosphere of dread which one shouldn't be feeling where one should be comfortable. His design team's strange use of a glass model of a human head which is stuffed and wrapped with what appears to be gauze that is lit from beneath is truly creepy and would look at home in *The Texas Chainsaw Massacre*.

An important part of the visual theme and aesthetic of Argento's canon is insects and animals and *Trauma* is no exception. In this film the predator/prey relationship among the human world around him is shown writ large by a natural act of survival. The nosy neighborhood child played by Cory Garvin is out one day studying butterflies when he spies a gecko eating one. This "simple" shot was anything but as Billy Jett told me about the difficulties of raising butterflies and dealing with the geckos to make this happen.

Well, without getting the society of lizard protection after me, we had to keep the geckos at certain temperatures. We didn't have an animal wrangler on this film. I had to build a butterfly habitat in our office. I lost a whole crop when someone left the door open where the habitat was. They are very delicate, and one day I came to work and they were all dead. The geckos, we learned are terrible, they bite you. We had them in coolers at various temperatures so

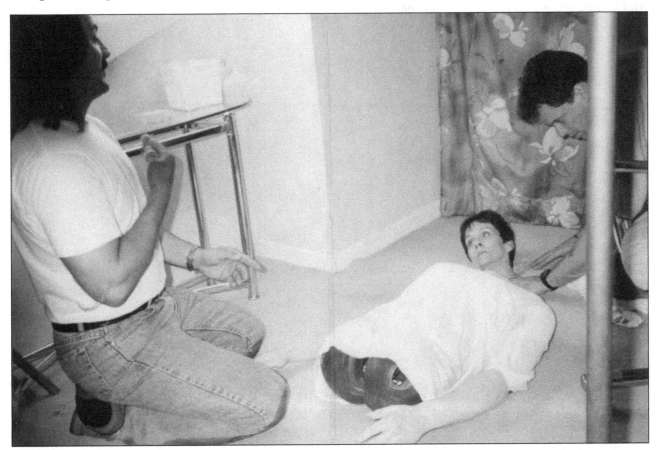

Hope Alexander-Willis readies for her close-up while Tom Savini explains the setup. COURTESY HOPE ALEXANDER-WILLIS.

they would be easier to work with. But that shot of the gecko eating the butterfly was just a straight ahead second unit bit. We lucked out and got it. There was no effect; we just had to make it happen. He [Dario] is the maestro and things would just pop into his head and it's a challenge for us to make them happen.

In his second collaboration with Argento, Pino Donaggio provides a very energetic and at-odds score that doesn't consistently match the visuals like some of Morricone's "experimental" work on *Four Flies on Grey Velvet* and much of Goblin's output for Argento. Donaggio does contribute his Herrmann winking "swirling" cues a few times, and overall, it's a good composition, especially when experienced apart from the film. The work print of the film is temp scored with some familiar music ranging from pieces of Danny Elfman's *Beetlejuice* score to Enya's *On Your Shore* — during the scene in which David jumps into the lake behind his house after he fears Aura has drowned herself.

In *Broken Mirrors, Broken Minds*, Maitland McDonagh writes, "Overall, Argento seems to be reaching back with *Trauma*, trying to rework elements that have succeeded in the past and give them a contemporary gloss. But he's treading water, rehashing material without revitalizing it." At the time, that may have been the case, however, time has been kind to the film. I feel its neo noir visuals and "family friendly" gore factor set it apart from much of Argento's later work — *The Card Player* being equally as bloodless as an exception. *Trauma's* story is intriguing with some very strange characters, and, if nothing else, it is notable for the fact that it is the first time Argento directed his younger daughter in some very troubling situations. After his second experiment in America, Argento would return home to Italy and produce what is arguably the best film of his later career, starring Asia again: 1996's *The Stendhal Syndrome*.

INTERVIEW

BILLY JETT

(Production Designer, Trauma)

Billy Jett is the production designer on Trauma and has worked behind the scenes as production designer and art director on projects on the small and big screen. Jett has had a long working relationship with Charles Band on many films from *Demonic Toys* (1992) and the newer film, *Ooga Booga* (2012). In television he has worked on the TV series *On the Lot,* and *Unsolved Mysteries.*

DB: So how did you get involved with the Italian film industry?

BJ: It was Ovidio Assonitis, who made *The Curse* and its sequel. Then I worked on *Sonny Boy.* These got me in with a group of Italian filmmakers who did quite a few films over in the U.S. Prior to that, I had worked on bigger budget things as a set dresser and prop masters. What the Italians did was they let me become an art director. Prior to that, I was headed toward bigger budget union films as a set decorator; I would work as the props person, the art department in general.

DB: Tell me a little about *The Curse* and its sequel. I noticed they were released as a double feature here in the U.S. on DVD.

BJ: *The Curse 2* was radioactive snakes and Screaming Mad George did the FX on that. Prior to those was *Sonny Boy*; David Carradine plays a woman in drag. Brad Dourif was in it as well. It was very disturbing; a lot of people list it as a cult film. These people steal a baby and raise it in the desert. We shot that in New Mexico. A lot of great filmmakers from Italy would come over here and knock these things out really fast and then go back home and work for Bertolucci. I learned a lot from these guys just about color and lighting and the process of filmmaking; they had a very different way of looking at things.

DB: Do you recall how you got the job working on *Trauma*?

BJ: David Pash was the executive producer and I think he got my name through some of the Italian filmmakers I had worked with previously. Typically, the executive producers are the money people, but David was really hands on. I don't have a clear recollection of the process of me being hired. I know that Dario, when asked why I got the job, is because he had seen other horror films I had worked on and other people he was looking at for the job didn't have the experience with horror movies.

DB: For a horror movie and for what Dario does, *Trauma* looks like all the life is drained out of it. Like making a black and white movie in color. Can you talk about the overall look of it?

BJ: We all worked closely together on all of that as far as the look. It was shot on location in Minneapolis. Other than the basements, they were existing places that we dressed. It was reality based. All of our sets were steeped in reality as opposed to a fantasy setting. Everything was talked about in those terms of being as it would be in the real world. I think the art department did a good job and the local crew was all very good. It was interesting in that there were things we did that maybe weren't noticed. This is something I've never done before for a film: I raised butterflies. Dario wanted butterflies and it wasn't the season for that. How do you get butterflies? The close up shot of the gecko eating the butterfly, I thought that was pretty amazing. That we pulled that off was amazing. It was very difficult to do.

DB: How do you make that happen? How can you set that shot up?

BJ: Well, without getting the society of lizard protection after me, we had to keep the geckos at certain temperatures. We didn't have an animal wrangler on this film. I had to build a butterfly habitat in our office. I lost a whole crop. They are very delicate and one day, I came to work and they were all dead. The geckos, we learned, are terrible; they bite you. We had them in coolers in various temperatures so they would be easier to work with. But that shot of the gecko eating the butterfly was just a straight ahead second unit bit. We lucked out and got it. There was no effect; we just had to make it happen.

He is the maestro and things would just pop into his head and it's a challenge for us. He puts it on the table and asks if we can do it. Can we rise to the challenge? Piper Laurie's head after she gets decapitated was another challenge. We did it on an elevated platform and it was pretty effective. She was under the floor to get that shot. The basement, we wanted that harsh look. There was so much light pumped into that space, I recall the wood almost burning, it was so hot. Dario wanted this certain look, this bright sunlight coming through the windows, it was all a set on a stage. We wanted to accommodate.

DB: In terms of your collaboration of working with Rafaelle Mertes, how did that conversation go? Would you do your work first and then he would lay out how he wanted to light it?

BJ: Traditionally, I throw everything into the hands of the DP across the board after talking to the director. Film is light, so I have to provide the opportunities in my design to allow them to light. And when we talked about the amount of the light coming in, I had to adjust some of the structural pieces. The windows had to match up with what would really be there on that house.

DB: The interior of Frederic Forrest's office, he's holding that glass head and above him, there is another head sitting there that is lit from within. It's really creepy and looks as if it has skin.

BJ: You're starting to notice some stuff, then. There were subtle things we tried to pop in there, the set dresser Jackie Jacobson. She went on to be a successful set decorator in New York. She would find pieces that would pop up and that would be it. Forrest had some input on that. He wanted to throw in his two cents, which we then had to accommodate.

DB: Do you remember what that head was supposed to be? Do you recall the reason for it being there?

BJ: We tried to add something to his personality; it was there to fit his character. It was something a little odd. I do it all the time; it may not make a whole lot of sense, but maybe it catches the light. In the case of that, we tried to keep up with the head motif. So that glowing head just seemed to work. Jackie scoured the town. There aren't prop houses there, so you really have to get out and hunt around. I keep a lot of things dark and I've gotten work because people say that I really know how to work with the dark. Especially now with HD, I think things are darker in my work because of lighting skin tones. But then it just felt like the way to

go with that house, the séance scene. I remember that beautiful tablecloth in that room.

DB: That set, the way it's shot, if you look into the corners, you can't really see anything. But it looks like a nicely dressed set, the details. But you never really see it because it's in the dark.

BJ: But see, that's OK because it's not a theatrical-looking film. I didn't want it to look like a cliché of a horror movie. That was a beautiful house to work in. And you didn't want to make anything look out of place in the set. We just wanted to keep it real. It's all about the characters and we know where we are; it doesn't need subtitling to explain it.

DB: It's a nice set because they're immigrants and how they would live is a nice contrast in the outside world. You see things there that you wouldn't see anywhere else in the film.

BJ: You said it better than I could. It's a collaborative effort at that point. We're trying to make it happen and find these things and you don't always know if they're going to show up.

DB: The house where the lesbian couple lives, there is a statue of a naked woman's torso in the front yard. In the film, that statue tells you they're a couple.

BJ: It was subtly there and it asks the question for you just like you said. And not many people notice things that like. Another thing I did was I stuck some subway signs around the streets and there is no subway in Minneapolis, but again, we're trying to create this "anywhere" environment. And they were put there to confuse you a little. There is also a scene where Asia and Chris are in the diner and we put the subway signs there, too.

DB: Do you recall who created the guillotine diorama that opens the movie?

BJ: That was Nancy Darby, who was the Art Director. I worked with her and my crew to construct that. It came out really nice; it's really interesting.

DB: Was that meant to be used anywhere else or was it strictly for the credit sequence?

BJ: It was made just for that bit. Dario is very specific with things like that. There is the scene with the curtains with the embroidery on it that was not scripted, but something he thought up; he said it came from a dream. And we had to create it. It was a nice scene. It came out beautiful.

DB: Well, you bring that up, it's a very bright, white scene and you contrast that with the rest of the movie, which is really brown and drab.

BJ: A lot of that was just organic to the location, the woods and the interior of that house. So we decided to visually make the entire film look natural.

DB: The decapitation of Hope Alexander, was that an actual location?

BJ: Yes, it was completely done on site at the hotel, just dressed the room with a fake water sprinkler and the false floor. We flooded that room a bit, actually. So the people that were in that suite the next day had a great surprise. It was a big suite that we kinda just cut in half. And Hope was a trooper; there was water everywhere, down her throat, up her nose, in her eyes. It had to be rough on her. She was basically being water boarded. I was in that room that day doing the water gag myself. She was down under that floor for a while. You try and make those false floors as comfortable as you can, but you're in a big box and sometimes you can't do that much with it.

INTERVIEW

HOPE ALEXANDER-WILLIS

(Linda Quirk, *Trauma*)

A longtime devotee of the theater, Hope Willis has an impressive resume on the stage, having worked with Tennessee Williams, John Houseman, and John Astin in various capacities. On the screen she has been in such features as *The Other Sister* (1999), *Frankie and Johnnie* (1991), and both *The Princess Diaries* films (2001 and 2004). She now directs and teaches theater in the Chatanooga, Tennessee area.

DB: How did you get involved in this project?

HW: It was just your standard audition. Dario and the producers liked me, so I got the role. Then they flew me out to Minneapolis to make the movie.

DB: With your theater background, had you worked with any of the other actors?

HW: Just Fred [Frederic Forrest] from a previous job. So that was fun.

DB: Just to clarify, you have watched the movie?

HW: Yes, when it first came out, so it's been a while. I didn't really like it. But mainly because I don't like horror movies; I don't like to be scared. However, my son, when he found out I was working with Dario, totally flipped out. He was wildly excited; he loves the genre, so yeah, it was big points.

DB: Did you take your son to the set or to meet him?

HW: No, he grew up in the industry, so he's met a lot of people. That doesn't faze him.

DB: What were Piper Laurie and Brad Dourif like to work with? They seem very high energy and really intense.

HW: Well, Piper was great. A few of us in the film are theater people, so that was our hook into each other. Dominique, he's with an extraordinary theater company in Minneapolis, so a lot of us sat around talking about theater.

DB: Since several of you came from the theater, was there any kind of feeling among you that this wasn't "high art?"

HW: Not at all; just because you're doing theater doesn't mean you're doing "high art." I've done a lot of bad plays. I think what people forget is this is a business, so you're lucky if you have a remarkable experience with something or you feel like you've contributed something to the culture through your art. Most of the time, it's business. Some days are good, some are bad. Sometimes it goes well, sometimes not. But it isn't always an inspiring, life-affirming thing.

DB: Piper Laurie's performance in this alludes to Margaret White in *Carrie*, of course, but her performance here is so nuts.

HW: That's working with Dario; he encourages you to go over the top. But off camera, there's none of that. There's nothing "out of the box" about her; she's very professional.

DB: Well, some of them are much more subdued. Chris Rydell is very much the straight guy and he plays it very mellow. And Asia seems a bit skittish and nervous.

HW: I think she was intimidated by Piper.

DB: So about your role and the actress who played your girlfriend? Some people that I've watched the movie with aren't totally convinced you're anything but roommates.

HW: Funny, when I would tell people about the movie, I would tell them I play a lesbian who gets beheaded. And my head talks after I'm dead!

DB: So let's talk about your murder scene.

HW: OK, so here's what happened. I gotta tell you, I'm beyond claustrophobic. And I get on set; they had built this prosthesis for my neck. So the assistant director says to me, "You need to crawl on your stomach under this platform and put your head through this hole in the floor." So they put me in a situation where I can't move my arms and legs. I was panicking. I asked if they could lower the floor onto me instead of having to crawl into place. Well, Dario fucking flips out! Finally, he convinces me to do it. And he says that if something

goes wrong or I get really uncomfortable, they would lift the floor off of me so I wouldn't have to crawl back out. And I believed them, but I don't think they would have done this. I don't think Dario cared about my mental state at this point. So again, I agreed to this, but I said someone had to be down in there with me holding my hand. So this poor grip is trapped under this thing with me and the floor was only built up a few feet off the ground. So I keep thinking "Don't fart, don't fart…" This poor guy is under there six inches from my ass and I'm thinking, "I'm going to kill this man." So then we get into position and Dario puts all this blood on me. Then they start the water. The water is hitting my face and my eyes and it's making me blink. And Dario screams, "Cut, no, no, no you can't blink!" But the water is hitting my eyes and I can't help it but to blink. And Dario is screaming, "She needs more blood on her! Give me the blood!" This went on for quite a while, the blinking, the water, and the blood. And that water wasn't heated and then with the blood, it would go down into that hole and into my clothes. After a while, I was laying in the cold, sticky pool of yuck. And then finally, it was done and as promised, they lifted the floor off of me.

DB: How long would you estimate this took?

HW: A few hours; it was awful. But what can you do? It's a job. I shot a series in Europe, in Germany for a month and Budapest for a few more, and I swore I would never go to Germany, but you don't turn down work.

DB: So let me ask you about Dario as a director. You said he got pretty upset about this whole situation. I've never seen him lose his cool; maybe it was the language barrier with the crew, wasn't helping things?

HW: Well, he was just very Italian. I wouldn't even call it temper or whatever. He was just very expressive in Italian. And he has the energy of a kid, very much like a kid.

DB: So do you have any other memories of the shoot other than your own trauma of being trapped under that floor?

HW: Not really. I think the biggest thing was that when you're an actor, nobody says to you, "Do you want to do this? Can you do this?" It's just assumed that since you're an actor, and this is one reason I stopped acting and started directing, it's assumed you're just going to do it. It was surprising how little empathy there was. Although I understand that and again, as a director now, I certainly understand it a lot more than I used to. He wasn't really asking me to do that much. When I was working in Hungary, I had a director who wanted me to go up onto a window ledge of an old fifteenth century castle. So going underneath a constructed floor isn't that bad compared to that.

DB: So did you go out onto that ledge?

HW: No, I learned to say "Fuck you, actors aren't props" in Hungarian. I've unfortunately forgotten how to say that over time. But then it was handy.

DB: Well, you say that "actors aren't props" and that's something leveled at Dario fairly often. That he doesn't really care about actors. And the camera is really what matters. Did you get this impression?

HW: Not really, no, but you have to remember that film is a director's medium, not an actor's medium. Editors and producers also have a lot of control. But no, I never thought that was the case at all. I thought he respected us even though he could be very strict and controlling at times about certain things.

LA SINDROME DI STENDHAL
THE STENDHAL SYNDROME

After an attempt at cracking the U.S. market with *Two Evil Eyes* and *Trauma*, Argento returned to Italy to make a complex, abstract, and challenging film that stands as a unique piece of art from a newly invigorated filmmaker. *The Stendhal Syndrome* is suggested by the writing of Dr. Graziella Margherini, an Italian psychoanalyst and psychiatrist who was the director of the mental health services of the Florence City Center. She would see many tourists come into the hospital suffering from the same symptoms: panic attacks, depression, and excitement. Some even had "a misperception of reality…reality had become threatening, scary, causing insomnia and a need to be cured," according to Margherini.

The patients also often suffered from "a crisis of identity, a loss of one's self. The motivating causes were the journey, being far away from home, an intense artistic sensibility and the encounter with great works of art, that is the power of images." Margherini was the first person to give the syndrome a name, inspired by the writings of the French writer Stendhal, who, in a journal titled *From Milan to Reggio Calabria* on January 17, 1817, wrote that when he entered the church of Santa Croce, a strong emotion overtook him, and that he felt himself lose his balance. This caused him to leave the church and retire to a nearby bench. He explained that the only thing capable of calming him down was the writing of Ugo Foscolo, who conveyed the difficult feelings of fainting. Something in this indirect commiseration allowed Stendhal to regroup and later write about the experience.

After the initial attempt by Argento to shoot the film in the U.S., it was decided to shoot in Italy, partially due to both of the leading actresses backing out of the project: first Bridget Fonda and then, reportedly, Daryl Hannah. Dario decided to take a huge risk and hang the entire film on his daughter, Asia, after she had done him well in *Trauma*. She had also, at that point, starred in the critically acclaimed film by Patrice Chéreau, *La Reine Margot*, alongside her soon-to-be costar Thomas Kretschmann and *Suspiria*'s Miguel Bosé.

Forgoing his hometown of Rome and his home away from home, Turin, as the singular location for the film, Argento jumps all over the country, shooting in Rome, Florence, and Viterbo. Florence is especially important, not only because of the Uffizi Gallery but also the Arno River and the Ponte Vecchio, providing a rich cultural and historical texture that had really only been present in any prominent way in *Opera*. With *The Stendhal Syndrome*, Argento really embraces his country's heritage, showing off the living museum that is Florence while also turning us on to its darker side as well, as is typical in his visions of hell that are Rome and Turin in many of his films.

Italy is a largely Catholic country, and even though the church's grasp is loosening as time goes on as Europe becomes less religious, it's interesting there are so few religious allusions in the film, seeing as Italy is drowning in religious art. One of the more "blasphemous" moments comes when Anna runs from Alfredo's car, and instead of chasing her, he gets out of the car, gun in hand, pants partially undone, and stretches out his arms in a crucified Christ-like pose. This is echoed in the ending when Anna is carried away by a group of police in a reflection of Michelangelo's *Pieta*, arguably one of the most famous pieces of religious sculpture.

Catholicism is replaced by psychology, the religion of the mind. After Anna's initial trauma, she doesn't run to the church or seek the aid of a priest for spiritual and emotional guidance. She solely seeks the aid of Dr. Cavanna (Paolo Bonacelli) at the behest of the police department. Bonacelli famously appeared in Pasolini's film *Salò* as "The Duke," one of the "Fascist Four" who torture and abuse a group of teenagers for their own amusement. Strangely, in an inversion of roles, Argento plays the mad aggressor here and Bonacelli the gentle caregiver.

For his opening credit sequence, Argento chose a series of distinct paintings from artists as diverse as Andy Warhol to Rembrandt, scrolling along the right side of the frame and it sets a disquieting mood. Morricone's hypnotic and haunting theme, easing the viewer into this strange new world, transitions the scene from the credits to following a yet unnamed Anna (Asia Argento) walking through a crowd outside the Uffizi Gallery in Florence. As she passes a statue, the point of view is obtuse — an impossibility given that she is walking straight past it. Yet, from her perspective, it is frightening and distorted. The Stendhal

Syndrome is already taking hold of her and the audience collectively.

Once Anna steps into the museum, its labyrinth-like layout mirrors her mental state, which begins to collapse as the frescoed ceilings come alive. They begin to cause her to forget why she is even there in the first place. She journeys farther and farther into the museum, the score becoming more and more circuitous, echoing Anna's weakening inner self. Once she pauses in front of *Federico da Montefeltro and his Wife* by Piero della Francesca, she is literally beginning to splinter as the framed diptych behind her head suggests: the male and female emerging or invading. The image also predicts what will become of Anna's later psychotic male/female mental struggle.

After nearly eight minutes of a dialogue-free sequence, Anna is stunned by Caravaggio's *Medusa*, its seeming emergence from the canvas causing her to faint and hallucinate herself into *The Landscape and the Fall of Icarus* by Bruegel, where she hits her head on the ocean floor. As she swims back up, she encounters a giant grouper fish with a human face, which she kisses. Maitland McDonagh writes in the expanded edition of

Argento and Argento at the Uffizi Gallery in Florence, Italy, shooting The Stendhal Syndrome. COURTESY THE DEL VALLE ARCHIVES.

Broken Mirrors, Broken Minds of this sequence: "Bizarre to begin with, the image becomes grotesquely significant in light of the fact that many types of grouper are 'protogynous hermaphrodites,' creatures that grow up female and then become male."

Gender issues strike an interesting note in the characters concerned in the film's love triangle between Anna, Marco, and Marie. After Alfredo's first attack, Anna cuts off her hair at the hospital in an attempt to transform herself into somebody else, become potentially "less attractive," and put some distance between her older, abused self and bring about a new woman, as she becomes physically more "male." Both her brother and Marco comment on her new look, driving her deeper into herself.

One night, while Marco (Marco Leonardi) is over at Anna's house, she snaps at the mere suggestion of anything sexual, turns him around, and dry humps him, saying, "You want to fuck me? I'm fucking you!" as he begs her to stop. Although she later tells her doctor that the idea of sex disgusts her, she has found analogues for the sexual act in eating chocolate, which she never liked before, and cutting herself because, as she says, "It makes me feel alive."

Alfredo Grossi (Thomas Kretschmann) stands as one of Argento's most interesting characters to date. He is married and by all counts lives a very normal life; to look at him, it would be hard for anyone to not be attracted to him. When Anna first meets him outside of the Uffizi Gallery, he is quite gallant, checking after her wellbeing and even offering to pay for her cab ride. However, as their next encounter proves, he is nothing but a monster in a nice suit. Yet he is convinced that he is doing Anna some good in torturing her and that she is deriving some pleasure from this. "Come with me," he pleads as he is raping her the first time. He is driven by pure hatred, it seems, and has no motive for what he does. There is no conversation to understand his mentality, he doesn't make any excuses, and he clearly relishes the pain he inflicts.

In contrast to Alfredo, Anna is rather meek and insecure, a young and naïve detective who feels her lack of experience betray her once she is attacked by the object of her hunt. Argento turns the audience's expectations inside out by giving us a hero who is anything but, yet we are still on her side, even when it is revealed that she has been murdering people. Call it the "Norman Bates Effect." It's interesting how easy it

Asia Argento applies another layer to her delusion. COURTESY MAITLAND MCDONAGH/MEDUSA.

can be to manipulate the thinking of your audience. As long as you set up enough humanity in someone, you can forgive almost anything.

William Friedkin's controversial film, *Cruising*, has Al Pacino playing a character, Steve Burns, who is very similar to Anna. He, too, is a young cop sent out on assignment to investigate a murder and like Anna, he gets lost in his investigation and becomes someone, in time, neither he nor his girlfriend recognize. Steve, previously strictly heterosexual as far as we are concerned in the story, becomes deeply entrenched in the gay S&M subculture of New York City in a capacity that far exceeds "research." Both of these characters have not only their conscious minds and lives twisted into something new but their entire sexual being morphs them into something and someone else. As the previously mentioned scene with Marco's "rape" at the hands of Anna's aggressive exorcism of her damage, Steve goes home to his girlfriend (Karen Allen) and has some unexpectedly rough sex with her in much the same manner.

Jung said, "Woman is compensated by a masculine element and therefore her unconscious has, so to speak, a masculine imprint. This results in a considerable psychological difference between men and women, and accordingly I have called the projection-making factor in women the animus, which means mind or spirit." Anna's animus comes to the fore once she has killed Alfredo. In taking his life to avenge her own pain and suffering, she has absorbed his pathology. Her "shadow" self and her animus meld, creating yet another person inside of her. This new male self must be disguised because she is female, so she wears a long blond wig, reminiscent of his hair, takes to wearing long, white, flowing gowns, like the clean white suit she first sees him wearing at the gallery and even the white tank top he wears while raping her. In becoming a new "Anna/Alfredo," she has transformed into a Grecian goddess, a vision of the epitome of female beauty. Anna's newly discovered aggressive sexuality springs to life when she meets a young art student named Marie Beyle (the given name of Stendhal was Henri Marie-Beyle) in an art store while the two are looking at prints. She slams the rack into his hand and laughs, enjoying that she has caused him some pain through the flirting.

Anna's malefic unraveling begins even before the first attack by Alfredo in her hotel room at the Albergo Porta Rossa (Hotel Red Door). Argento, setting the action at that specific hotel, at least in name, brings to mind a place of violence and evil, a portal to hell, perhaps even illicit sexual encounters, not rest and relaxation. After taking a few pills to help her sleep, Anna has a terrible dream — or is it a hallucination — in which she exits the hotel room through a copy of Rembrandt's *Night Watch* to get us into a scene that explains why Anna is in Florence: to hunt down a rapist and murderer.

The Porta Rossa district, where the hotel sits, has a long history of being an artistic and social center of town for centuries. And Florence itself has had a prominence in art, ranging wildly from the works of the Renaissance Masters to Ridley Scott's film *Hannibal*. In Puccini's comic opera *Gianni Schicchi*, the aria "O Mio Babbino Caro" is sung by a young woman, Lauretta, in mourning over a relationship that her father doesn't approve of. Lauretta begs her father to give his blessing and threatens to throw herself from the Ponte Vecchio into the Arno River after saying she will go to the Porto Rossa to buy her own wedding ring! Italian art is full of violence and overblown emotional reactions, and Dario's film is no exception. The Stendhal Syndrome itself is an oversensitivity to artwork, often causing violent reactions. Could it also be seen as a comment on art inspiring violence, as many parental watch groups are so apt to shout when the social winds are blowing in the right direction?

"Maybe I should try to paint something myself," Anna tells her doctor in an attempt at some exposure therapy. Anna decides upon returning to the "warmth" of home in Viterbo and the site of her first bout of The Stendhal Syndrome at the Etruscan museum as a child, to paint to confront this demon that haunts her. After covering herself in paint instead of putting it to canvas, she lies on the floor, curled into a fetal position, suggesting a rebirth of sorts or the first steps of her transformation into Anna/Alfredo. The next time we see her room, it is full of paintings, all of the same thing: a screaming face with tears running down it.

The film is overrun by male characters, but ruled by a single woman. Anna allows almost every man to come and go as she feels the need to use them to her own ends. Her boyfriend falls by the wayside after her trauma, and she completely forgets about him once she meets Marie. Dr. Cavanna and Marco become victims of her lust for power and aggression. In a scene during the film's conclusion, Dr. Cavanna tells her, "It's time to shake off the lies like you would an old winter coat when summer comes," which strangely causes a confession to bubble up out of her. Visually, she is lit in a strangely film-noir-like manner, her eyes limned in a sliver of light similar to the shadows of the Venetian blinds in Dr. Cavanna's office — another noir callback. Again, is this merely a doctor's office or a confessor's box?

As the romance with Marie (Julien Lambroschini) heats up, her relationship with Marco cools considerably, to the point where she sneaks out of her own apartment to see Marie at the museum where he works as an assistant. This pivotal scene that starts as a romantic meeting turns ugly, when he is murdered while cleaning up and readying to leave for the evening out with Anna. The depth of Anna's deception to others and herself is illuminated when it is revealed that she is the one who murdered Marie. It seems there is a switch hidden in her that she cannot control when around a man, whether he is desired or reviled. She simply cannot help herself but to continue feeding the vengeance demon that lurks inside her fractured psyche. Anna's new ego cannot handle the contradiction of her selves, so she has to eliminate him and every male who she now sees as a potential threat.

From the earliest days of his career, Argento has been pegged the "Italian Hitchcock" and nowhere is that more evident psychologically than in this film. The two sides of Anna can be read as kindred spirits to the two Kim Novaks in *Vertigo* — Madeleine and Judy. In both cases, a male force creates the two sides of the same woman. Apart from the psychology of the female figure, both films have prominent scenes in museums, The Legion of Honor in San Francisco and the Uffizi Gallery in Florence, which bring to question the mental state and identity of our female protagonist. In *Vertigo*, Bernard Herrmann's score creates a swirling and dizzying mood as Kim Novak sits in front of a portrait of the mysterious Carlotta, creating a vortex of confusion and intrigue. *The Stendhal Syndrome* features Ennio Morricone's similarly circular theme with Anna wandering through the Uffizi, and the audience has no idea who she is. She has no identity and she is a huge question mark, much like Madeleine at that equal scene in *Vertigo*.

The Stendhal Syndrome constitutes a welcome change from the watered down work Argento turned in during his creative stay in the United States. It is a brave, strange, and challenging film that has no equal in anything Argento has created, standing as a singular achievement by an established and exalted genre veteran. For his next outing, Argento would tackle Gaston Leroux's *The Phantom of the Opera*, his first period horror film.

The two Kim Novaks being threatened by an unknown male assailant…James Stewart, perhaps? COURTESY THE DEL VALLE ARCHIVES/PARAMOUNT PICTURES.

IL FANTASMA DELL'OPERA
THE PHANTOM OF THE OPERA

"Isn't it strange to watch this story and it's *not* a musical?" My grandmother, with whom I watched *The Phantom of the Opera* the first time I saw it, said to me from across the couch in her living room. As a fan of the Webber musical since childhood, every version of the story gets measured with that musically infective yardstick. In place of the iconic white half mask as worn by Michael Crawford in the original production of the show in London in 1986, Argento's Phantom is the first in film and stage history to not don a mask, but in its place a long, waist length blond wig. It is a puzzling characterization decision that is intended to highlight the "horrors inside," laying everything bare and perhaps attempting to make this Phantom a heavy metal anti-hero.

Christine Daae (Asia Argento) is a young singer in the Paris Opera, currently the understudy of Carlotta (Nadia Rinaldi), the resident diva of the company. One night, Christine meets a mysterious man (Julian Sands) in a hallway in the theater, and they have an instant psychic connection. Soon, Christine is devoted to this mysterious man; she spurns the advances of Baron Raoul De Chagny (Andrea Di Stefano) and is oblivious to the attentions of her handmaiden Honorine (Coralina Cataldi-Tassoni). While this sordid love story unfolds, the legend of "The Phantom" grows, as various people disappear or show up dead. Little does Christine know that her mysterious stranger, with whom she is having a psychic and sexual affair at the expense of everything, is the "Phantom" in question. And by the time she figures it out, she has passed the point of no return.

The Phantom of the Opera has a rich cinematic history, going back to 1916 with a German film, which is now lost, written by Greta Schroder, who also appeared in Murnau's *Nosferatu*. The legendary silent film released in 1925 (the Lon Chaney vehicle directed by Rupert Julien) is, so far, the most faithful adaptation of Gaston Leroux's serialized novel. The film was a huge artistic and commercial success for Universal, giving birth to the "Universal Monster" with *Dracula* and *Frankenstein* to follow within the next six years. Chaney's makeup, which he designed himself, would become so iconic that every subsequent version to hit the stage or screen would shy away from attempting to emulate it in any way — apart from an odd animated film from Ireland's Emerald City Productions in 1988, which has the phantom looking quite a bit like the Chaney incarnation. Interestingly enough, this cartoon follows the novel about on par with the silent film, but begins the story after Christine has taken the lead from Carlotta, to keep the running time down to a "kid friendly" fifty minutes.

Claude Rains would be the next actor to portray the titular character in Universal's updated version of the novel in 1943. Shot in "blazing Technicolor," as the advertising materials promised, and boasting a "cast of thousands" — a tagline ripped from the promotional materials of the first film — this newer *Phantom* started the trend of deviating greatly from the source material in favor of new inventions with the characters and plot. In this instance — in one version of the script — the phantom, as Christine's father, was a wronged musician who had acid thrown in his face by a music publisher's secretary! Argento has gone on record many times, stating that this particular version of the story struck a chord with him as a young boy, he had wanted to do his own version of it for years, and it was the first horror film he remembers seeing as a child.

England's Hammer Studios would jump into the game next, with their 1962 film, which did poorly in the U.K. but was quite successful in the U.S. Much like the previous film, The Phantom (Herbert Lom) is a wronged composer who had a splash of acid to the face, thus confining him to live in the sewers of London. According to Marcus Hearn in his book, *The Hammer Vault*:

> *Censorship was once again largely to blame and many of the explicit shocks that were Hammer's stock in trade were sacrificed to attain the "A" certificate required by British distributor, Rank. Director Terence Fisher seemed surprisingly unconcerned… in a 1964 interview with Films and Filming magazine, Fisher actually defended the censorship that prevented audiences getting a clear view of the tormented Phantom's face. "There was no reason to show his face here, you'd seen the acid go into his face, you knew how pitifully he was in agony all the time."*

The film eschews any horror for a romance between Heather Sears's Christine Charles and Edward de Souza's Harry (the Raoul analogue), and it contains unnecessary plots such as Michael Gough trying to bed Sears after offering her the lead in his new opera, as well as the phantom having a servant/henchman to do his dirty work.

Brian De Palma would try his hand next at retelling the story in 1974 with a modern twist. Set in the music industry, *Phantom of the Paradise* tells the story of a hapless composer, Winslow Leach (William Finley) who has his music stolen (that bit again!) by the duplicitous Swan (Paul Williams). This rock musical, very much in line with *The Rocky Horror Show* — which had been a huge hit on the London stage — pulls references from countless films and literary sources, from Alfred Hitchcock's *Psycho* to the Faust legend, to knit together a "hip" version of Leroux's timeless story. Of note is Jessica Harper as Leach's muse, Phoenix, whom Argento would cast in *Suspiria* two years later.

It would be fifteen years before another feature film would be attempted with Robert Englund as the Phantom and Jill Schoelen as Christine. In 1983, a TV film starring Jane Seymour and Maximillian Schell surfaced and quickly disappeared back into the depths. 1989's feature film of *Phantom* is decidedly gorier than all of the previous versions combined, and it seems

Chaney shocked audiences worldwide with his portrayal of The Phantom in Rupert Julien's film. COURTESY THE DEL VALLE ARCHIVES/UNIVERSAL PICTURES.

Rains as the second Phantom from Universal. COURTESY THE DEL VALLE ARCHIVES/UNIVERSAL PICTURES.

to be carried on the back of the success of Englund in the *A Nightmare on Elm Street* series of films. The Phantom's "mask" takes a nod from *The Abominable Dr. Phibes,* as Erik reconstructs his face by sewing skin over his burned visage (Krueger again), the result of a Faustian pact with the devil to have the ability to create music the world would love.

This blood-soaked take on the tale seems to have laid the groundwork for a more horrific version of the familiar story when Argento took the reins. Dwight Little's production has Joseph Buquet skinned alive and stuck in Carlotta's dressing room wardrobe; a theater critic is murdered in a Turkish bath (this scene has considerably less nudity than Argento's) and poor Carlotta becomes part of dinner at the masquerade ball.

In between the Robert Englund feature and Julian Sands eventually taking on the role for Argento, a TV miniseries was produced for NBC in the United States, starring Charles Dance and Teri Polo. Taken from the stage play by Arthur Kopit and Maury Yeston, the miniseries removed the musical numbers but retained the plot, which has the former owner of the Paris Opera (Burt Lancaster) revealed to be Erik/The Phantom's father. Curiously, this miniseries is what

prompted the musical to eventually be staged, due to its success on television. Inarguably the biggest coup for this film was the use of the Paris Opera as the primary location for the project, lending it an authenticity the other films lacked.

Upon its release, critics almost universally panned Argento's *Phantom,* and audiences did not seem to respond well either. Julian Sands is sadly unable to do much with this collection of reactionary tics that masquerades as a character. Usually a capable actor, I was mesmerized by his one-man show, *A Celebration of Harold Pinter* (in a strange coincidence, it was produced by Jill Schoelen, Robert Englund's "Christine" in the 1989 film), but here, he isn't able to create a believable character from the hackneyed and nonsensical script. Asia Argento doesn't fare much better as the leading lady everyone seems to be madly in love with. Again, she is a good actress, given good material, but frankly, I couldn't understand why everyone was in love with her. Doing what she is told, Coralina Cataldi-Tassoni (as the lesbian maid Honorine) gives the character the emotional maturity of a teenager, all jealous carping one second and moony-eyed optimism at the slightest hint of hope. Tassoni has corroborated

Promotional art for the Hammer version of Phantom.
COURTESY THE DEL VALLE ARCHIVES/HAMMER.

Brian DePalma directs a swingin' version of the classic story. COURTESY THE DEL VALLE ARCHIVES/20TH CENTURY FOX.

what I suspected: that the lesbian subtext was there on the page from the beginning.

Nadia Rinaldi (as the opera diva Carlotta) gives possibly the best performance in the film, as she seems to be the only one aware of the ridiculousness of her role and that the character is fairly one note and should be played to the hilt. Rinaldi had only seen a few of Argento's films before accepting the role, which is her first English language performance, and she is surprisingly not dubbed. Nadia told me she sees Carlotta not as campy, but "a grotesque, an exaggeration." And she truly is in every way, and that is why her performance is able to stand out — it's self-aware, but not self-conscious.

Davide D'Ingeo — who plays Alfred, the man who works in the flies in the theater — told me that Argento originally asked him to grow out his beard for a few months for the part. But, when he arrived on set, Argento said the beard appeared fake, so he insisted he be clean-shaven for the role. D'Ingeo is also quite proud of his death in the film and doesn't see it as a bad thing that his role is small because "In a Dario Argento film, it is always better to die. And my death is a good one!" The death of D'Ingeo's character is accompanied by the demise of his girlfriend, Paulette (Kitty Keri), a wash woman in the theater, who has her tongue bitten out — surely a reference to Sands's earlier film, *Warlock*, in which he bites out a character's tongue and spits it into a frying pan.

In telling this gothic romance/horror tale, Argento seems to always have his focus in the wrong place. His penchant for goofy humor is evident in the scenes with the rat catcher and his dwarf assistant. That rat catching vehicle/machine with its Rolls-Royce-like hood ornament is utterly ridiculous, which is the point, but it doesn't fit into this film. Likewise, the idea that rats raised the Phantom, that they protect him, and then pile on that he seems to masturbate while covered in them, is just disgusting and silly in equal measure.

After such an amazing reunion with Ennio Morricone for *The Stendhal Syndrome*, it only made sense that Argento ask him to score this gothic "horror romance," which he seems so fit for, especially in light of his classic work on *The Mission* and the "Gabriel's Oboe" theme, which is so beautifully romantic, lush, and haunting. Indeed, Morricone doesn't disappoint. The main theme, "Sighs and Sighs," is a great start to set the mood, but sadly, the film never reaches the highs of the score.

Ronnie Taylor's cinematography is top notch. The film is beautiful, and he captures the period details nicely. The scenes in the phantom's lair are especially lovely with all of the firelight and shadows. The production design, courtesy of Antonello Geleng, and the costumes by Agnes Gyarmathy are all surprisingly lush for a film made for five million Euros. The film wisely puts every dollar where it belongs.

When a story has been filmed as often as this, the question of necessity must arise, and the film doesn't add enough to the legend to warrant its existence; Argento's *Phantom of the Opera* should be looked upon as an experiment and nothing more. Yes, it is overtly sexual and it is appropriately vicious. But, at the end of the day, does the inclusion of Edgar Degas painting the dancers in the Corps du Ballet, some gory killings, and a needless pedophilic subplot justify another film of this tale? Julian Sands told me that "Argento is a psycho…a beautiful, genius psycho." Wisely, Argento would unleash that psycho in his return to his roots for his next project: A pastiche of older themes and plot points with a "modern" slant, the neo-giallo, *Non Ho Sonno*.

Julian Sands in Argento's Phantom. COURTESY MAITLAND MCDONAGH/MEDUSA.

NON HO SONNO
SLEEPLESS

Upon the dawning of a new millennium and the almost universal panning of *The Phantom of the Opera* two years prior, this 2000 offering is a neo-giallo that again adhered to some of Argento's favorite themes, while bringing the police procedural into the mix with uneven results. Before meeting Max Von Sydow's Officer Moretti, the camera takes the point of view of someone sitting in the passenger seat of a car looking out the windshield and into the rearview mirror concurrently. In a single shot, the thesis of the film is presented: moving forward into the future of the giallo while looking back at what had come before, at the hand of the man who made the genre his own in the 1970s and further honed it into the 1980s. I had managed to see the film at the 2001 American Film Market in Santa Monica in a packed theater; there were even a few people standing in the back. As with many Argento films, there was some "inappropriate" laughter during a few scenes, and at the end, I heard a guy in a suit, who I assume was in acquisitions, say, "That wasn't bad for *that* kind of movie, but it could lose about fifteen or twenty minutes."

Non Ho Sonno is an interesting cornucopia of old themes and ideas revved up for a modern audience. At the hands of Ronnie Taylor, it has a clean, almost sterile look, with bold splashes of primary color that dominate the landscape. This visual scheme makes sense, since this is a film obsessed with childhood. It should look like the interior of a daycare from hell. Centrally, the film boasts an interesting performance by Max Von Sydow, who is one of the last people I would ever think to be in an Argento film. Everyone acquits themselves nicely, with the usual assortment of cinematic oddities Dario often gives us; some silly overacting sits

alongside some more solid craft. Stefano Dionisi as Giacomo is a performance that can only be appreciated in the Italian version, and Chiara Caselli also comes off as much more likeable and real — although near the end, her character becomes quite unkind to Giacomo out of fear of his presumed destructive behavior. The English language track buries her performance perhaps more than anyone else's. The only native actor, it seems, to provide his own voice is Roberto Zibetti as Lorenzo. Zibetti provides the film with a truly bizarre performance: cold and calculating one minute, too affectionate the next, and bouncing-off-the-walls insane at the end.

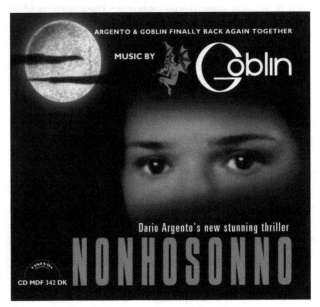

CD jacket for the Italian release of the film's score heralding the movie as "Dario Argento's new stunning thriller." COURTESY THE AUTHOR'S COLLECTION/ CINEVOX.

With Argento's much-hyped reunion with Goblin — they disbanded again immediately after — the score is truly fantastic and rocks along at a great clip. It matches the film nearly flawlessly at every turn, highlighting one odd thing after another and never letting the audience breathe. The film's overly long running time is aided greatly by the fantastic music by Simonetti and Company. This is probably the prime example of an Argento film being carried by its score. *Suspiria* could get away with all of its cinematic awe-inspiring garishness because of its atmosphere and artistry; the newer, more "realistic" giallo of *Non Ho Sonno* needs the support of this score to keep itself afloat, especially as the middle is much too slow.

Non Ho Sonno begins in 1983, with a young boy being questioned by Officer Moretti (Max Von Sydow) after his mother has been murdered before his eyes. He assures the boy he will find who did this, "Even if it takes me all my life." Flash forward to Torino, "Today," as the title card informs us, and we see an overly made up young woman talking on a cell phone to arrange a sexual liaison. I bring up this minor scene solely because of the camera work and the way in which the camera moves, beginning with her breasts and then roaming over her face, one eye at a time, while ending the shot on her mouth. It's unlike anything Argento has ever done, and I can only theorize that the shot is designed in such a way to subconsciously suggest the conclusion of the film, where the killer's head is blown clean off in a reference, intentional or not, to the shotgun blast to the face of the little girl in Lucio Fulci's *The Beyond*. *Non Ho Sonno* is a psychological minefield, and the story proper begins with the series of close-ups on one victim and ends with the killer's destruction. The physical proximity of the camera to the woman's face is also far more intimate than is comfortable for most and creates a sense of claustrophobia and forced intimacy.

The opening train murder of Angela is clearly Argento's attempt to recapture the intensity of the now classic opening scene in *Suspiria*. It also brings to mind *The Night Train Murders*, starring Irene Miracle of *Inferno* and Macha Meril of *Deep Red*. In this "new school" giallo, it is interesting that he would reach back into his first supernatural film for inspiration. And by the time Angela loses her fingers in an echo of *Tenebrae*'s arm chopping, she is bathed in primary-colored lighting that harkens back to *Suspiria*, but with a very mid-'80s Brian De Palma feeling. The scene feels as if it could fit right into *Body Double*. As interesting and impressive as a scene like this is to open the film,

it causes a problem structurally for the rest of the film as it simply can't keep up with the relentlessness of the opening, consequently, all of the character development and plot wrangling sags in comparison.

With the reintroduction of Moretti in the present day, the film steps back into nostalgia as he reminds us repeatedly of the way things "used to be." In a very clumsy piece of dialogue, he is told, "You guys didn't keep written reports; you kept it all in your heads." When was there a time when the police force didn't keep reports? Once Moretti is put back in touch with Giacomo (Stefano Dionisi), the past comes rushing back to him as well, as he is reconnected with his childhood friends Lorenzo (Roberto Zibetti) and Gloria (Chiara Caselli).

Giacomo isn't only the protagonist of the film but is also the center of this trio of childhood friends, as the story alludes he has been sexually involved with both of them. There is the love scene between Gloria and Giacomo we are privy to, which is oddly interrupted by a phone call from Moretti, which allows us to see the answering machine more intimately than we see the young couple in the throes of passion. In regards to Giacomo and Lorenzo's relationship, it is very clear they were close when they were younger; just how close depends on how much you want to read into it. Lorenzo's father's (Gabriele Lavia) disapproving and suspicious glances at the two of them whenever he is in their presence gives the impression that they are, or were, up to something. This is verified during a scene where the young men are sitting across from each other in the kitchen of Lorenzo's apartment, catching up on each other's lives since they last saw each other as kids. They divulge they were equally disappointing to their respective parents, Lorenzo in particular. Strangely, Lorenzo has his shirt off and Giacomo has his unbuttoned and open. Surely it's not just the balmy Italian heat explaining their state of dress.

This love "triangle" only hints at the sexuality in the film, which is brewing violently below the surface. The killer, in his early "sexual" encounter with the prostitute, clues us in to the fact that the murderer is interested in anything but vanilla sex, as the client — we never see him — propositions her with some "disgusting thing" that she won't do until he waves more money at her. She then suggests they play one of her "special games" while twirling her hair like a lamely flirting schoolgirl. The prostitute, played by Barbara Lerici, recalls the gender confusion casting of Eva Robins to play the "girl on the beach" in *Tenebrae* and Geraldine Hooper portraying

Massimo Ricci in *Deep Red*. Perhaps Argento cast Lerici in this role due her androgynous appearance, thus giving the audience something to think about in terms of the mysterious killer's sexual orientation. Is this someone who is into fetishistic heterosexual sex as is perhaps suggested by these "disgusting things" she wouldn't do or is it something more "deviant?" Is this mysterious man into girls-who-used-to-be-guys or those that still are? Either way, it is never explained, and the character remains an enigma until the very end — even though he has a "girlfriend" with whom he has only had the most perfunctory of conversations, and there is very little affection between them.

It is entirely doubtful, then, that Lorenzo, when later revealed to be the killer, has ever had sex with his girlfriend or with anyone but Giacomo, as he is clearly obsessed with him. At the end of the film, he says, "It was a game between you and I, like when we were kids." Surely these childhood games he refers to in the final scene also involved sexual experimentation, as is natural with children, as Giacomo had no complicity in the murders committed when they were children. There is more than a passing resemblance here to the Miguel Arteta film *Chuck and Buck* with Michael White playing Buck. Buck is an adult who never matured beyond his childhood homosexual relations with his best friend Charlie — where they played "Chuck and Buck, suck and fuck" — and with who he is now obsessed as an adult, clinging desperately to this childhood memory that, sadly, his life has never equaled.

Turning to his tried and true theme of childhood trauma and the havoc it wreaks into adulthood, the film is packed with terrible parents. Lorenzo's overbearing father ultimately does whatever he can to save his son from being brought down for his crimes. "Lorenzo, it's not my fault," he says at the film's close. But does this mean that he is finally admitting that he couldn't have possibly created this monster, or is he hinting that he did everything he could to protect him and he's sorry he got caught? Poor Giacomo didn't fare any better with his mother being murdered while he watched, only to land on his father's doorstep for a brief period before being raised by other family members. Vincenzo's all-too-loving mother, Laura De Fabritiis (Rosella Falk), was willing to kill her only child to protect him from scrutiny and scorn, not taking into account her culpability for his murder all these years later. Yet, when she finally tries to come clean, she is murdered at the family home by Lorenzo after he played a particularly cruel trick with one of his puppets

and led her to foolishly hope for an instant that her son may still be alive.

Lorenzo's modus operandi is unusually complicated. *Deep Red*'s murderer also shared the need for a trigger from the past in the form of a childhood song or rhyme to meet specific requirements. "These nursery rhymes are notoriously expressive," Patrick Macnee's Dr. Caleb informs us in Francis Ford Coppola's *Dementia 13*. Coppola's debut film also shares a similar plot device to *Non Ho Sonno*'s "Animal Farm" rhyme, as the killer takes a childhood rhyme literally, much like Lorenzo, and places a body on a meat hook as a method of hiding it from prying eyes. "Fishy, fishy in the brook. Daddy caught you on a hook," Dr. Caleb repeats to himself after hearing the rhyme from the mouth of the man he suspects of committing the terrible deeds.

Whereas *Deep Red* had the "bad mother," *Non Ho Sonno* has the inverse at its core, a father who is "protecting" his murderous son, yet continuing to put many more lives at risk by not turning him in. The film also brings to mind the nature vs. nurture creation of a "monster." Was Lorenzo's privileged childhood so awful in some way, that he felt compelled to kill animals and then people for attention? Or maybe there was more going on with Vincenzo reading the kids his stories than was remembered by the children, their parents caught on, and that's why, as Giacomo says, "My mother put a stop to that."

Asia Argento told me, in regards to *Non Ho Sonno*, "I have great admiration towards my dad. I don't think he'll ever 'go back' to anything; his path is always to go forward, so this giallo will be a totally new thing." In some regards, Asia's observations bear fruit, as in many ways the film is a modern reworking of Argento's beloved giallo. However, the same problems he has always faced, mainly stiff dialogue and poor acting and dubbing from his supporting players, are still here. However, the film's tight, intricate plot is intriguing, but in typical Argento fashion, leaves many psychological and character threads dangling.

Audiences responded happily to the film, which pleased Argento greatly, he told me. Beyond being a success in Italy and in most territories abroad, it did fair business on video, allowing the film far greater reach. Dario's next film was meant to be a vehicle for Asia Argento, reprising her character from *The Stendhal Syndrome*. It would be dropped in favor of another script titled *Il Cartaio/The Card Player*, and would, ultimately, star Stefania Rocca in the female lead.

a film by

DARIO ARGENTO

SLEEPLESS

GORIAL

Marketing material from a screening at the American Film Market. FROM THE AUTHOR'S COLLECTION.

LA DOLCE GIALLO

To quote Sam Dalmas in *The Bird with the Crystal Plumage*: "Go to Italy, they say, nothing interesting ever happens there." So I did. I was to visit Dario in Italy in May of 2000. I had the approved six weeks off of work, and I wanted to see as much of Europe as I could, as it would be my first trip outside of the U.S. My original itinerary was a dream to me. I was going to start in France and make my way through to Italy, stopping in every country along the way for several days, doing whatever I wanted. Sure, I'd be sleeping in hostels and whatever cheap shack I could afford, but I didn't care. I was going to Europe!

As luck would have it, my employer at the time decided to cut my time off from six to two weeks. Well, there went my dream European vacation. But I was still going, that was the important part. So, with a little change of plans, I decided to just spend the nearly two weeks abroad in Italy alone. With this truncated time frame, I had the idea to ask my mother, who had never been anywhere outside of the U.S. besides Mexico, if she wanted to accompany me. She seemed interested, but had no intention of sleeping in hostels or shacks, and this actually worked in my favor as now I was able to sleep in hotel rooms instead of rooms shared by twenty college students sleeping on their possessions. And private bathrooms — the luxury!

Rome was the first destination of a three-city tour, including Florence and then on to Turin, where *Non Ho Sonno* was being filmed. Sleep wasn't an option during the first few days in Rome. At night, I would wander around the city by myself, enjoying the stillness of the empty streets, going back to the hotel to get a few hours sleep, only to get up and do it again the next day. I was trying to find the Rome of Dario Argento's films in my nighttime excursions, but sadly never felt like I could find it, as I was surrounded by the usual tourist destinations no matter where I went in trying to escape them in order to find the true heart of Rome. I wanted to experience the Rome that Tony Musante reveled in, the Rome John Saxon slunk through, and only found the tacky representation in *Mother of Tears*. A coworker back in San Francisco had told me that Italy was a place you should walk everywhere possible, so I adopted this mindset when planning the itinerary from day to day. These first few days in Rome, I managed to see a great exhibit of Salvador Dali's work and an amazing show of Monet's paintings, which up to that time had been the largest single collected exhibition anywhere, with pieces borrowed from all over the globe. Everyone has seen those water lilies in some form or another, but I wasn't prepared for just how many of them he had painted and the technique used made them sparkle: they were breathtaking. There's something about being surrounded by beautiful art that makes me feel truly alive and free, somehow.

By day three in Rome, we had seen quite a lot: the coliseum, the pantheon, and the usual spots. It's a great city to just, pardon the pun, roam around and do nothing, letting its historical essence talk to you and guide you from place to place. I'm by no means Catholic or religious in any way, but I had to visit the Vatican while in town, which I did by myself. The museum was quite extraordinary, only to be topped by the gift shop, where the Pope's face was plastered on anything and everything they could possibly put it on, from dinner plates to t-shirts. I found it all quite humorous and a little disrespectful and cheap, to be honest. If Catholic doctrine didn't decry the use of condoms, I am sure they would have put his holiness's likeness on those, too!

One afternoon back home, before leaving for Italy, I received an email from my friend Simone Arrighi, the then president of Asia Argento's fan club, informing me that Asia had invited me to the Rome premiere of her film *Scarlet Diva*. A few months prior to meeting Dario in San Jose, I had struck up an e-mail correspondence with Asia through her website because I was writing a paper on Dario's films for a class in college. So we had an acquaintanceship, and she had been very sweet to me. Needless to say, I was very excited to finally meet her.

The day of the premiere, I was so anxious as it was my first exposure to the "glamour" of the film business. The day couldn't have gone by more slowly. I had brought over my nicest clothes and shoes for the event, and my mother got dressed up as well. Did I really want to wear a dress shirt and slacks in this heat? Better to chance that, I thought, than be underdressed for the occasion. An hour before the screening, we headed over to the theater. Along the way, my poor mom got the heel of her shoe caught in a cobblestone in the street, falling to her knees and scraping them up pretty well.

After some first aid, courtesy of a restaurant employee, she decided to forgo the film and go back to the hotel, causing me quite a bit of guilt for leaving her alone and in pain, to which she insisted that I stay because this was one of the reasons we had come.

Sending Mom off in a cab and hoping she would get back to the hotel safely, I spent a good half hour outside that theater by myself, waiting for something to happen. It wasn't long before a few members of Asia's fan club started arriving at the theater and that's when it hit me. Damn, I was really overdressed! Not only that but, for some reason, they all knew who I was! "Oh, you're the American here to see Asia and Dario," one told me. "Can I take a picture with you?" asked another. This was getting weird.

One of them even had a video camera and was recording all of this for posterity, although I don't think much was happening yet. All that changed as Asia appeared on the scene with a few photographers who appeared out of nowhere. As if I had a sign on my back, she made a line straight for me, gave me a hug, and said, "Derek, you're here!"

With Asia Argento at the Rome premiere of Scarlet Diva. FROM THE AUTHOR'S COLLECTION.

I leaned into her, "Of course, I wouldn't have missed it. Thank you so much for the invite." "Of course! Have you seen my dad yet?"

"No, that's in another week. We're going to Florence next."

"Who are you here with? I thought you came alone." she said with almost suspicious curiosity.

"I invited my mom along. She's never been to Europe."

With an unexpected fear in her eyes, Asia looked like a shocked child. "Your mom is here!?"

"Back at the hotel, yeah, she got hurt in the street and went back. I feel bad."

Relieved, a smile came back to her face. "Tell her I'm sorry, but I'm glad she's not here. I couldn't explain this movie to your mother."

I couldn't help but start laughing at this. She was afraid of *my* mother seeing this movie when her uncle was producing it and her father had been advising in the sound mix. They had seen everything and were in more of an awkward place than someone she didn't even know. Her unexpected modesty was quite charming.

"But I have to ask you, why do these people know who I am? Not by name, but I've been dubbed 'The American guy who is here to see you.'" "I sent a message out to people in the fan club to come to the screening tonight and I think it's Simone who told some of them to say hi to you." She smiled and gave me a kiss.

By now, I'm sure I was blushing, but I stammered, "I should have figured that out. It's fine, just unexpected. I'm excited to watch the movie tonight." "Well, I hope you like it. It's almost time to start, so I should go in. I'll see you in a bit."

With another hug, she was gone, so I decided to hang around outside and watch the people coming in. I've always thought that the books you read and the movies you like say a lot about who you are. And I'm a people watcher, so this was intriguing to me: a way to learn what "kind" of Italians are into films outside the mainstream of imported fare and all the knockabout Italian comedies and serious international award fare. Everyone I spoke to was very nice, and I even ran into Vera Gemma, one of the actors in the film and daughter of Giuliano Gemma, star of *Tenebrae*.

Anyone that has seen *Scarlet Diva* can attest to its bravura, no-holds-barred attitude, whether you like the film or not. Well, imagine watching it in Italian, having only to rely on the images to convey this story. I could follow it for the most part, but was eluded by the subtlety and the humor in it, as the audience was

laughing at things that I couldn't understand. And that opening where Asia is having sex in her trailer on a film set is something I'm glad I didn't have to endure with my mother along. I would have been as equally embarrassed as Asia suggested she may have been.

When the film was over, Asia called all of the creative team that was present up to the front of the theater to take a few bows and do a short talk to the audience. You could hear the pride in her voice at having created this rather raucous and unique film. I had made my way outside of the theater when Asia found me again and asked me what I thought of it. I didn't really know how to respond to this as I couldn't understand much of the dialogue. I just responded with, "I'll have to wait and reserve judgment until I can see it subtitled."

Turning my attention to a blonde woman beside her, Asia said to me, "Derek, I want to introduce you to my sister." I'm embarrassed to say I very casually asked, "Where is she? I would love to meet her," and poor Fiore said a little defensively, "Right in front of you!"

I wanted that cliché of a hole to open up in the ground and swallow me right there. I don't think I'd ever been so embarrassed in my life, but luckily she wasn't bothered by my gaffe and shook my hand. We had a rather pleasant conversation about my trip and how I knew Asia and Dario, while Asia looked on. After taking a few photos together, it was time to wrap up the evening, so after saying goodbye to Asia, I stuck around with Fiore a bit, where she was with a few friends. They invited me out to a bar to have a drink, and I said that I didn't have a car or any way to get around, to which Fiore said to me, "Oh you can ride with me on the back of my scooter."

Being the good son that I am, I was thinking of how my mother was alone and injured, so I begged off, and if I have any regrets from that trip, that is it. How often was Fiore Argento going to ask me to go have a drink in Rome? But familial loyalty being what it is, I caved to its pressures. Nevertheless, it was a fantastic evening I will always cherish. What a great way to wrap up my trip to the eternal city!

The next day, Mom, still hobbling a bit, hauled her luggage alongside yours truly doing the same, while cursing the cobblestone streets. The city was not made for luggage on wheels is all I have to say! But we were soon on a train bound for Florence. The city was nothing I could ever be prepared for. It is beautiful beyond description, even with a thousand motor scooters whizzing by at earsplitting volume all hours of the day and night. The town sounds like it has been taken over by gardeners with leaf blowers.

We soon settled into our hotel and, as this was the city with the least time on our schedule, began to venture out shortly after. One thing must be said for Italy. If you don't like anything else, this is a country that knows how to eat. We found this amazing restaurant that I believe was a portion of the lower level section of a centuries-old monastery. Oh, risotto, how I love thee! This restaurant also introduced me to tiramisu, which, naturally, I have never had this good anywhere, ever. A great memory, but annoying in trying to recreate the taste of it when coming up against watery, overly espresso-soaked and often frozen, tiramisu in the States.

I spent the next day and a half in a blur of sightseeing, eating excessively, and dying from the awful humidity. My tour was capped off by seeing Michelangelo's David in a near-empty Academy and a trip to the Uffizi gallery with Morricone's score to *The Stendhal Syndrome* playing on my portable CD player while I was in the Boticelli room.

From Florence, we went on to Turin, and the train ride was great. Roughly four hours looking at the amazing Italian countryside, all the little villages that dotted the landscape seemed so exotic, like film locations yet to be discovered. Our hotel in Turin was like nothing I had ever experienced. This building had to have been at least three hundred years old, and the door to our room weighed about a hundred pounds. The lock must have been from the Middle Ages because the keys to the room were quite heavy and they were almost humorous in their size, looking like a prop from a Hammer film. I half expected Peter Cushing to greet us at some point, and I wouldn't have been surprised to see Barbara Shelley in our bathroom.

The next morning, I woke up in my tiny hotel room in Turin. The humidity made the air physically dense, and, being from California, I had only experienced weather like this in Florida. At least it wasn't raining and, well, I was in Italy, so I really couldn't complain.

The earth didn't swallow me whole. With Fiore Argento. FROM THE AUTHOR'S COLLECTION.

Being my first full day in Turin, I was anxious to get things underway. After all, this was the main reason I had come to Italy, to see Dario Argento. Honestly, I don't remember much about the start of the day except walking out of the hotel to find my way to the location where Argento and company were shooting. His assistant, Carla, who was also the production secretary on this film, had given me an address, and now I had to figure out how to get there. On a map it looked fairly close, so I hit the street with my mother, and we started walking over to where we assumed the location was. After about a half hour of walking around and not really knowing if we were getting any closer, I approached a woman on the street and, in my mangled Italian, attempted to ask her directions. She very quickly called her brother out of her home, and he came out and spoke the most beautiful English. At least, it sounded that way to me because I was desperate to be where I was going that day.

Thanks to the kind gentleman, we found the shooting location within a few minutes. I knew we had arrived when we were greeted at the curb in front of a large house by a faceless puppet dressed like a midget pimp wearing a snappy suit, reminding me of the similarly "faceless" killer in Bava's *Blood and Black Lace*. On the other side of the street, there were a few transportation trucks and a group of people standing around and watching a lot of nothing happen.

We were standing outside of this probably centuries-old home in awe, admiring the architecture that resembled nothing I had ever seen back home. Claudio Argento was the first person I ran into outside of the house that was being used as the location where the "killer dwarf" lived in the film. After a brief introduction to Claudio, he disappeared into the house and Dario came out and greeted me with a smile and a hug. "Oh, you're here! Fantastic. This weather is not good." No, no it wasn't. I introduced my mother to him, and he was quite sweet about the whole thing. He somehow sensed she wouldn't have much to say to him, as she had never seen any of his movies, and he quickly tried to make her comfortable by asking her about our trip so far. I will never forget his comment to my mother upon this initial meeting, "Janice," he said with a nod and a smile, "that is a very nice name. Like Janis Joplin!" Being a great fan of Joplin, my mother laughed and seemed surprised that he knew who she was. Ah, music, the international icebreaker.

Once the introductions were out of the way, Dario took us on a short tour of the house, explaining that it used to belong to the man who invented the X-ray and was a registered historic landmark. The house had been roughed up some for the shoot to make it look abandoned and dirty, but it couldn't diminish how amazing this place was. Ava Gardner in *The Sentinel* couldn't have sold us on the place any better. After this little guided walk, it was back to work, as Stefano Dionisi was shooting his side of a telephone conversation. With the rain machine going and light playing the reflection of the storm onto the ceiling, it was interesting to watch this being shot as Dionisi speaks very little English and it just made him all the cuter, watching him struggle with the language.

I hadn't met Ronnie Taylor yet, but to hear him reading Gloria's side of this phone call was hilarious. This specific portion of the scene was when Gloria had called Giacomo on Moretti's cell phone, and she was explaining her part in the ballet, and that she was "dressed like a swan." It's hard to describe how funny it was to hear these words come out of Taylor's mouth in his very male and very British voice.

Once this short scene had been completed, Argento called me outside to where the crew had been prepping a crane for the shot where the camera glides along the ground a bit, goes up the side of the house, and up along the roofline, echoing that much more elaborate roof crawl in *Tenebrae*. As I made my way out of the house into the backyard, I could hear a few words screamed in Italian and realized I was the one being yelled at! I backed up and back into the house, and the screaming continued until one of the crewmembers gave me the evil eye and got on his hands and knees to smooth out the ground I had just made footprints in!

Walking very carefully around this newly cleaned up patch of dirt, I made my way over to where Dario was sitting and, of course, he was laughing at my predicament the entire time. Taking a seat alongside Dario on a low stone wall, he explained to me what he was planning to do with the camera. As a lifelong lover of films and filmmaking and a huge fan of Argento's work in particular, I have no words to explain the bliss I was in at this moment sitting next to Dario, his script binder and storyboards at hand, getting a lesson from a master.

Seeing Dario work is an interesting experience as he has a sort of Jekyll and Hyde temperament, depending on what is happening. Granted, I haven't worked with him as an actor or crew member, only as an observer, but he seems to spend so much time in his head that when it's time to get these ideas out to his actors and crew, it's somewhat unpredictable what Argento you will get. This isn't to say that he was ever mean or cruel to anyone — quite the opposite. I only imply that at times he is quite calm and you can barely hear him speak, and at other times, he is so energized that he is jumping up and down and yelling happily at what he is seeing on set.

Cinematographer Ronnie Taylor, who had worked with Argento previously on *Opera* and *Phantom of the Opera*, became a touchstone of sorts for me on the set, being one of the few people who spoke English. Claudio Argento was always busy putting out some fire or another on the set, so he was unavailable much of the time, although I did have a brief conversation with him that for the life of me I cannot recall. I didn't have a conversation with Taylor about anything, as such, as we traded anecdotes about being in Italy and just how different it was from our respective countries.

"The prostitutes here are much louder than back home," he said with a laugh. "I'm not joking. The other night at our hotel, they kept me up until all hours going on about their business in the alley right below my room. I yelled down to them to shut up and go fuck somewhere else. But they stayed put until they were done."

"Well, I didn't see any of that," I said, "but in Rome, we saw a naked homeless woman almost daily. I named her 'Little Suzy homemaker.' She would stand in the middle of the street and yell at cars. I thought she was going to get killed. Nobody seemed to pay any attention to her. I was tempted to call the police and see if she could be picked up. But the police scared me; they all stand around with semiautomatic weapons strapped to their chests. And what the hell is with the women on patrol wearing skirts and heels?"

"That's Italy, my boy. Everything and everyone are just a little bit crazy. And that's why I love it so."

I'm saddened that I didn't get to spend more time with Taylor; he was a really warm, funny personality without an ounce of "I've won an Academy Award" pretension or bullshit about him. But I can see why he and Argento were so loyal to each other. They genuinely like each other and get along well, even with the language barrier. The language of cinema is universal and they both speak it fluently.

This first day on the set, my mother had an experience only a foreigner who was visiting Dario Argento would have. We had seen Massimo Sarchielli — who plays "Leone" in the film — milling around the set, dressed very nattily, looking every inch the homeless tramp he was meant to be. During a break during shooting, I was with my mother and Dario out near the front of the house, as was Sarchielli. My poor mother couldn't understand anything anyone was saying, and she had no idea who anyone was, so when Sarchielli tried to talk to her, she was a little nervous, assuming he was a bum off the street, not knowing he was an actor in the film. With a rather distressed look on her face while trying to be polite, she began inching herself away from him. After a "safe" distance, my mother exclaimed, "Great, the only Italian man to flirt with me and he's a bum!"

"Mom, I think he's *in* the movie," I replied with a little embarrassment.

"Oh, well, there are all those people just standing around in the street. He could have been anybody."

Around lunchtime, Argento took us to the craft service table and insisted we eat something. Now, this table, I have to explain, was not much of a table, but a couple of sawhorses and a plank of wood. Resting rather precariously on top of this was an espresso/coffeemaker like none I had ever seen. It was a massive, ornate brass affair and I was waiting for the makeshift table to buckle under its weight, sending the entire spread, which included a whole lot of cookies, crashing to the ground. Next to this "table" was a cooler full of ice and beer and other alcoholic drinks. Dario explained with a smile that it was someone's birthday on the crew and once the day's shoot was done, they were going to have a celebration on set, which he invited us to attend.

Sad to say, we didn't stay for the party as my mother was becoming increasingly anxious to go back to the hotel, and we were both getting tired after walking for days on end everywhere we went, which enabled us to soak up as much of Italy as possible. Who wants to sit in cars or subway trains when you're in such a beautiful place?

After a much-needed night's rest and ravaging the continental breakfast at the hotel, which consisted of blood orange juice, pastry, and fruit, on an endless horizon of buffet tables, it was off to the second day of shooting at an enormous hospital, which was only partially in use as a retirement home of sorts. You can see a very brief exterior shot of the place in the film, with Stefano Dionisi and Chiara Caselli walking down a breezeway after they leave Roberto Zibetti in the hospital.

Gaining entry into that enormous brick and glass building was a bizarre experience and was like checking *in* to the hospital! We had to go up to the front desk, be checked off a list, and tell them we were there to see Dario. Like a scene from a movie, a nurse came out of nowhere and walked us down into the sub, sub basement of the building, where they were shooting the drowning of the disco dancer. Crammed into this dank, dark space were a good fifty plus people, and, again, it was almost uncomfortably hot down in that musty room, but I was there to witness the magic of the day.

Dario seemed to be in good spirits and greeted us warmly, as he did the previous day. However, this day seemed much more frantic and I don't know if it was because a murder was being filmed or time was an issue, which I'm sure it was, but Dario appeared frazzled.

The day's shoot was taking place in a corner of this basement level and a makeshift enclosure was created with duvetyn, darkening the space surrounding the pool where the "cat" was to be drowned. With this arrangement, I wasn't able to see exactly what they were doing, but I had access to the monitor at Dario's director's chair, so I could watch from there. I could sense something wasn't right though, and it didn't take long for frustrations to mount. This poor girl couldn't "drown" properly, and they were having to do several takes of this, which required that she be dried off and her makeup reapplied, which would of course take up more time — and time is money.

In a break during this scene, Dario came out to where I was watching the monitor, and he told me to relax and sit in his chair. Out of respect, I tried to beg off and tell him that I was fine standing, but he insisted, "No, sit, it's warm, relax. Have something to drink. I would let you in to watch, but it's too crowded in there."

Well, I didn't want to seem rude, so I spend a good chunk of the day sitting in his chair. When I say "his chair," I mean that his name had been written on a piece of fabric, which was pinned to the back of the chair. This isn't Hollywood, where money is wasted printing chair backs with people's names on them. Printed or pinned, it was still equally surreal and very exciting.

Elena Marchesini, the actress playing the character of "Mel," really took a beating this particular day of shooting. Not only did they have to do multiple takes of this drowning but also she just seemed really uncomfortable because I think she felt she let Dario down. It has to be said that many of these young Italian actors are so excited to work with Argento because his of his reputation and legend. At one point in a break during shooting, she came over to where I was sitting, the costume assistant put a robe on her, and

she just started talking to me. Well, trying to, anyhow. Moments like this, I'm sorry my Italian is nearly non-existent, as Elena seemed a bit upset that she wasn't able to "die" properly, and she seemed in need of a bit of comfort, if even from a stranger.

After everything was reset, Elena gave it another go, and this take resulted in a bit of clapping when it was over, and Dario emerged with Elena, all smiles, and he gave her a hug. The process of creating a piece of art is a great thing to witness when it goes well because you can feel the excitement and pride it produces in people involved in its creation. And this set always seemed a rather nice place because Dario never screamed or lost his patience outwardly, and being surrounded by a young and eager crew seemed to feed his energy as well. If you've never been a witness to it, there is a bit of childish glee in Argento when he feels things are pleasing to him creatively. He smiles a lot and his eyes just light up from the inside.

As the day wore on, the staff of the hospital slowly started trickling down into the basement to watch the shoot, and soon it was white nurse uniforms as far as the eye could see, which made me wonder who was attending to the patients upstairs. As soon as the hospital staff cleared up, Susy Mattolini, the costumer on the film who I had been talking to a bit, along with her husband, invited me and my mother out to a late lunch the next day.

Arriving on time at the Best Western in Turin right on time, Susy and her husband took my mother and me to a small café, where we were met by a few of the crew members and the actor Giancarlo Colia, who played Adolfo Farina in the film. While we were having a small lunch of salad and bread, Signore Colia was getting a bit too comfortable with my mother. And, not speaking any Italian, she didn't know how to respond to this, except to smile and be polite. Susy turned to my mother and said, "It's OK, he's like that with everyone."

After the meal was over, my mother decided to go back to the hotel to call her real estate agent as she was trying to sell her house. Before she left, she said to me, "You should try to see if Dario can have dinner or something with us tonight. It's our last night here." With that, she went back to the hotel, and I stayed behind with Susy and the group.

No more than three minutes had passed when who should come join us at the table but Dario. Oh, great, my mother was going to love this. The second she leaves, who should show up? I was pleasantly surprised to see him again as I was afraid the set would have been the last time I would get to talk to him, and he was so busy, there just wasn't much time to talk. Well, here it was, my chance. Dario took the chair next to me, we said our hellos, and I asked him what he was doing here. "I am editing the film," he said, pointing to the building he had just walked out of. "It's hot up there, no air conditioning. I came down to get something to drink and take a break."

After I asked him how the shoot was coming along, he looked down at my arm and began to pinch me and smile. He laughed a bit. "The mosquitoes love you, bites everywhere. It's because you're so white! You are Portuguese; why are you so pale?" Well, I guess the Irish genes dominated, but what about this was so funny?

He kept pinching me and laughing. Yes, it's true, I looked as if I were afflicted with some skin disorder, but what could be done? This would be one of my fondest memories of the trip, Dario Argento laughing at my misfortune around a table full of people while we drank and ate as the mosquitoes feasted. It was like a scene out of *Phenomena*; at last, my love of his movies was merging with reality. La Dolce Giallo!

SCARLET DIVA

THE HEART IS DECEITFUL ABOVE ALL THINGS

"I don't think Scarlet D[iva] is the right film for American audiences; it is too tough, lots of nudity, drugs, and rude language (But not to shock—spontaneous stuff)," Asia told me while she was in postproduction on the film. Anyone that has seen *Scarlet Diva* can attest to its bravura, no-holds-barred attitude, whether you like the film or not. Well, imagine watching it in Italian, having only to rely on the images to convey this story. I could follow it for the most part, but was eluded by the subtlety and the humor in it, as the audience was laughing at things that I couldn't understand. And the opening of the film where Asia is having sex in her trailer on a film set is something I'm glad I didn't have to endure with my mother along. I would have been as equally embarrassed as Asia suggested she may have been.

Asia Argento's first film as a director is an interesting semi-autobiographical "vanity" project, but in a completely less-than-flattering manner as would befit a true vanity project. She is all too eager to be perceived as terrible and look equally as awful.

Anna Battista (Asia Argento) is an actress whose life is a series of unfortunate events. Whether she's rescuing a friend from an abusive boyfriend, falling in love with a man she will never see again, or doing drugs while pregnant, this woman is spinning out of control. Or is this the only way she can feel in control? While her life plummets steadily downward, she is trying to write a screenplay titled "Scarlet Diva" based on her own life.

This open wound of a film has an interesting heritage. "After working with [Abel] Ferrara, one of my favorite directors, everything seemed dull," Asia told me. "I was agoraphobic and barely left my home. So I started writing a book [*I Love You Kirk*]. My father read a few pages and told me he saw a movie there. So I began writing it. Reality and fiction merged into my creative process."

The film opens, post credits, with Anna in a trailer on a film set, having sex with a man. When they are interrupted, she goes into the bathroom and mumbles to herself, "Damn, I didn't come," and this prompts a memory from childhood — when she was interrupted by her mother while masturbating. This scene sets the tone for the entire film, the foibles and pitfalls of adulthood as they are reflected and shaped by childhood experience. Later, Anna watches her older brother, whom she still bathes with, making out with a girl, and she begins to give purchase to her own sexuality.

As an adult, sex and the simple desire to be loved and, more importantly, needed, drives Anna through her whirlwind existence. That being said, she is completely self-centered and blind to what she is doing to everyone around her and, more importantly, to her unborn child. Argento has created a complex and challenging character that refuses to be any one thing at any given time. In one instance, she is obliging to some overbearing male fans who spot her in a gas station. She gives them the autographs and the photos they request, but it isn't enough. She hops into her car, drives away in a hurry, but still takes the time and energy to wave goodbye to them, as if to not leave them completely let down by being ditched. Later, when she is propositioned by a sleazy film producer

(Joe Coleman), against her better judgment, she goes up to his hotel room to look at a script and even agrees to give him a massage right after telling him that she is tired of the Italian film industry's treatment of women: "I want to become a directress as I said tonight because actresses in Italy are bitches. It's terrible to be an actress in Italy; you have to show your tits in covers, always be sexy in films, it's bullshit. Enough of this."

Anna's rejection of the unfortunate state of female affairs in the Italian film industry is a not-so-thinly veiled indictment of the status quo in Asia's life, as well as an actress. Although she knows it is wrong and she wants to change the rules, she knows she has to continue playing the game to some extent to get ahead. As well, she knows whereof she speaks, as she has been acting since childhood, her first role alongside her mother, Daria Nicolodi, in the TV miniseries *Sogni e Bisogni*.

The complexity and contradiction of women in the film is perhaps personified by the character of Veronica, Anna's best friend who is in a relationship with a sadistic man, whom Anna tries to protect her from. This comes to a climax when Anna visits her friend in Paris and discovers her gagged and bound to her bed. However, the more we learn about Veronica, it's not so clear that Anna's intervention is needed or desired. Vera Gemma, Asia's friend in real life, plays Veronica, and had this to say about her chacter: Yes, she wrote it for me. She always thought I had a masochistic attitude in love, in a more psychological than physical way, as in the movie. She wrote this exaggerated woman who loved to be beaten, and thinks that love and pain are the same thing. This was an amazingly funny and ironic character. My father [Giuliano Gemma] was uncomfortable when he went to see the movie alone one afternoon in Rome. He came home and said, "Why did you do this? Don't play any more characters like this!" Of course I thought it was cool!

As Anna wends her way through life fueled by her obsessive, destructive love for Kirk — a man who claims Elvis Presley is his father — Anna builds up just as many injurious fantasies about what their life will be once they meet again. She is hell-bent on pursuing this "impossible love," which she romanticizes yet, somewhere inside herself, she must know will never come to pass. Jean Shepard as the rock star whom Anna falls in love with is the perfect emotional foil in his detached coldness against Anna's rapidly clinging nature.

Once Anna realizes she is pregnant, she doesn't take the maternal route and do anything to protect

the life of the child inside her. Instead, she insists on abusing herself, and now her unborn child, to drown out the reality she cannot face. In a literally and figuratively revealing scene, Anna stands in front of the bathroom mirror nude, shaving her armpits and then putting on make up, only to smear it all over her face while crying and making a grotesquerie of herself. This visual representation of her inner self is mirrored in some of the "hideous" artwork that she draws of herself in her "Book of Sorrows." In one illustration, her nose is exaggerated, her face a strange funhouse mirror view that only someone who hates their inner self so much that their outer self has to match, no matter the reality.

To quote Anthony Franciosa in *Tenebrae*, "If you remove all the boring parts, you have a bestseller." Exaggeration is the film's modus operandi as there is truth buried beneath the film's nearly operatic self-destruction. As Asia said in a documentary about the production of the film, "I look for the truth in the

Asia during a quiet moment on the set. PHOTOGRAPH BY SIMONE ARRIGHI.

biggest lies." The statement of the real-life actor and director can be reflected back to the fictional one, as Anna's darkest truth, which is fiction, does illuminate Asia's true self. Yet it would be foolish to try and gauge just how much truth lies in these overblown falsities. It all goes back to the human attraction to pain and suffering.

Asia's second film as director, *The Heart is Deceitful Above All Things*, is completely reliant on such lies and delusion. It is based on a collection of loosely connected stories published under the nom de plume J.T. Leroy. Leroy — who purported to be a gay male who was an HIV positive, transsexual teenage runaway who had worked as a truck stop prostitute — in reality, was a middle-aged female writer named Laura Albert. When the "scandal" broke that there was no real J.T. Leroy and a woman named Savannah was posing as the elusive and mild-mannered author, many celebrities who were struck by the young man's honesty and voice quickly changed their tune.

Asia said of the scandal and the film:

I felt quite relieved when I learned the story wasn't a real one, an autobiography. Even though, unfortunately, stories like these really happen in this world. It was so hard to play that character, the evil mother. My daughter was two years old. It was a demon that possessed me and it took so long to expel it. Maybe if I had known it was fiction, I wouldn't have been so loyal to the book (such a great book), but I would have changed it a bit. It's a good thing that I didn't. I thought I was doing psychodrama, that the movie would help J.T. overcome his horrible childhood.

I can't help but think that most of the people who claimed to be shocked by this admission knew this was a hoax all along, or at least had some kind of inkling something wasn't right. It's all just too crazy to believe in the first place. I had my doubts about Leroy when

Asia or Anna? PHOTOGRAPH BY SIMONE ARRIGHI.

I first read his novel *Sarah*, the follow-up to *The Heart is Deceitful Above All Things*. Regardless of the truth behind the "truth," Asia read Leroy's short stories and was compelled to make this film.

Maitland McDonagh adds:

> I have a lot of reservations about the source material. But I can see what appealed to her. It's also about a child who is hauled into an adult world and has to figure out a way of surviving in a very chaotic environment. And I think casting herself as the mother was something that shows she may have a vanity about what she is willing to do. But she has no vanity about what she will do, if you see what I'm saying. She's willing to play a horrible character and look like shit. A lot of people find the glamour in the drug culture. It's like the Saint Augustine thing: just wallow in all of the destructive glamour in it and then clean up from it at the end. You never get that sense of that from her. There is no underlying moralizing to the way that she treats that character. Which is very much, I think, what that material needs.

At the end of *Scarlet Diva*, Anna lays on the ground, pregnant, helpless, wondering about the life inside of her. Suddenly, she hallucinates a new man, glowing, a possible savior figure, her own Jesus Christ in silver metallic pants. *The Heart is Deceitful Above All Things* opens with Sarah (Asia Argento) being reunited with her son, Jeremiah (Jimmy Bennett), who she put up for adoption when he was born. Sarah's completely selfish and self-centered act mirrors Anna's behavior in the first film.

Sarah, born to an Italian mother and raised in boarding schools in Italy, now lives in the Southern United States, running from one drug-fueled and abusive situation to the next, dragging her young son along for the ride. The episodic nature of the narrative mirrors *Scarlet Diva*'s as well, as there is no real plot to speak of, only the increasingly destructive misadventures of this Courtney Love lookalike-cum stripper-cum truck stop whore.

Although this mother is anything but, Asia is able to give this monster enough pathos to almost make you feel for her, despite her cruelty. Yet this self-absorbed, attention-seeking beast is too hyper-sexualized and awful to someone she should love unconditionally that you just want this kid to either kill her or run away. At one point, the child does run away, only to be picked up by the police. Sarah is able to charm the police into handing him over to her instead of investigating the child's grievances if any were expressed. But it's obvious to anyone he is deathly afraid of this woman. It isn't until she starts making him feel guilty for even being alive that he absorbs all of her self-esteem issues and they become a self-actualizing, codependent mirror of one another that the film becomes truly mesmerizing.

Jimmy Bennet and the Sprouse twins, Dylan and Cole, play little Jeremiah at different ages in the film. The Sprouses and the solo Bennett are fantastic performers. I can't imagine their parents being thrilled with the material because it's so tough, but it is a showcase for their talents. When I attended the Los Angeles Film Festival premiere of the film with "J.T. Leroy" in attendance, the Sprouse twins were running around causing havoc as any boisterous kids would. I couldn't help but think it was strange their parents would even let them watch this film considering what it contained. Although they participated in these scenes, they are shot in a way that took the actions out of context, but once they are reconstructed, it's nothing short of brutal for much of the running time.

With these two films under her belt, Asia Argento has become heir to the Argento film dynasty. Yes, she will carry on the family name in cinema, but in a completely different way than her father, and she will undoubtedly influence an entirely different audience. Female film directors are a sadly small lot, and to have one with such a unique pedigree and with such a distinctly raw voice is refreshing, but hardly commercial. Yet that doesn't seem to bother Asia as she once told me, "I'm not comfortable in groups. I would rather be alone, writing."

INTERVIEW

ASIA ARGENTO

Never one to rest on her laurels and be famous for fame's sake, Asia has carved out her own distinct identity as a writer/actress/director/artist/DJ and as some may not be aware, a musician. She has recently released an album comprised of music written and recorded over the last decade titled *Total Entropy* and has a new film titled *Misunderstood* slated for release in 2014.

DB: Can you tell me about your first memory of watching a movie? What did cinema do that other art forms didn't for you at a young age?

AA: My parents told me that when I was born, as a celebration, they screened *Gone with the Wind* for three days in a row. I used to love that movie as a kid and still do. Cinema has always been my great escape.

DB: What was your first memory of a film set? I would assume you grew up on your father's.

AA: The first time I visited my father on a set was during *Tenebrae*. I didn't grow up on film sets. I didn't visit one of my father's until I was nine and started working in movies. My father didn't like his daughters around; I think he thought we might be distracting. My first memory is someone shouting "SILENCE PLEASE!" and I'm holding my breath for the whole take because I am afraid to make noise.

DB: What was school like? I'm assuming most people in Italy knew who you were because of your parents. Did this make anything difficult for you?

AA: I think kids were intrigued and they loved our horror Betamax video collection. We made a pact that if they came over to watch a scary movie, they weren't allowed to tell their parents.

DB: You've been writing pretty much your entire life. When did you start and what were you writing?

AA: I've been writing poetry since I was five years old. At age nine, I published a small book.

Asia Argento, the inner eye. PHOTO BY SIMONE ARRIGHI.

DB: What writers influenced you then and now? And why did/do they resonate with you?

AA: I used to love Robert Walser and Colette growing up, Baudelaire in my teens. Then I moved to Russian literature, which pretty much stole my heart forever. The idea of penitence and redemption in Dostoevsky is so absolute.

DB: *Sogni e Bisogni*, the TV miniseries, was your first acting role and alongside your mother. Did you pursue acting as a way to get your parents attention or to prove to them that you could do what they do?

AA: I started doing it because the director, Sergio Citti, came to the house and liked my little androgynous scoundrel face and asked me to play in his movie. The idea hadn't crossed my mind before. I wanted to be a writer. But when I started doing it, I realized it was a great way to be the center of attention, not so much my parents, who wouldn't accompany me on the set, but of grownups in general.

DB: Did your parents ever push you toward anything when you were younger? Did they want you to stay out of acting and anything entertainment related?

AA: My mother wasn't into the idea of me acting. She always said she didn't want to look like Brooke Shield's mom. My father was proud of me. Every time I started a new movie, he would come to the set the first day and take a Polaroid of me.

DB: Next, you acted in *Demons 2*; do you have any strong memories of this shoot?

AA: I remember being in a car with fire and demons all around…and feeling a little scared.

DB: Around this time, your father made *Phenomena*. Fiore was in it. Did you have any desire to be in the film?

AA: No, but I dubbed the voice of the child assassin for the Italian version of the movie.

DB: Did you make friends with Jennifer Connelly at all?

AA: Yes. I was very young, so she was closer to Fiore, but she was so lovely and kind.

DB: What was this shoot like as an observer for you? It's a crazy film.

AA: I went to the set only once, when Fiore was getting her hand stabbed by a scissor. I remember feeling bad for her because my father made her repeat the take a number of times.

DB: *The Church* came next. Although you were young, can you tell me anything about working with Soavi? He's a unique talent and creates some interesting visuals and set pieces, but not in the way your father does.

AA: He was very gentle and fun to work with. I don't remember so much of the shoot, but there were other kids and we were in Budapest and we had a lot of fun watching soft-core porn on the hotel pay-TV.

DB: After two horror movies in a row, you did a few dramatic roles (*Zoo* and *Friends of the Heart*). What were these experiences like after being in such fantastic and dark films as a young actor? Did you have to use part of yourself as an actor you hadn't used up to this point?

AA: When I shot *Zoo*, I was 11 and it was my first lead role. I felt an immense pressure and responsibility. I won many awards for that movie. Shooting *Palombella Rossa* with Nanni Moretti was very hard because I was far from home and didn't have my family with me and felt very lonely. I would barely leave the hotel room. People thought I was a spoiled brat, but I was only depressed. I stopped acting in movies because of the shock until I did *Friends at Heart* at age 16. That was a big turning point for me. That's when I realized for the first time this was the job I wanted to do in life.

DB: Finally, your father put you in one of his films when you made *Trauma*. Since you had grown up watching your father work, do you think that prepared you for the type of director he would be?

AA: I was afraid he'd be severe. I was afraid to disappoint. But the experience was great and it brought us very close.

DB: Were you able to separate the familial relationship from the professional one at this point? Can you explain what this did to your relationship, working on this movie?

AA: We became friends. We were no longer father and daughter.

DB: Did you feel any reticence from the rest of the cast since you were Dario's daughter?

AA: Luckily not.

DB: After a few more films, you made *La Reine Margot*, which was a big success worldwide and was the first film I ever saw you in. Can you tell me about this film and what it did for your career and for you personally as an actor?

AA: When I tested for the movie, I had no idea it would be such a big production. It was my first French language movie and I didn't speak French. I am not sure what it did to my career; I never know what movies do to career/life.

DB: Most people outside Italy, myself included, have never seen *DeGenerazione*. Can you tell me a bit about this project?

AA: It was a collective movie directed by young upcoming directors of horror/fantasy. It was the first short movie I ever directed. It was pretty weird and I don't know how it fit with the rest. Mine was surreal, a dream about masturbation.

DB: *The Stendhal Syndrome* I consider to be one of your father's best films and my favorite of everything you have done together so far. It's a very rough journey your character takes. What was it like preparing to become this person who then becomes someone and something else entirely?

AA: It's my favorite movie that we shot together and the most challenging role. Maybe I was too young to play it (I turned 20 on the shoot).

DB: How much input did you have in the way your character looked in either guise?

AA: I didn't like the costumes very much and the wigs were a bit over the top.

DB: The film is really harmed in the English dub without your voice and your English, even in *Trauma*, was fine. Were you hurt when your vocal track was thrown out?

AA: Yeah, that didn't feel good. I remember when we presented the movie in the States, we'd always walk out of the screening when my character starts talking after the long sequence in the Uffizi museum.

DB: *Stendhal's* final shot of you in the arms of the police being carried away. What were you processing during this scene? It's very intense and poetic. It reminds me of Michelangelo's "Pieta."

AA: I was processing the loss of my sister. Especially that primal scream when the police catch her. The final image came to my father's mind just the day before we shot. I improvised the part of the dialogue when the character is making plans for her future before she gets caught.

DB: *Traveling Companion* and *Viola Kisses Everybody* got you some more international exposure and *Traveling Companion* won a lot of praise for your performance. Again, after working with your father, how were these two projects for you?

AA: *Traveling Companion* remains to this day one of my favorite movies I've ever done. Working with a master like Michel Piccoli was such a great lesson of cinema. *Viola Kisses Everybody* was a comedy, which became a big hit in Italy. It was very challenging to play in such a different genre of movies.

DB: *Phantom of the Opera*…when you read that script and your father approached you about it, were you hesitant? That story has been filmed so many times. What do you think your father brought to it that is special or unique?

AA: No, I was very enthusiastic. He had never done a movie like that before, a classic, a story that wasn't his. What my father brought was the opposite of Andrew Lloyd Webber.

DB: Was the lesbian innuendo between your character and Coralina's intentional? And can you explain what your father was doing with this dynamic between the characters?

AA: It's just a hint. My father loved the idea that my character was desired by everyone because of her innocence.

DB: What was Julian Sands like to work with?

AA: Very mysterious guy, very smart.

DB: You cast Davide d'Ingeo in *Scarlet Diva* after *Phantom*; is this where you met? And if so, I assume you hit it off right away. Can you tell me a bit about him and what you saw in him that made you want to cast him in *Diva*?

AA: We became friends and I saw his great potential. I wanted to give him a role that was different from the other things he had done.

DB: *B Monkey* had a pretty big release worldwide and they even reprinted the novel to tie into the film here in the U.S. Can you tell me a bit about the film and what the process was like?

AA: It was my first big English language movie. It was quite terrifying and once again, I felt an enormous responsibility. It was like starting from zero because no one knew who I was. But my inner warrior came out and I didn't let my fears have the best of me.

DB: There were some fairly extensive reshoots. Can you talk about this?

AA: Excruciating. Too many producers, too many opinions, too long of a shoot.

DB: And what were Rupert Everett, Jared Harris, and Jonathan Myers like? There were rumors you dated Myers. Is this true?

AA: Oh well...I also kissed Rupert.

DB: I know Abel Ferrara is a huge influence on your work and it shows in *Scarlet Diva*. What do you admire so much about Ferrara and how does his word drive yours?

AA: Working with Ferrara, for the first time, I didn't have to follow the camera, but the camera followed me. I encountered for the first time the joys of improvisation. Abel really pushes you to the limit. He makes you think you're coming up with something, but he's manipulated your mind so you're doing what he wants from you. I loved how he directed actors and learned a great deal from him.

Christine and Raoul in Phantom. COURTESY MAITLAND MCDONAGH/MEDUSA.

DB: *Diva* is a very personal film. What was the impetus behind it?

AA: After working with Ferrara, one of my favorite directors, everything seemed dull. I was agoraphobic and barely left my home. So I started writing a book. My father read a few pages and told me he saw a movie there. So I began writing it. Reality and fiction merged into my creative process.

DB: When we first met, you told me that you thought the film wasn't right for U.S. audiences and it was too rough and full of sex and drugs and unpleasant things that audiences here may not like. So once it was released here, what did you think of its reception?

AA: I was very flattered and surprised it had a release and the reception went beyond my wildest dreams.

DB: How did you writing the rhyme in *Non Ho Sonno* come about?

AA: My father asked me to write it. It came to me very naturally. It was like going back to write my childhood poetry.

DB: *The Heart is Deceitful Above All Things* is a polarizing film to say the least. But I think it shows a lot of growth in you as an artist. After the J.T. Leroy scandal, do you think the film is tarnished in any way?

AA: I felt quite relieved when I learned the story wasn't a real one, an autobiography. Even though, unfortunately, stories like these really happen in this world. It was so hard to play that character, the evil mother. My daughter was two years old. It was a demon that possessed me and it took so long to expel it. Maybe if I had known it was fiction, I wouldn't have been so loyal to the book (such a great book), but I would have changed it a bit. It's a good thing that I didn't. I thought I was doing psychodrama, that the movie would help J.T. overcome his horrible childhood.

DB: Do you see *Scarlet Diva* and *The Heart is Deceitful Above All Things* as companion pieces in any way?

AA: I think the two movies are completely different. Only the director is the same.

DB: Can you talk about this new script you've just finished?

AA: Not yet!

DB: Now that you have children, do you want them to follow into the family business? Anna is old enough to be acting and asking to do this kind of thing. What have you told her about it? Has she shown any interest?

AA: Anna Lou wants to be a rapper!

Asia and I, along with a few friends in San Francisco, California 2002. FROM THE AUTHOR'S COLLECTION.

DB: What prompted the desire to release a record? Did you ever have any serious intent to perform or record music?

AA: I started recording music 2 months after Anna was born, in 2001 with my beloved friend composer-producer Hector Zazou, RIP...I never stopped since. Music and literature, not movies are my real obsession since I was a little girl.

DB: The album is stylistically all over the place. Your film career and the roles you have taken reflect a similar attitude. Was there a conscious effort to make the songs as different from each other as possible?

AA: I listen to all sorts of music, mostly 60's and 70's, even though I DJ electronic music from early 90's and until 2005. I read mostly novels from the past, the so-called classics. My favorite movies are from the silent era till 1975. I guess I know music better than most musicians I know. Since I collaborated with many different musicians on the record I sort of adapted my poetry to their vibes.

DB: Working with Morgan...you made Anna together. And now music, how is the relationship the same or different? You are married now, is there any awkwardness jamming with your ex?

AA: Me and Morgan are best friends forever, always had been(even though we went through some rough times we are all set now), and always will...especially because of the art we started making together. Lately we have a newfound harmony prompted from making music again and concerts too. As far as my 'husband' [Michele Civetta] goes, I am happily separated since April.

DB: Have you given up acting? I saw a comment somewhere and you referred to yourself as an ex actress.

AA: Yes. I have given up that humiliating, degrading shit. I haven't enjoyed acting for 8 years. After my son Nicola was born in 2008 (except for the movie I have done with Fanny Ardant last winter) I never took acting gigs that lasted longer that 2 weeks.

DB: Can you give any details on the new film?

AA: Details will come soon. It's a story about children, set in 1984. My favorite actress in the world will play the role of the protagonist mother's. What I do is secret. SECRET.

DB: Lastly, how do you want to be remembered? As an actress, a director? A mother?

AA: As someone who has opened and walked through many doors.

IL CARTAIO
THE CARD PLAYER

After the almost universal praise of *Non Ho Sonno*, at least among most fans, Argento began work on its follow-up fairly quickly. In his first full-blown police procedural outside of "The Tram" episode of *Door Into Darkness*, Argento returns to his hometown of Rome to film *The Card Player*. The film's title brings to mind the series of paintings by Cézanne depicting French peasants playing cards and smoking. *The Card Player* is a surprisingly emotionally warm giallo inside of a sterile and, at times, adrift and cold "Policier" from a director experimenting with yet another visual style fairly late in his career.

Argento reaches into the past with the hook weapon from "The Tram" episode from *Door into Darkness* with Remo's death, the sound recording clue taken from *The Bird with the Crystal Plumage*, and naming a character "Professor Terzi" from *The Cat O' Nine Tails*. Bringing the giallo into the "now," the ever-present black-gloved killer lovingly strokes the keyboard of a computer he uses to ensnare his victims as he shows off his handiwork via webcam. William Malone's film *Feardotcom* from 2002 also used murders via webcam motif, and in both cases, it has rendered the films a bit dated right out of the gate.

Anna Mari (Stefania Rocca) is a police inspector who is on the trail of a killer who hides behind the Internet to force the authorities into games of "high stakes" online poker in a bid for the victims' lives. An Irish detective, John Brennan (Liam Cunningham), shows up on the scene on behalf of a British tourist who was murdered, and the two team up professionally and personally while they hunt down the killer.

Part of the police procedural is, of course, dissecting and examining dead bodies for clues — typically something Argento wasn't too keen on in the past. His attitude toward police and their work seems to lean toward the Hitchcock model in that it isn't terribly interesting to watch or it is something to be laughed at as in *Deep Red* with the police always eating or, in *The Cat O' Nine Tails*, exchanging recipes. *The Card Player* does, however, contain several moments that hew to the worn formula of the subgenre. In one scene, Anna and John are probing a corpse taken out of a river, only to be shown by the medical examiner that a playing card, the joker more precisely, had been inserted into the woman's vagina. John explains that perhaps the card is sending the message that he wants the police to know he's crazy, that he will do anything.

Back to "The Monster of Florence," one of his victims, Stefania Pettini, had a grape vine stuck in her vagina after her murder. These murders were so highly publicized in Italy, and even worldwide, for so long that it isn't surprising they could have perhaps seeped into Argento and Ferrini's writing. The unsolved murders that were credited to the so-called "Monster of Florence" were all couples out in public places, in parked cars, having romantic trysts. Criminologists have tried finding anything that points to the potential reasoning behind the grape vine being inserted into the woman's vagina. One theory was that it is a biblical allusion to the grapevine: "I am the vine, ye *are* the branches: He that abideth in me, and I in him, the same bringeth forth much fruit: for without me ye can do nothing."

Could the killer be saying that "He" is the judge that will bring down sentence on these people? The woman is being punished for her misdeeds and must pay with her life, and now he has made her reproductive organs useless. In several cases, the killer had removed the women's reproductive organs much like Jack the Ripper, also rendering their womanhood fallow in a symbolic gesture outside of taking their lives. In the same scene, while examining the corpse, John finds a seed from an unusual plant in the victim's nose. It would obviously have to have been planted there intentionally and has obvious parallels to Jody Foster finding the moth cocoon in the woman's throat in Ted Demme's *The Silence of the Lambs*.

Credited as "Victim 3," Vera Gemma makes her second appearance in an Argento film after a small role in *The Stendhal Syndrome* as the police woman who assists Anna after she is raped in Alfredo's car. Her role in *The Card Player,* is brief, but a bit more memorable as she is a victim this time. Gemma's enthusiasm for the role was evident: "I requested a small role but I wanted to be a victim. If you don't die in an Argento movie you don't exist. It's important! All the actors want to be in the movies, they all want to die! Dario strapped me to that chair for about a half an hour and

left me there to make me feel nervous. He wanted to make me feel angry, so when we would shoot I would really be trying to fight for my life. He doesn't talk a lot to actors, but he likes to put you in these situations so you feel like you're a victim. He wants to create these big, tense moments…"

In a film that is visually cold and sterile, dealing with the very technical day-to-day business of Anna and John's police work, there is an unexpected focus on the psychology of Anna and, in turn, her relationship with John. There are several instances of Argento showing the back or the top of Anna's head, almost suggesting that we are "entering" her mind. When the first poker game is being played, Anna turns away from the game being played, and the camera lingers on the back of her head. She is in effect turning away from her father, his gambling that ultimately took his life, and she is refusing to face herself and the possibility she may have to play the dreaded card game for fear of becoming like her him.

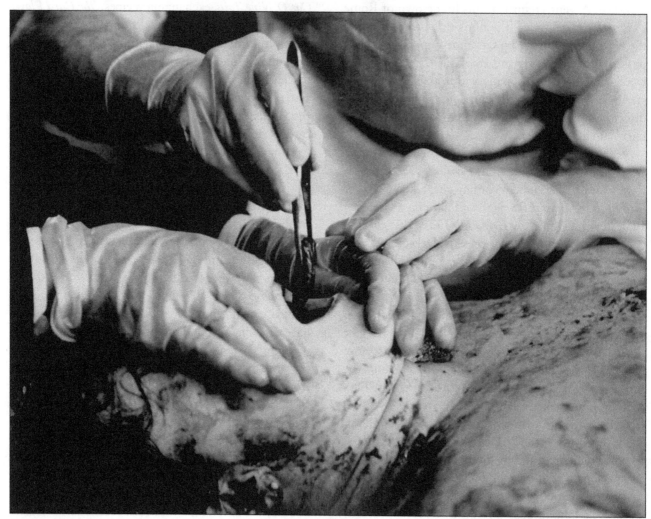

Jodie Foster discovers a disturbing clue in Silence of the Lambs. COURTESY THE DEL VALLE ARCHIVES/ORION.

The film's most striking set piece reveals a bit of Anna's insecurity, after she chases an intruder out of her home. Benoît Debie photographs Anna from overhead as she moves through her pitch black apartment, the room lit with intermittent shards of light through the windows. Once she reaches the backyard and jumps up on the fence, she castigates herself for not shooting him. "Shoot him; what are you waiting for?" she says to herself.

One gets the impression that Anna has never really given herself permission to have any kind of relationship outside of work with anyone. She has no friends to speak of, and so when John comes along, she is hesitant to open herself up to him — yet, despite her better judgment, she does so. Their sex scene in the film is possibly the most soap opera moment in any Argento film; it lacks any edge that most of the previous sex scenes display. Their handguns are shown lying together on the bedside table. Even Stefano

Dionisi and Chiara Caselli's love scene in *Non Ho Sonno* is intercut with Moretti's phone message.

As the film following *Non Ho Sonno*, *The Card Player* follows a logical line in being another "neo giallo," yet it already feels out of date because it depends so much on the online poker angle. The influence of the "torture porn" subgenre can also be seen in the way the victims are held hostage and their appendages being removed, albeit off camera. The traps set around the killer's home are also reminiscent of the *Hostel* variety of films and, out in the real world, the traps set by domestic terrorists to keep the police out of their homes.

Much can be said of Argento's thematic repetition and visual elements that he uses time and time again, and *The Card Player* doesn't do anything to quiet his critics. Unfortunately, the film, despite having some solid performances, is a bit flat. It's honorable for Argento to experiment with a new, sleeker feel for a project, but the script just isn't terribly interesting

Liam Cunningham as Det. John Brennan. COURTESY MEDUSA.

and the seemingly endless poker game scenes stop the film dead in its tracks.

On the sonic side of things, I am probably in the minority in thinking Simonetti's score for *The Card Player* to be one of his best solo efforts. Simonetti has completely embraced the inherent cheesiness of the online poker bit and created a soundtrack that is equally exciting and corny at times. A completely electronic effort, the creepier bits are truly effective, as when Anna is hunted down in her apartment by the killer. Things are just as entertaining and true when Anna shoots out the car stereo at the film's climax because the music is making her crazy — a shadow of Tilde in *Tenebrae* being menaced by the record being played upstairs before she shouts to have it turned down.

At this juncture in Argento's career, after so many theatrical features, it would seem somewhat strange for him to return to television, but that is exactly what he did with his follow-up, *Do You Like Hitchcock?* It's another giallo of sorts, only this time, an homage to the venerated British master of suspense from Italy's master of suspense and the "Italian Alfred Hitchcock," no less. To borrow a quote from the inspiration for his next project, I will defend Argento from his critics with a quote from Alfred Hitchcock, "Self-plagiarism is style."

TI PIACE HITCHCOCK?
DO YOU LIKE HITCHCOCK?

"Maybe I have inherited Hitchcock's audience, but certainly not his themes. Between me and Hitchcock there are differences of morality and neurosis. Hitchcock is a puritan while I am an anarchist, even too anarchist for my own good," Dario Argento is quoted as saying in the book *Dario Argento: il brivido, il sangue, il thrilling* (Edizione Dedalo, Fabio Giovannini 1986). And he isn't alone is separating the two. Mimsy Farmer, in an interview for Video Watchdog (issue 161), said, "I certainly wouldn't put Argento in the class with Hitchcock, but he hasn't done any harm to suspense movies, he's just done it differently. It's a different style."*Do You Like Hitchcock?* is the first of Argento's work for television since *Door Into Darkness* in the early 1970s, outside of a few commercials for Fiat, a household cleaner, and a rather amusing sugar commercial in which the product is so sweet it can chase even Dario Argento's monsters away. In what was a planned series of films for Italian television, Argento's appears to be the only one that was ever completed. Early in his career, Argento had the "Italian Hitchcock" label slapped onto him because of *The Bird with the Crystal Plumage*, and now, it seems, he has answered those critics directly with this "homage." Although the title asks an obvious question, the answer is not so simple, as it adds many other directors and filmic references to the response.

Alfred Hitchcock famously had two television shows, *Alfred Hitchcock Presents*, which ran for ten years, and then *The Alfred Hitchcock Hour*, which went for another four years. In turn, Argento had a short-lived variety show of sorts called simply *Giallo* — cohosted by Coralina Cataldi-Tassoni, in one episode wearing a matador-like outfit — which showed short horror films and interviews with various people associated with Argento's films, while the rather well-dressed audience clapped on cue.

Giulio (Elio Germano) is a film student living and studying in Turin. When he should be working on his thesis, he is instead spying on his neighbors and one rather attractive one across the way in particular. After the young woman's mother is murdered, Giulio is convinced that the girl is somehow involved in the crime. Inspired by the movies of Hitchcock, naturally, he is determined to get to the bottom of the mystery.

Giulio is working on a thesis not about Hitchcock, as the title would lead you to believe, but about German Expressionism, which is not, ironically, the school of film where Argento's favorite filmmakers, Lang and Murnau, did their most famous work. Hitchcock only really comes in when Sasha (Elisabetta Rochetti) and Federica (Chiara Conti) are in a video store with Giulio and he "spies" them arguing over who will rent the last copy of *Strangers on a Train*. Would this ever actually happen? No, but it's part of the setup. I'm sure they have been watching him as much as he's been watching them.

Allusions to *Rear Window* abound as Giulio and his girlfriend, Arianna, are both involved in the detection, much like James Stewart and Grace Kelly. The business with the house key is reminiscent of the key from *Notorious*, but, unlike here, the key actually has some bearing on the plot. Argento takes to referencing Brian DePalma as well, when Sasha does a seductive peep show in front of her window for Giulio, much like Holly Body (Melanie Griffith) in *Body Double*.

Damaged children and their parents factor here as well. Giulio's mother is overbearing but in a genuinely caring way. She only wants her son to be happy and be a better man than his father, while hoping her son will accept her new boyfriend. Sasha, on the other hand, has a harridan of a mother — at least from Sasha's point of view, as we are only privy to her "attacking" her daughter over watching TV too loud and showing concern for some reckless behavior.

Pino Dinaggio's score is a really nice touch, as it echoes Hermann's work. There is a strings piece like the main theme in *Psycho*, a circular-sounding theme that recalls *Vertigo*. Dinaggio borrows from his own work on various films he has scored for DePalma. Interestingly, there is some music in *Mother of Tears* written by Claudio Simonetti that sounds a bit like some of the music here.

For the first time, Argento uses a white-gloved killer as opposed to the trademark black gloves of gialli past. His own self-referencing continues with close-ups of the mechanisms of locks, much like in *Inferno*. It goes so far as to have *The Card Player* and *Scarlet Diva* advertised in the video shop where Giulio rents movies and first meets Sasha and Federica.

The central character of Giulio is reflective of Hitchcock's "everyman" heroes, who aren't heroic in the least and are only trying to figure out the mystery and stay alive in the process. Unlike Hitchcock, Argento doesn't make his leading men romantic figures. They are all highly flawed people for the most part, and Giulio is no exception. In one scene with Arianna, Giulio is quite rude to her and tells her that he has gotten rid of everything of hers in his apartment. But, in the end, the two kiss and make up, and Arianna is there to help Giulio out of his predicament once Federica is revealed to be the killer in a scene on a rooftop, which echoes *Vertigo*.

Argento's return to television has yielded his strongest work post-*Non Ho Sonno*, excepting *The Card Player*. The cheap and nasty thrills of his later work seem to fit better into the medium of television than the underfunded and overly ambitious films he has been trudging through. Ironically, the inverse would be expected, as most directors don't bode well with the prescribed restrictions of television. However, in the case of *Do You Like Hitchcock?*, it doesn't suffer from the smaller budget. He has reigned-in the grander excesses that fall flat in *Mother of Tears*, while hinting at what is possible with *Jenifer* and *Pelts* — his episodes for the Mick Garris-created *Masters of Horror* — when he is challenged with smaller budgets and tight shooting schedules.

Giulio's new neighbor is reading Mary Roberts Rinehart's *A Light in the Window*. Rinehart was an American writer known for her murder mysteries, most famously *The Bat*, which was a huge success on stage and then was made into two films. Rinehart also wrote *The Yellow Room*, which could have also been a fun in-joke. But the title *A Light in the Window* is a nice pun; it is that light in the window which draws Giulio in and causes all this trouble. Will he be able to stay away in the future?

INTERVIEW

WALTER FASANO

(Editor, *The Card Player, Do You Like Hitchcock?,*
Mother of Tears; co-writer *Mother of Tears.*)

Fasano is has been a professional editor since the 1990's and has worked on narrative and non-narrative projects alike. He has also contributed to films as composer, writer, and director.

DB: You first worked with Asia on *Your Tongue on My Heart.* How did that job come about? And what was the experience like working with her?

WF: I had already met Asia a few years before working together on *Your Tongue on My Heart.* When she was asked to direct and star in this music video, she invited me to work with her and I happily agreed. I was assistant director and editor. Shooting and editing was delightful. We shot a couple of days, including burning a stuffed animal, a panther, in her flat. We edited the video in three days.

DB: The first film you edited for Dario was *The Card Player.* Did you get this job because of your work with Asia or did Argento already know you in a professional capacity?

WF: I had met Dario before, but it was only for *The Card Player* that I was invited to work with him. He was looking for a new editor and I knew his assistant director, Roy Bava (son of Lamberto, nephew of Mario); I think he suggested Dario to meet me. I had dinner with him and his brother Claudio in a small trattoria in Rome in a break during a night shoot. We spoke about the movies of the Dardenne Brothers and his Belgian DP Benoit Debie. Being a cinephile, I was very interested in the subject matter and I knew Dario was a cinephile. So after this talk… well, I got the job.

DB: The editing job on *The Card Player,* there is a great montage under the opening credits of Stefania Rocca getting to work in the morning and starting her day; was this your concept or Dario's?

WF: The concept was Dario's and I tried to make it the best I could.

DB: Simonetti's music in this scene is a nice way, along with your montage, to set the mood for the film. How was the music laid in? Did you edit to music or was the score done to your edit?

WF: Both. I made a rough cut without music (I often cut sequences without sound), then laid a temp track, then selected a track between Claudio's original ones for the movie. Then he post-produced his track. Claudio is great; it's great fun working with him. After so many years with Dario, he's still more passionate and serious. He named a track of *The Card Player* "Fasan Techno" after me!

DB: Simonetti has said that he writes the music sometimes without even seeing anything shot. Have you had this experience working with Argento and Simonetti? That you have to edit to his music?

WF: Yes, he did this in *The Card Player.* I had 4 or 5 tracks to start working with. He had written these tracks reading the script. I cut some sequences to his tracks and sometimes cut his music on "my" sequences.

DB: *Do You Like Hitchcock?* has a great scene with the scooter chase. How much would you say of the editing was Argento, how much is you?

WF: The vision is often Dario; the technique and fine tuning is mine.

DB: Did Pino Donaggio's score for *Hitchcock* influence your editing? And what do you think are the biggest differences to an editor's eye and ear between Simonetti and Donaggio in terms of what they deliver?

WF: Pino scored the movie after we finished the rough cut. We already had temp-tracked the rough cut with some of his music, some of Bernard Herrman's. Donaggio was not present in the sound mix, whereas Simonetti is usually there. Pino is a very nice person to work with, collaborative, interesting.

DB: What was the biggest challenge of this *Mother of Tears*?

WF: The biggest challenge was surely the short post-production time we had for delivering the movie and the small budget for the vfx that were made in Canada, completely different time zone, conference calls at night…

DB: How does working with Argento as a director differ from others you have worked alongside as an editor?

WF: Dario cuts movies very fast. He has got clear ideas, arrives early in the morning, goes away at mid-afternoon so that the editor can fine-tune all the work done during the day. I assembled his movies very fast (5 weeks for *The Card Player*) and asked him for four more days to work on it to get to the final cut. He likes to watch the rough cut with temporary music and sound effects. Then there are some weeks for working on the movie until we felt it was ok. With me, he was always kind and focused. He follows every phase of the post-production.

DB: What is your favorite part of editing a film?

WF: I like every part of it.

DB: Do you have a favorite film of Argento's? Did you grow up watching his work? If so, what is it like to work with someone whose work you have been a fan of?

WF: I definitely grew up watching Dario's movies. *Profondo Rosso*, *Suspiria*, and *Inferno* are all-time favourites for me. I knew them almost by heart before meeting him and this surely helped me in finding a good way to communicate with him, including also the fact that he's a cinephile, and we share a lot of common ground.

MASTERS OF HORROR

A two-season horror anthology show created by Mick Garris and then licensed to Showtime Networks in the United States, *Masters of Horror*, was a welcome inclusion into the long tradition of horror on television, taking its cues from such classic shows as *Thriller*, hosted by Boris Karloff, *The Twilight Zone*, and, more recently, *Tales from the Crypt*. Garris was tasked with gathering creative talent for the series and was able to pull together an impressive, if uneven, roster of directors for the series.

With a collection of directors ranging from Stuart Gordon to Takashi Miike, Garris wanted the show to have an international appeal, and when it came time to find a European director, he said, "He was our first choice. He is the great European horror director. Who do you go to except Dario Argento?" With that mindset, a few stories were given to Dario for his first season episode and he settled on *Jenifer*, based on a story by Bruce Jones and illustrated by Bernie Wrightson from *Creepy* magazine. Steven Weber wrote the script and Argento summarily removed some of the more comedic material along with a good portion of the dialogue, according to Garris.

"He [Argento] really liked the sensual and sexual aspects of this irresistible monster." Garris told me. "I mean, from the head up, she's hideous, but there's a hypnotic quality about her. And from the neck down, anybody would find it difficult to resist this goddess, you know. And he loved the dichotomy of the ugly and the beauty. Beauty and the Beast; he always referred to Jenifer as being both."

Frank Spivey (Steven Weber) is a cop on a lunch break with his partner when they spot a guy about to knife a girl to death. Spivey shoots the man, but only after he shouts a warning, "Go away, you don't know what she is! You have no idea!" Spivey rushes over to him as he utters his last word: "Jenifer." The girl, who doesn't speak and is seemingly deformed, is taken to a state mental hospital for the once over, and Spivey discovers she is a Jane Doe with nowhere to go. So, being the Good Samaritan he is, he decides to take her in for a while like a lost puppy. And it doesn't take long for his decision to have rather dire ramifications.

Weber, as the victim of this succubus, turns in a fine performance and seems to be channeling a bit of his performance as Jack Torrance from Mick Garris's miniseries of Stephen King's *The Shining*. Speaking of King, Argento claims King had approached him a few times to adapt his work and Dario declined, afraid he would not be able to do the material justice. Carrie Fleming gives a near silent performance outside of some cries and moans and does a fantastic job with the role. The moment where she thinks she has pleased him by stuffing that circus owner in the refrigerator is especially memorable, given the character's base knowledge of human emotion. He is laughing, so he must be happy, right?

Possibly the most interesting aspect of this film is the sexuality it exudes, or I should say oozes, and it is almost always nearly repulsive and is unlike anything Argento had ever done before. From the frigid relationship between husband and wife to the insatiable appetite of the creature, Argento really seems to go all out with every opportunity for these characters to have sex. But it also must be noted that in Steven Weber's character, there is another instance of the impotent male who falls victim to the wills of a woman. His life revolves around this entity in the hopes of saving something in himself, since the relationship with this wife is in shambles and he needs the validation. And he is addicted to it and her, like a drug. Or is he under the spell of some unseen force within Jenifer?

Claudio Simonetti's score begins with a child's lullaby, much like the opening of *Deep Red*, to relate the innocence of the Jenifer character. Much like Carlo from *Deep Red*, she is a victim of circumstance, and they only act according to situations and environments they are placed in to survive and little more. As if he were suffering a hangover from *The Card Player*, certain cues feel inspired by the feeling of that work, especially the young boy chasing Jenifer through the woods. In a few instances, the score even resembles portions of Hermann's work for *Psycho*, but overall, it is not terribly consistent with the visuals.

Argento returned for the second season with the superior *Pelts*, based on a short story by F. Paul Wilson. Jake Feldman (Meatloaf as Meatloaf Aday) is a sleazy fur trader obsessed with two things: making the perfect fur coat for a trade show, and a stripper at a local club. One will help him get the other, but at what price? Speaking of *Pelts*, Mick Garris told me, "He went back to the full primary color palette with *Pelts*, with the stuff in the strip club especially. It's our wettest episode, blood, not seminal fluid. It's incredibly grotesque in a wonderfully over the top way and I expect nothing less from Dario."

Meatloaf in the lead role is a nice surprise, having liked some of his work in the past — his turn in *Fight Club* is unforgettable and, of course, his Eddie in *The Rocky Horror Picture Show* is memorable. He has never been asked to carry a film to my knowledge, but he is more than up to the challenge here. He is a compelling screen presence, even though he is a completely pathetic and unlikable bully. Ellen Ewusie is beautiful to look at, and she's a feisty actress who imbues Shanna with some fire when warranted, but also with a desperation that is palpable.

Argento appears to have had more confidence with this second outing than the first as there is more for him to play with in terms of the characters and overall story. *Jenifer* was a very straightforward and simple story, yet they both share a common weak male in the service of a woman to, in turn, get something from her. Also like *Jenifer*, this film is obsessed with sex and what people will do to get it and try to keep it. Jake is a fur trader who has found the most amazing pelts from a seemingly rare breed of raccoon. His first thought is to make a coat for Shanna, a stripper he visits and harasses frequently at the club where she works. But she puts up with it because he always pays her well.

Their dynamic is interesting because they are both in the business of selling their respective "pelts" — Jake with this animal fur and Shanna with her own, which is a rather lascivious visual pun. There is another level to this innuendo, as Jake is attracted to these "coon pelts" and, not to be racially insensitive, but he is after Shanna's "coon pelt" as well. I cannot help but think this tacky joke is intentional, and if it's not, it's a rather perverse coincidence. It must be noted that Argento reveals Shanna to be a lesbian, or at least bisexual, in a scene where she is having sex with a woman in an office at the club. He seems to be treading Jess Franco territory, cramming as many breasts into a one hour film as he can and capping it off with a girl-on-girl sex scene.

The visual design of the film seems to also reflect a bit more of Argento's previous work, whereas *Jenifer* was drained of life, much like its lead character. The strip club where Shanna works it gaudily lit in the front, and the back halls and rooms look like something out of *Suspiria* with blood red walls and black doors. To be more precise, the walls appear to have had blood thrown on them and it dried as it ran down.

Shanna's apartment, when we finally get inside along with Jake, looks like something out of Bava's "A Drop of Water" segment from *Black Sabbath*.

Off of the visual and on to the aural: Claudio Simonetti turns in an average score that gets the job done without any memorable cues. There is a theme that sounds a bit like the love theme from *Non Ho Sonno* that is played during the sex scene with Stefano Dionisi and Chiara Caselli. Simonetti would join Argento on his next feature film, *Mother of Tears*, the conclusion to the "Three Mothers Trilogy" that began in 1977 with *Suspiria*.

Jenifer seduces her prey in a page from *Creepy* magazine, illustrated by Bernie Wrightson.

ISSUE 63, 1974. WARREN PUBLISHING.

INTERVIEW

MICK GARRIS

(Producer, *Masters of Horror*)

Having begun has career in film producing behind the scenes films for Avco Embassy, Garris soon caught the eye of Steven Spielberg, who hired him to write on the TV show *Amazing Stories*. Since then, Mick has written and directed many adaptations of Stephen King's work; the theatrical film *Sleepwalkers* (1992), the mini-series of *The Stand* (1994) arguably being the most successful and the mini-series of *The Shining* (1997) being the most controversial among fans. Beyond the two Stev(ph)ens, he has also contributed on *Hocus Pocus* (1993), with the story credit, directed *Psycho IV: The Beginning* (1990), and continued on with *Masters of Horror* as a network TV series *Fear Itself* in 2008. His wife Cynthia has worked on several projects with him as an actress, and appeared in Argento's *Masters of Horror* episode, "Jenifer."

DB: How do you feel Argento fits into the horror genre as a film director?

MG: Well, what's great about Argento and just about everything he has done fits into that mode is that they have their own sense of dream logic. You don't go to an Argento film thinking about structure and beginning, middle, and end or classical American storytelling. They tap into something far richer and deeper and more subconscious. They have their sense of nightmare, dream logic. And he uses this really wonderful palette of primary colors. And a fluid camera that you never know what it's capable of doing; it floats around and really is your psyche at work unconsciously. Dario is a great artist in that regard. Not everything in his movies makes literal sense, but they're not supposed to. The early gialli maybe do. But as they became more sophisticated…*Suspiria* was really a launching point of this style of color and madness and bizarreness and wet stuff like crazy! He's probably the leading proponent of this kind of imagery.

DB: Speaking of this dream logic, is there any particular moment or set piece that really stands out for you?

MG: The scene in *Inferno* where the entire room is underwater and you are floating through that. That is probably one of the deepest, most beautiful realizations of the subconscious I have ever seen on film. It's

really quite spectacular and innovative. Neil Jordan did something similar in one of his movies, but, of course, Dario did it first.

DB: As a filmmaker, in what way do you see his influence being felt most?

MG: Well, I think his influence is enormous and mostly in the complete fearlessness of what he's doing. Just the total commitment that if it's going to be grotesque, then by God, it's really going to be grotesque and not being limited by traditional logic. And to some, that would be a criticism, but to me, it's a freeing of the artistic soul. And his influence, starting with *Suspiria*, mostly, I think, has been felt in horror films internationally. I've been going to a lot of film festivals around the world with Masters of Horror and seeing reactions to the episodes and in Italy at the Torino film festival, I told Dario, "You're the Beatles! It's John, Paul George, and Dario!" So the reaction to him in Europe is that he's a superstar. He's only known by the cult here in the U.S. But around the world, he's seen as quite an amazing guy.

(Cynthia Garris comes in…)

DB: How were you cast in *Jenifer*?

CG: I got cast in the role of the mother of the teenage boy in *Jenifer* because my wonderful husband suggested it to Dario Argento. He did require me to audition for it. But he did hire me and it was really exciting to be hired by him. I've always loved him, oh, *Suspiria*. I saw that when it first came out. And I always loved that movie so much. It was a dream to be able to work with him.

DB: Was it strange to be cast via the Internet?

CG: I had to go to a casting office and I had to audition in front of a camera and they sent my audition to Italy for Dario to view. And I'm told he said, "She'll work out, just don't make her look so rich." I wasn't wearing any jewelry…I toned it down. But I guess I just have that look!

DB: What was it like working with him since Dario's English is somewhat limited?

CG: Working with Dario was a completely unique experience. I only worked one very long day. Most of my scenes were with Steve Weber, who is an old friend from working together before. Dario is like this joyous child. There's just something about him…his enthusiasm…I was never intimidated by him. I thought I would be because of the great Argento. But he giggles a lot and nothing seems to bother him at all. The day went smoothly. Although he has a unique style of directing! He likes to edit while he directs, so there's a lot of stopping in the middle of scenes and turning the camera around, a way that we're not used to here. But he was delightful and I know just one or two words in Italian, so I kept hurling them at him all day. I do know some vulgar words and I was very careful not to use them. I think I kept asking him where the toilet was over and over again…among other things.

DB: There is a rumor I've heard for years that Dario doesn't like working with actors; did you get any impression of this?

CG: My impression of him is that he loves actors. I don't know what kind of fits he may throw in his own country when he can fully express himself through his native language. All I know is he was delightful. In fact, I was nervous about working that day and Steve Weber was really off his game, I don't know if he was staying in character all day or what. Between the three of us, I think he was just magnificent. And he held it all together. He even just smiled and let me go on this laughing jag about nine hours into trying to understand what he wanted me to do in this one scene. It was very hard for him and his interpreter to get me to understand what he wanted me to do and I just kinda lost it. I did that thing that would show up on a blooper reel if I were more famous. I just couldn't stop laughing, but he didn't get mad. He just let me laugh and laugh and blow a few takes. So I think he's wonderful to work with. Dario did a lot of kissing of my hands. He is very European. You know, there was almost subservience about him, a kind of gratitude. He was lovely and not intimidating at all. I've worked with some directors that can be very intimidating. But not my husband!

(Cynthia leaves.)

DB: Has Dario had any direct influence on you as a filmmaker?

MG: Probably not so much as a writer, but it's hard to not be inspired by someone who is visually creative. And he has made so many films that have gone so visually adventurous that I would say definitely there are moments in *Valerie on the Stairs* that could have antecedents in Dario's work. Maybe *The Shining* had some influence as well. In *The Shining*, I did some theatrical kind of lighting changes within shots that are not really traditional in modern filmmaking, but Dario's done a lot of that and the palate of going to primary colors in *Quicksilver Highway* was inspired by *Suspiria*.

DB: Let's talk about *Masters of Horror*; it really is your baby.

MG: Well, I may have been the facilitator, but it wouldn't have existed without these incredible people who have decades of experience in guiding the whole horror genre. Modern horror really was created by these guys. I would love to take credit for it, but I was just the guy who was able to round up the masters.

DB: Can you talk about the genesis of *Masters of Horror*?

MG: A lot of us are friends. A lot of the filmmakers in the genre are friendly and we run into each other at conventions or socially or at film festivals, that sort of thing. And there would always be the, "We should all get together for dinner sometime and wouldn't that be great?" And I realized after a few years of this that nobody was going to do anything about it unless I did. So I spent about a week contacting a bunch of the guys that I knew and it was really complicated trying to pin them down for a date and so I spent a full week trying to do that. And we had a dinner with a dozen of us: it was me, John Carpenter and John Landis, Tobe Hooper and Larry Cohen, and William Malone, Guillermo Del Toro. And we had a great time. Everybody really had fun; you're not doing interviews, you're not doing anything for the press or doing sound bites or talking about movies you're trying to promote. It was just kind of a let your hair down…no friends, no spouses, no girlfriends, boyfriends, things like that. And it was just a really good time with a bunch of people with a lot of shared experiences. So we have done six or seven of them now over the last couple of years. And we would basically talk about how great it would be to do work of our own without interference from anybody else and that led to " Hey kids, let's put our own show on!"

And so I got everyone to commit to the concept of one-hour movies that were completely up to the director creatively. How they wanted to handle it. Give them creative control. If we could find a network that would license it and someone to finance it. And so IDT, the company that owned Anchor Bay, jumped right in. We pitched to three companies and all of them wanted it. Anchor Bay said, "Fine, when do we start?" and "How much will it cost?" and we were off and running.

DB: When did Showtime get involved then?

MG: Well, we would have made the show with or without a network because it was financed by a DVD company. But we knew it would be a lot better if we could take it to a network. Showtime wasn't looking for a series at the time, but they knew how smart an idea it was to get this show. They had never had a *Tales from the Crypt* or anything like that. John Carpenter had made *Body Bags* and that was a pilot for an anthology series that Tobe Hooper worked on with him, but that was several years back. Because we were making it, they wouldn't have any ownership in it, but they could license it at a very low fee and it was a very low fee. So they jumped at the chance. They came onboard and it was a really good partnership. They didn't spend much money for the license or much on promotion, but it became their second highest-rated series. It was a great relationship for everyone involved.

DB: How were the stories chosen and then given to the directors?

MG: The directors got the material from two sources: my producer and I would meet with writers and get pitches from them or we would search through short stories we thought would be interesting. We also developed a bunch of scripts from freelance writers or I would write something. And about half of the directors chose from those scripts. We would give them everything and give them a choice. Sometimes we would choose a few that we thought would be appealing to a certain director because of their own style or taste in material. Half of them would come in with their own material or write it themselves or bring in a writing partner. Joe Dante brought in *Homecoming* that he had written with Sam Hamm. John Landis and his son, Max, wrote *Deer Woman* together.

DB: How was Dario's episode developed?

MG: That was one we developed. I was working on *Desperation* with Steven Weber and it looked like

Masters of Horror was getting close to happening. Weber came up with a story from the early 70s that Bernie Wrightson illustrated and Bruce Jones and written [that appeared in *Creepy* magazine]. It was one of a couple we sent to Dario because we thought they would really appeal to him. We sent him the comic story as well and he ended up recreating some of the panels from it in the show. We were right; it really appealed to him and hit him right where he lives.

DB: Do you recall anything specific about it that he commented on when you presented it to him?

MG: He seemed to like the madness of it. He really liked the sensual and sexual aspects of this irresistible monster. I mean, from the head up, she's hideous, but there's a hypnotic quality about her. And from the neck down, anybody would find it difficult to resist this goddess, you know. And he loved the dichotomy of the ugly and the beauty. Beauty and the Beast; he always referred to Jenifer as being both. It was interesting because Weber had written the script and starred in it, but yet had to hand it over to Dario, but had total creative control. Weber is a very verbal writer. There was a lot of humor and dialogue in it that Dario didn't want to deal with. He pulled out I think a third of the dialogue that Weber had written. He wanted it to be more visual than aural.

DB: You mentioned the fact that Weber wrote it. Dario usually writes all his own material.

MG: Well, Dario really liked the script and it was an opportunity to make an American film. He rarely works outside of Italy. It was a thrill for us. We always wanted the show to be international. Both years, we had an episode shot in Japan and Dario was our bid for the European director. He was our first choice. He is the great European horror director. Who do you go to except Dario Argento? He really liked the story and the comic. But he definitely came in and made it his own. And Weber, as Cynthia mentioned, was a little off his game or upset, I think, because a lot of his quite clever dialogue wasn't in it anymore. He is a huge horror fan and was thrilled when Dario became involved in working with him. All of his qualms were put to bed immediately when he saw how well it was received with audiences.

DB: In regards to the episodes, how much freedom were the directors given to do what they wanted?

MG: On *Masters of Horror*, the directors are given total freedom…now that doesn't mean you can do anything because there are broadcast standards and especially in the wake of Janet Jackson showing her nipple and destroying the youth of America. The FCC has been really nasty in the Bush Administration, which is only appropriate since it is the nastiest administration in our history. When we were shooting, and I know what you're getting at…there is a scene in which Jenifer bites off a sixteen-year-old boy's penis. We knew when we were shooting that this makes it hardcore and that it was going beyond the pale, even beyond what you can do on pay TV. There are a lot of stores that won't sell things that are X-rated or unrated. And if you have someone with a penis in her mouth, even if it's for violent purposes rather than erotic purposes, you are violating standards. And Dario knew while we were shooting that it wouldn't be broadcast that way. But he said, "You know, let's do it anyway. Nobody's ever done this before and maybe it will go on the European DVD." And nobody thought it would end up on the supplements of the U.S. DVD. But it's there to be seen.

DB: *Jenifer* is much more sexual than anything Argento has done in the past, probably more than all his previous films combined.

MG: There has always been an erotic element to his movies, but I really think he got excited to do a story that was so decidedly erotic. With *Pelts*, this is even more so. When I saw him on the set of *Mother of Tears* in Torino, he said to me the *Masters of Horror* experience unlocked his creativity and that was fantastic! Here are two scripts written by two people other than Dario and he had a lot of input obviously… they challenged him and brought out these wonderful explosions of creativity. And I think the eroticism of them is what he really responded to. When Venne wrote *Pelts*, he wrote it with Dario attached. But he really wanted to go as far as he could in the sex and violence. It was great to see him do that. When we were reading women for the part of Jenifer, it was great to watch. I was in a hotel room with one of my producers and Dario and he would be down on the floor on all fours, miming, "No, do it like cat! Very sexy!" It was just great to watch him to it and show her what he wanted. It was just an incredible sense of dedication and the art of making movies. And working with actors, it was great to watch him. He loves actors. I don't know where it had been said that he doesn't. It's not like Hitchcock

and the cattle; he kind of blossoms around them. He is very fatherly and kind and loves it when they bring something to it themselves.

DB: I have to say your impression of Dario is pretty good!

MG: He's so filled with enthusiasm. It's hard to not be filled with affection for him. I first met him years ago at the Saturn Awards for the Science Fiction Academy. I was introduced to him as the guy who did *The Stand*. He was actually approached to make it after George Romero was attached to it for so long. He said to me, "*The Stand* it is, it's big!" One of the greatest things in doing *Masters of Horror* was becoming friends with Dario. He's a very loving, affectionate friend. Seeing him on the set of *Mother of Tears*, he came up to me, gave me a hug,, and said, "Mick, I love you!" To have Dario Argento tell you he loves you is a very humbling experience because he's such a great guy.

DB: As a producer, what was it like working with him?

MG: Well, I wasn't around much. I would be there a few days and really just left the directors alone unless there was a major problem that needed to be resolved. Dario works very quickly; he knows exactly what he wants. And he does shoot in a way that is foreign to Northern American filmmaking. You'll usually do a master, a close-up, over the shoulder, a reverse. He would start out with what he wanted of the master. Then he would go "cut," then do the end. Then do a close-up for a few lines, an insert here or there. We shot with two cameras most of the time. He likes to work fast. And he wasn't feeling well making *Jenifer*; he had been sick, was having back pain. On *Pelts*, he was not having these problems. *Pelts* is gorgeously shot; with *Jenifer*, it was more of a muted palette because the comic was in black and white and he was emulating that. He went back to the full primary color palette with *Pelts*, with the stuff in the strip club especially. It's our wettest episode, blood, not seminal fluid. It's incredibly grotesque in a wonderfully over the top way and I expect nothing less from Dario. He works in a way that is unconventional to us, but is more common overseas. Just puzzle pieces. Bogdanovich once said filmmaking is making pieces of time and putting them together. And it's really evident in the way he [Dario] works.

DB: What was pre-production like on these episodes?

MG: Well, for *Pelts*, he and Matt Venne (the screenwriter) did a lot of back and forth with revisions. Usually, you have to deal with notes from networks, studios, and producers. We, the producers, would give him notes, but it was up to him if he wanted to use them or not. The pre-production was relatively short. It's only seven days and ten of shooting. There would be things going on before that, of course. But the pre-production with Dario in Vancouver was very fast. There would be meetings of the department heads and those various groups and they were off!

DB: Was there anything in *Pelts* that he couldn't do since *Jenifer* had the penis eating removed?

MG: No, he got everything he wanted there. For example, Miike's episode, Showtime couldn't even edit it down, it was so aggressively nasty. So they decided to just not show it at all. And I like that better than "OK, cut this, trim that." It's better that there be no creative intrusion on a filmmaker. But there were a few rules that Showtime laid down, but just because *Imprint* was so nasty, they just decided to not show it even though it didn't break any of Showtime's rules. Although it was released theatrically in Japan, in the U.K., it was aired. So it just goes to show the differences in what countries will accept.

DB: What do you think would be the greatest cultural divide between the U.S. and the rest of the world in terms of horror movies then?

MG: I think the big thing is the logic gap. Here, we need things laid out in a way we can accept. It's never been that way with a lot of European or Japanese films. In Japan, all the ghost stories, there is a kind of nightmare logic. The whole idea that everything needs to be wrapped up by the end of the movie is a very American attitude; not so in Europe. Opera, Italian opera, is so big and overblown that it influenced all of the cultural pursuits in Italy and maybe throughout Europe. So that sense that you don't have to tie everything up by the end may be the biggest difference between American and European films, especially Argento because they revel in the weird logic and the nightmare dreamscapes. We want the directors to bring that international sense to the outing and Argento certainly did.

LA TERZA MADRE
MOTHER OF TEARS

Mother of Tears was screening at the USC campus, and in attendance were Jace Anderson and Adam Gierasch, who wrote the screenplay with Argento. You could definitely feel the curiosity and electricity in the air as the film started, especially since it was introduced via a video from Argento himself. If I remember correctly, he said a professor at USC was going to be teaching a course on his work and that he was excited to come visit the school and audit the class.

The audience's response to the film that night was hard to gauge, as people were laughing throughout the film at almost everything that happened, whether it was meant to be humorous or not. During the "spike through the vagina" scene, one older woman got up in a huff and exclaimed, "I've had enough!" and left the theater. The demon at Asia's bedside did garner some gasps and jumps, and some of the weirder ritualistic sex by the witches made a few go "Eew." By the time the closing credits rolled, there was some clapping and laughing, but I mostly remember a guy next to me, upon hearing that dreadful song by Simonetti and Dani Filth, scream, "What is this shit?" I couldn't agree more. That song works about as well as the random reggae band at the end of *Trauma* and the Kim Wilde song tacked onto U.S. prints of *Tenebrae*.

"I can't take anymore. I feel like I'm going crazy," Asia Argento's character, Sarah Mandy, says to Udo Kier's Father Johannes. Trust me, Asia, I can relate. After almost three decades since *Inferno*, it is a sad state of affairs that this is the conclusion to the trilogy set up with *Suspiria* back in 1977. The films before it had a mystery and grace to them that were singular to the world Argento had created with the duo of films that began the tale of the three mothers.

With so much anticipation riding on this project, there really is no way Argento could have won this one, so I can cut him some slack. But when you take the time to build a world over the course of two films, only to completely abandon it when you make the third, it just feels like a lazy and nonsensical way to approach things in the eyes of the fans that have been waiting years for some kind of conclusion to this story. It may have done him well to look back on *Suspiria* and *Inferno* for reference to create a piece that would fit into the puzzle he has been creating all these years. Instead, we get a cheap-looking, badly acted film that name-drops elements of the previous two, while totally dismissing what made them a marvel to experience.

Argento has surrounded himself with many familiar names: Asia plays our "hero" Sarah Mandy (Sienna Miller was considered for the role as well), and she is not a terribly likeable character. Coralina Cataldi-Tassoni plays her friend and coworker, Giselle; Udo Kier plays a deliciously campy priest; and Daria Nicolodi cameos as Asia's mother, just as she did in *Scarlet Diva* a decade prior. Massimo Sarchielli, who was Leone in *Non Ho Sonno*, shows up here as a homeless man, acting as a sort of sentry, who is living in the villa of the Mother of Tears. Offscreen, Argento is reunited with Frederic Fasano, who he had worked with previously on *Do You Like Hitchcock?* Fasano's photography is almost completely uninspired, but he's only following orders. I understand that Dario didn't want to completely reproduce the candy-colored environments of *Suspiria* and *Inferno*, but *Mother of Tears* is so drab and realistic-looking that it only resembles the other films in brief glimpses: at the exterior of the lair of the titular witch and her followers as they torture citizens of Rome, and each other, in a prolonged sexual orgy, in shots that are scattered through the film.

Claudio Simonetti's score is much less of an assault than it was in the other films he scored for Argento, with or without Goblin, as the music isn't as prevalent in the sound mix as it was in the past. The standout piece of music here is in the scene when Sarah is in the cab on her way to the lair of the Third Mother. It cleverly echoes both cab rides in *Suspiria* and *Inferno* — the only thing missing is Fulvio Mingozzi driving the car. On almost every front, the music seems to be nothing more than a decent addition, rather than something to experience. It is largely driven by a classical influence with a choir that appears throughout. There is a song over the end credits cowritten by Dani Filth — of the British rock group, Cradle of Filth — that is just terrible in every conceivable way. The opening titles theme is one of the better pieces of music, and it is accompanied by some interesting imagery, most notably some detail of several Hieronymus Bosch paintings.

Seeing as the opening to *Suspiria* is such an exercise in excess, it's only fitting that the opening to the finale to the trilogy be over the top as well. However, the original opening was much more intense, with a scene that comes before the cemetery scene that opens the film now. Deep in the catacombs, where three witches hold their rites, a small group of robed figures are seen at an elegant table setting, enjoying a meal consisting of a teenage boy, whom they are eating while he is still alive.

The way the film opens now, with the odd cemetery excavation — I still don't understand why they were rooting around back there — and the digging up of that coffin and stone box, it's just a rush to get to the violent bits. It doesn't take Giselle long to open up Satan's toy box by cutting open the wax seal that the Monsignore has applied to keep the evil captive. Of course, she cuts her finger because this thing needs blood, as per usual. In a ridiculous leap of logic, Giselle handles these centuries-old artifacts with her bare hands, one of them bleeding, while telling Sarah to be careful. My favorite part of this entire scene has to be the unveiling of this magical "talisman" which gives the "Model of Tears" her power: a t-shirt made of what looks like sackcloth dyed purple and accented with a gold glitter pen from a craft store. It's the newest

Shadows of death. COURTESY MYRIAD PICTURES.

centuries-old "artifact" I've ever seen. Also contained within the box are, conveniently, a jeweled knife and three statues that remind me of the "hear no evil, speak no evil, see no evil" monkeys that my grandmother had in her house when I was a child.

Jace Anderson told me that when it came to the witch's familiar, the little monkey that chases Sarah in this scenewho shows up repeatedly in the film, that once Dario read this initial draft, he loved the monkey and they (Jace and Adam) "went monkey crazy"in later drafts of the script until the monkey's screen time was truncated dramatically due to logistics.. Indeed they did go "monkey crazy", as there was a lengthy sequence in the subway station where Sarah is chased by the monkey and she falls on a moving sidewalk platform, then gets stuck in an escalator, which pulls a chunk of her hair out, only to have her hiding from the monkey in the maintenance room of the station, where she encounters her mother again. And, surprise, the monkey shows up again!

Before you know it, Giselle is being pinned to a table, and those little statues have turned into demons and are cramming some crazy corkscrew from hell into her mouth to break her jaw open. This bit of oral cavity violence is a nod to Tassoni's memorable death in *Opera*, where she inexplicably swallows a bracelet and the killer cuts it out of her with a pair of upholstery shears. Of course, these monk-robed demons aren't content to just crack open her face, so one of them takes that ever-so-handy jeweled knife of yesteryear — its value shot to hell now — and eviscerates her. As she stumbles around with her insides hanging out and pouring onto the floor, one of the demons grabs her and strangles her with her own intestines. If you're wondering why the trio of demons that attack Tassoni can barely be seen, Argento didn't care for the way they looked on film when looking at the dailies, so they reshot a portion of the sequence and optically darkened them out, as is evident in the final product.

In a collection of poorly staged scenes to follow, Argento only manages to elicit laughter instead of the shock I am sure he was going for during the "big apocalypse" that is overtaking Rome. Sure, there is a small amount of surprise in seeing a woman throw her infant child off of a bridge, but when the obviously plastic doll's arm breaks off when it hits the side of the bridge, you may want to go for another take. And the various "crowd" scenes of violence are so sparsely populated that it's only embarrassing rather than effective.

I would attribute this, somewhat, to the fact that the small budget (around four million dollars) didn't allow them to stage bigger scenes of destruction as the movie went along, so we get a series of smaller ones piled on top of one another throughout. There is a truly terrible CGI burning of a church that looks as believable as a mid-nineties computer game.

Udo Kier's small role in the film is a breath of fresh air, as he seems to be the only one in on the joke. He doesn't speak his lines as much as yells them one second only to fall into a shaking fit and whisper the next. Is this caused by the supernatural goings on? Or the medical affliction that Marta gives him medication for? This scene where we meet Marta, an old friend of her parents and conveniently a psychic, and Johannes is really exposition 101 as we are brought up to speed on the events of *Suspiria* and *Inferno* with a dash of new information thrown in for good measure.

Marta is named Violetta in their first pass at the script, and she lives alone. This isolation only makes her murder sadder to me because she has nobody to share her final moments with, even though they are excruciating. Yes, she has to watch her girlfriend die in the film as it is, but the girlfriend is a wasted character because she is there, as Kim Newman puts it in Video Watchdog issue 147, "…to have a naked cuddle and get stabbed in the tit."

Asia's mother, Daria Nicolodi, appears among a group of "spirits" that look like the nylon-clad extras in George Romero's segment of *Two Evil Eyes*. Obi-Wan Nicolodi's appearance in this movie is just sad, for as good an actress as she is, to be reduced to this? For a long-dead parent who happens to be a "powerful" witch, she seems to have nothing to impart to her child, other than silly things like, "Fight, Sarah, you must fight!" or "Run, you must run now!" It's not as emotional as it's trying to be, and it just makes me chuckle.

Jun Ichikawa has a small role that was even smaller in the original draft of the script, only appearing specifically at the end of the film during the big destruction scene. Ichikawa told me:

Dario and I created that character together. I suggested she speak only Japanese to give her a sense of mystery because nobody would be able to understand her outside of the other witches. So it made the character more fearsome because nobody knew what she was threatening. I was really impressed with his energy and his ideas as a director. And when he suggested I wear a gold tooth, I loved it!

As for the rest of her friends, the witches in the film are all dressed like Madonna circa 1985, by way of Siouxsie and the Banshees. And they are a uniformly embarrassingly awkward bunch of cackling, "menacing" mid- to late-twenty-somethings who stalk around the screen, all big eyes and wonky expressions. My personal favorite moment with these evil beings, is in the brief montage of them descending, not by broom or anything magical, but by plane. As a small clutch of them walk through the airport in Rome, they very stupidly disrupt other people. One of them even utters a threatening cry at a passerby that made the audience at a USC screening howl with laughter.

At the direction of her mother, Sarah goes to find "that great Belgian thinker" DeWitt, who Marta had mentioned in the powder puff scene. Once arriving at his nicely appointed home, she is encountered by what can only be described as his houseboy — an attractive young man with blond hair and a very bad attitude (Paolo Stella) that comes in and out with the tide. No sooner does he tell her he won't admit her into the home because DeWitt won't know who she is, than he lets her in anyhow. He's a smart one! I'm sure Mr.

DeWitt doesn't keep him around for his conversation. As soon as Sarah is in the house, she is thrown onto a chair and is given some kind of paralytic agent. While Sarah is unable to move, DeWitt rolls a large glass lens over to her, lights a candle, and, like the revelation of the Wizard of Oz, becomes a glowing green head. He then proceeds to look "into" her via the glass, by examining the surface of her eye while his young charge holds Sarah's eye open with an eye speculum. It's a bizarre, compelling scene and fits well with the mysterious magic conjured up in *Supiria* and *Inferno*. Sadly, this is the only scene in this movie that completely works and has something interesting to present to the audience.

The casting of Stella to play DeWitt's assistant suggests an interesting relationship Argento has never toyed with in the past. It obviously brings to mind more than just a professional relationship between the two, and this character has obvious gay overtones. In the script, the character is just an assistant in the most platonic sense, but Stella told me that Argento wanted the character to have "…no personality. He was there to learn from DeWitt and assist him in his work. He

The Wizard of…oh wait, wrong movie! COURTESY MYRIAD PICTURES.

was the surrogate for this amazing mind whose body is limited." When I asked what Argento was like as a director, he said simply, "Dario is a perfectionist and pure instinct. He has a manic attention to detail. So if you trust him, you will do your best. He is the master of Italian horror. I'm not a fan of horror films particularly, but I respect his talent and his reputation. He was a great teacher and I was honored to work with him."

Once Sarah is given the requisite information in this scene to track down the home of Mater Lachrymarum, she wanders into the house with no trouble — with that cop that we have seen in two or three scenes, but he really isn't important. There is a little wall puzzle she has to solve, and Adam Gierasch and Jace Anderson reached back into the screenplay for their "remake" of *The Toolbox Murders* with this bit of business.

Down in the Mother's den, there was a scene, written for the film in the completed first draft, which Argento removed — I would assume due to budgetary restrictions. Once all of the witches have convened to worship Lachrymarum down in the lair, she is standing above them, drinking in their adoration and gaining in power. Suddenly, she opens her mouth and a shower of multicolored gemstones rain down upon the people below her, burning their skin as they land. Naturally, the revelers wail in orgasmic pain from being "touched" by their master.

In the film's only really impressive camera move, we follow Sarah in a single shot almost all the way through the villa and down into the underground lair that Lachrymarum calls home. In another bit of business excised from the first draft of the script, there was something especially nasty that Sarah encounters, and it is described thusly:

> *She backs against the wall, horrified. In the dim light, it's hard for her to make out everything, but what she can see is horrible. A man stands stooped over in the corridor, both his hands and feet imprisoned in the stone floor. His eyes are solid black and his mouth spasms with tics. A third arm extends out of his buttocks, the twitching hand holding a noose with a dead cat hanging from it.*

The end of the film was largely changed, I am sure, due to budgetary constraints. Sarah, in the original first draft of the script, entered the catacombs through a trompe l'oeil painting of a church, in the wall (as Suzy does in *Suspiria's* climax), after being hunted by that monkey once more. And once she was down there, she came upon basically what is in the film now, only the police officer who helps her is nowhere to be found and there is a Cardinal of the Catholic Church, who, it turns out, was in league with the witches to hold their rites in the bowels of this church.

Also in this original draft, Sarah is teamed up with DeWitt and his assistant in doing away with evil, and they both die for their efforts. Sarah ends up hiding in a burial niche in the wall, and the monkey tries to attack her again. Only, before anything can happen, the spire from the church comes through the ground and the enormous crucifix impales Mater Lachrymarum (echoing the murder of a pair of twin vampires in Hammer's *Vampire Circus* when one is impaled by a cross, killing them both because they can feel each other's pain) and causes a huge crevice to open up in the ground, which Sarah escapes into. She then makes it to the surface and emerges from the manhole surrounded by traffic.

I must admit I was "shocked" at the level of gross, ugly violence in this movie. And I mean shocked in that it's unfortunate that he has seemingly chosen to mistrust his unique vision and instead try to pace the trends. The murder of Marta and her lesbian lover specifically strikes me as something completely out of Adam Gierasch's head, and seems far more suited to his *Night of the Demons* remake than anything from Argento. I am not slighting Gierasch, but tonally it seems out of place in an Argento film. There is something about the American mind that doesn't integrate properly into Argento's world, as we shall discover with Argento's next film, *Giallo*.

INTERVIEW

JACE ANDERSON

(Co-writer, *Mother of Tears*)

Jace Anderson, a Harvard educated writer, along with her husband Adam Gierasch have written thirteen produced screenplays. Among them, three films for Tobe Hooper: *Crocodile* (2000), *The Toolbox Murders* (2004), and *Mortuary* (2005). Gierasch has directed four films written by the pair: *Autopsy* (2008), the remake of Kevin Tenney's *Night of the Demons* (2009), *Fertile Ground* (2011), and *Schism* (2013) which recently premiered at ScreamFest in Los Angeles.

DB: Even before you got this job to write *Mother of Tears*, I'm assuming you two were fans of his work? There is some stuff in *The Toolbox Murders* that is very Argento.

JA: Totally, huge fans!

DB: Was there anything when you were first exposed to his movies that really made you sit up and notice him as something special?

JA: Watching *Suspiria* the first time, I was just amazed. I was so terrified, but so enamored of its beauty. The set design, it's so incredible. The lighting, the score, and everything about it drew me in. We went on a big giallo kick years ago and watched a lot of those. *The Bird with the Crystal Plumage* is one of my favorite movies ever, actually.

DB: So let's go into a little bit of how the job on *Mother of Tears* came about. How did you first meet and all that?

JA: We met him because he was in town editing the "Jenifer" episode of *Masters of Horror*. Our friend Mike Williamson was the assistant editor and he invited us in to say hello. So we gathered up our DVDs and books and trotted down there. And we were just hoping for him to look up from the edit bay and say "Hi" and that's it. He was very nice and we started talking and Mike must have told him that we were screenwriters because Dario starts talking about what his next project is going to be and that is the final chapter of The Three Mothers trilogy. And he asked if we had something of ours that he could read. At this point, all our

DVDs and books were shoved behind us very quickly. I was sort of in shock. So Adam went into pitch mode and we went home and the next day, we brought back a script for him to read.

We got home and thought, this is going to be a great story, but that's it. And so, I don't know, a week or two later, we sent him an e-mail saying, "Nice meeting you, hope you enjoy the script." Maybe a month later, we send a follow up e-mail and again, nothing back. And then maybe a month or two later, we had just finished something else up and hadn't heard anything else, so on a whim, we send another e-mail saying, "We just finished a job and we're waiting to start working on a project with you." The next day, there was an e-mail back from Dario with three treatments he had written on *Mother of Tears* and could we give him a call. And he wanted us to do a pass on the treatment. We worked on this for weeks, going back and forth. We would write treatments and send them to him and then he would write notes and send things back. Meanwhile, our agents and lawyer are asking us what's going on; they're concerned that we're doing all this work and not getting paid. We just said, "It's Dario Argento; what are you talking about?"

And then Claudio Argento calls us up one day and says, "We were wondering if you could come to Rome and write the script." Gee, well, I think so; you don't have to twist our arms. So we're rushing around getting our passports renewed and our agents are screaming about contracts. And we're like, "We're getting on a plane in ten days; make one happen!" And the next thing you know, we're in this great apartment overlooking the old city wall. And Dario would come over to the apartment every day and discuss ideas and we're writing scenes. Then he would read them on the spot and give us feedback. It was just a great collaborative process.

DB: Were you two chained to a desk like good writer monkeys? And then Dario would come in at the end of the day and read your pages? That must have been nerve-wracking to say the least.

JA: We were sort of writer monkeys. There was one time we had a meeting with him and as he was leaving, he said, "You are my slaves; write, write!" But generally what would happen is that we had a treatment we had all worked out. We were writing from that and then Dario would come over and we would talk through scenes. It was so great because he would also be acting out the scenes, which is awesome! And what we would do is write and get a chunk of the script done and then it would be translated into Italian for Dario and he would read it. I remember one day the script translation had only been done right before he was due to come see us and he arrives with the script. Most people we had worked with in this kind of situation would take that away with them and come back later to give us notes. But no, Dario sat down on the couch, opened up the file on the computer, and read it with Adam and I there. We sat there petrified. When he was done, he gave us notes. Sometimes what he would do is take the Italian pages, add in his bits, and then translate that back into English and then we would clean up the dialogue into something that felt more true to the language. That was a great collaboration. And Dario told us writing is his favorite part of making a movie. He also gave us research assignments. He asked us to go see the Piazza Navona or take us to a set of catacombs. He wanted us to experience the city because the film is set there. And there were very specific parts of Rome he wanted us to see.

DB: As the movie was shot, were there any rewrites done?

JA: Well, there was when Myriad came onboard with the financing. They asked us to make some changes and some of those, Dario was unhappy with and I believe, if memory serves me right, we went back then to the original draft we had collaborated on together.

DB: Can you tell me anything that was there that didn't make it to the movie?

JA: It's been a long time and I don't recall anything offhand. But I think they wanted something on a much more apocalyptic scale, like all of Rome burning down. And at one point, now that I think about it, and this was one of my favorite things we lost, at one point, she was in the catacombs with her followers and she opens her mouth and showers them with jewels and they land on them, burning their skin. But they were ecstatically gathered around her. That was one of my cherished contributions to the script. But Dario really didn't want to do it. He felt it brought it into the realm of fairy tales.

DB: What?

JA: Yeah, if there was one thing that we could have put back in…He was also emphatic that he didn't want to repeat himself and do that color palette that he had done with *Suspiria*. And he talked about in the beginning doing a lot of red and having it start normal and having it get redder throughout.

DB: There is a scene in the behind the scenes video on the DVD where the Mother of Tears is peeing on her minions. But it's not in the movie, is it? I've watched this twice recently and don't recall seeing it.

JA: You know, I don't remember if it's in there or not. I know we wrote it at one point, though. But there is one thing we wrote; it was prepared, but never shot. Have you heard of the super long demon penis?

DB: No, I love demon cock!

JA: *(Laughs)* Who doesn't? So we were visiting during shooting and Sergio Stivaletti came to us with this box and lifts off the top and shows it to Claudio and Dario. They're all standing there marveling at this thing and Sergio lifts it out to show it. Oh, I don't remember how big it was, but when you unroll it, and they did, it must have been twelve, fifteen feet? It could have reached across the room. There was a scene where the demon unzips his fly and this huge thing comes flying out. Dario and Stivaletti were like, "This is going to be great." They asked a few people and they all said it was a bit much and Asia finally said to dad that yes, it was too comedic. But you could tell Dario really wanted to try the demon cock. I think he knew deep down it wasn't going to work, though.

DB: Stivaletti must have an obsession with big dicks because in *Stendhal*, there is that graffiti monster with the huge dick. With your contributions to the script, was there anything you fought for that he didn't want or vice versa?

JA: I forgot about that monster in *The Stendhal Syndrome*; interesting. Well, the end of the movie, Adam and I were really surprised at that. When they come out of the manhole cover, we wrote that exact action, but the tone of it was very different. There was water coming up out of it and dirt and the bones of the dead and cars were screeching to a stop. It was this feeling of barely surviving. And so when we saw this sort of laughter and beautiful sunset, it just totally threw me for a loop. And I still debate with myself, what is the meaning or idea behind this final image and their manic laughter? It's an interesting choice that Dario made. I do have to say when Dario decided to put the monkey in, I went a little monkey crazy on the first monkey draft. That monkey was running down the subway escalator railing, that thing was everywhere. And Claudio had to tell me to cut it down. He said, "I don't think we can afford this much monkey."

DB: Was that literally how he phrased it?

JA: *(Laughs)* I don't think that was his exact phrasing, but I did go a little monkey crazy in the script.

DB: One thing that feels really out of place to me is Asia's mother coming back as the ghost. Was that you guys or Dario?

JA: I'm glad you brought that up because that is another thing that was different. The way we described that in the script. There are two instances where she shows up, I think. There was one when she showed up in the script and it was supposed to be scary. She rushed out of the darkness and then retreated. And the second, it was just supposed to be a voice behind a door.

DB: Can you explain why she was supposed to be scary? Was she trying to frighten her daughter? Or was it like she was trying to scare something away to protect her?

JA: I don't remember. I think it was that the realm of the supernatural and the spirits is scary, period.

DB: And the coven of witches coming into town. They don't fly in on brooms; there is nothing supernatural about them. They just fly in or drive or take a train. Just get a ticket and go to Rome. And when we see them, as much as I love Dario, I think he kinda drove off a cliff with this and having them sneering and cackling at people. They look like rejects from a Siouxsie and the Banshees video via Madonna in the early 80s. And was there to be more with the witches, specifically Jun Ichikawa's character? She seems to be featured a bit more than the others.

JA: I don't know who came up with the way they look, but I actually like it; it's fun. We weren't specific about

the look of them at all. In the script, originally the witches, though, they weren't all young. There were some older, haggard ones. I remember the decision was made that they should all be young and "cool" looking. I have to say, though, I love Jun Ichikawa, she's so cool, and I know it's so random, but I just love her. I think she's great in it. I mean, *Mother of Tears*, it's a movie with a monkey and Japanese witches and demons and she's peeing on her followers. Because I have such love for the experience writing it, I recognize that there are flaws in it, but I have so much love in it at the same time. I have to go, OK, so they're crazy 80s witches, why not?

DB: Did the witches ever have more to do?

JA: I don't think so, but this makes me remember something else. When you asked about the changes Myriad wanted. They wanted a traditional story arc from Sarah. That she would come to recognize her powers as a witch and use them to defeat the evil. She would find a mentor and learn to use her powers to overcome the Mother of Tears. They (Myriad) wanted her to use magic. I remember talking to Dario and Claudio about how to make this work; we were sort of stuck between being told by the financiers what they wanted and what Dario wanted. We tried to explain that it's not about her being a witch, these movies are about humans interacting with witches, and it's not about becoming one. They were really opposed to going that way. I don't think we ever did a draft for them where she made things levitate or did anything magical like that.

DB: Udo Kier's character, was he meant to be in the movie more or was he just meant to be father exposition?

JA: There was an earlier draft that went in a slightly different direction. When her investigation took a different order. And his part was a little bigger because of this. But I don't remember the specifics.

DB: So I have to say, when I first saw the movie with a friend of mine, she was really offended by the murder of Marta and her girlfriend. Especially when Marta has the metal pike shoved into her girly bits. I've always defended Dario against the misogyny label because he kills men all the time, too, and I don't think he has any ill will. But this movie, the murder scenes aren't stylish, they aren't really creative, and they're just really mean and cruel. I really thought there was a level of ick to it that turned me off. So was this scene something you or Dario wrote? Not to get too PC on you, but the lesbian murder, I mean, were they punished for not being penetrated by men? And then you have this thug come in and penetrate them in the way he does.

JA: I don't even know how to answer this. I do know that Dario set out with this to make it the most violent of his movies. And I think he succeeded. I think it was Adam who came up with that (the vagina pike). And then Dario came up with the eyeball gouging of Marta's girlfriend. I mean, look, I contribute my share of nasty things, too. I wish I had a handy answer to that, but I have to say I do get conflicted sometimes about that. One on hand, I feel like I have to defend myself because people start talking and say that I'm betraying my gender and "Oh, how can she write that?" I start feeling like "Oh my God, I'm betraying my gender by participating in that." But at the same time, I like my job. I have yet to be on a film set where an actress did anything but laugh when filming a scene like that. And I think the symbolism, yeah, I think is icky. Frankly, I don't like it. And I didn't like it and I said when we were writing. But it's in and one of the reasons it's in is because it's effective. And the reason I objected is because it's effective and it got to me. And if the movie is supposed to be disturbing and it disturbs you the same way the eye one does, it's doing its job.

DB: I wanted to bring up my favorite scene in the movie. Let's lighten the mood a little here. I really love when Asia goes to visit "that great Belgian thinker" and his houseboy answers the door. They shove Asia into that chair and perform that exam. How did this scene come about? Do you recall?

JA: I don't completely; it was Dario's idea, I do remember that. But there is a lot of exposition in this movie and it's one of the hardest things to do is to hide exposition. So that's why the comic book sequence is there and this scene with the eye exam as well. And Dario had planned the comic book bit from the get go. But the eye exam scene I remember trying to put in to disguise the exposition of some action and that's where this comes in. The verification of who she is gives them a way to give her more information. There were so many scenes with talking heads. We had to find a way to break up the repetition.

DB: And of course, the eye speculum calls back to Betty in *Opera*.

So let's discuss the end of the movie. There is the orgy of murder and what some people may call sex. It's like Clive Barker's wet dreams, I would imagine.

JA: I have to say, that orgy scene at the end, Adam I were kind of crushed when we saw the size of it because it was written as massive. When we conceived it originally and what we had talked about with Dario, the three of us were constantly one-upping the other. We had talked about that Bosch painting, "The Garden of Earthly Delights," and there is a man bending over with a hand coming out of his ass with a noose coming out of it with a cat in the noose. Really messed up, fucked up things. So we would throw things out at Dario and then he would come back with something. It was supposed to be her passing a couple fornicating while wrapped up barbed wire and roses or people caged. Just think of all the horrific things in that painting and that was the inspiration. It's probably really hard to pull that off cinematically, so that didn't come to be. But that was the original idea.

DB: The idea of the magical purple t-shirt with the glitter on it that Asia just pulls off of her and everything is destroyed. The ending to the other two movies are just as abrupt and random, but I think the reason this one, at least to me, falls short is it's the end of the trilogy and maybe it should have been more?

JA: The original draft of the script, there was this massive thing where the spire cross from a church above the villa crashes into the earth, pierces it, and impales the mother of tears. The t-shirt removal only weakened her. Then the caverns flooded and Sarah killed the monkey and then goes up to the surface like it ends now.

DB: Symbolically and visually, that's much more interesting. Also, Asia in the flood of shit, was that a deliberate nod to the end of *Phenomena*?

JA: I don't think it was a deliberate *Phenomena* nod. Try saying that ten times fast! It was just what we wrote. But I do know that Dario was putting in nods to various movies in it.

DB: You made a new friend making this movie, Coralina.

JA: Yes, my flower sister.

DB: Did you hit it off right away?

JA: Yes, she's great.

DB: That scene when she is murdered, you were there when they shot all that?

JA: Yes.

DB: OK, not to be rude, but did nobody on the set not think it was odd that these employees of this museum would be touching centuries-old artifacts with their bare hands and then bleeding all over them?

JA: I never noticed that, but now it's going to bother me.

DB: I'm sorry; am I banished from the house now? I'm not blaming you, you didn't direct the movie, and it's just sloppy on Dario's part. His AD wasn't paying attention.

JA: No, no, but it's funny. I read a script the other day and two cops just scoop up some evidence in their bare hands in a scene and I thought, "God, what are these writers thinking?"

2012

GIALLO

On the heels of *Mother of Tears,* Argento decided to make a film from a screenplay written with another pair of Americans, Sean Keller and Jim Agnew. The script, titled *Yellow,* was a lean police procedural with a terribly unlikable "hero" at its center, Enzo Avolfi. On paper, the script may have had promise, but what resulted is a rather lackluster attempt to modernize a genre in a questionable manner by bringing in elements of the torture-porn craze and doing away with the mystery of who the killer is.

If the title is any indication, *Giallo* would appear to be an overt homage to the genre that Argento helped make famous, but it is much more a modern detective thriller with nods to the genre than an outright pastiche and even parody as some have suggested. It seems to have less of a sense of humor about itself than *Non Ho Sonno* and even *The Card Player,* the two last gialli in Argento's canon. "One of the things he [Dario Argento] said right off was that he loved the title," Sean Keller, one of the writers of the film, said. "He wanted to keep that and we were a little hesitant because it would open up a whole can of worms. But we're absolutely willing to go on this ride with Dario because he knows better than us."

Turin is caught in the grasp of a vicious and elusive serial killer whose single M.O. is the destruction of beauty. Celine (Elsa Pataky), a fashion model, is kidnapped in a taxi one night, en route to meet her sister, Linda (Emmanuelle Seigner). Linda teams up with Inspector Enzo Avolfi (Adrien Brody), a surly, rude, and seemingly dismissive detective, to help track down the killer against a ticking clock with few clues to light their way.

Giallo seemed a cursed production from the start, as Ray Liotta, Vincent Gallo, and Asia Argento were all slated to star, but, for various reasons, they all dropped out, sending the project into a temporary tailspin. Adrien Brody was sent the script, and he agreed to star as Enzo and expressed interest in playing "Yellow" as well. Being an Academy Award-winning actor who would also sign on to produce, it seemed a great opportunity for the project. This would turn out to be a mixed blessing, as Brody's name would lend some weight to the film, which surely meant a bigger budget, but it also meant less control for Argento.

"Well, the casting is very weird. It was written to be an Italian detective and two American girls," Keller explained, "and what we got was an American detective in Italy and a French woman and a Spaniard playing American sisters. And we changed them to Canadians, so they have a French Canadian accent or something." While it's true that many of Argento's gialli concern themselves with an outsider in Italy, fighting to solve a series of crimes and trying to stay alive in the process, this film gives us nothing but tourists and foreigners to cling to, loosening the film's grip on the country it claims sanctuary in. Keller continues, "But that aspect makes it true to the original concept of the giallo: the multicultural cast that's all shot M.O.S. and dubbed later. That's one thing I would have really loved is if the whole thing were dubbed. I think it really would have brought it to that level where everyone would really get it and realize it was a throwback."

"Yellow" as a character is possibly the most unthreatening, silly killer in any Argento film. First of all, he looks like Jim Nabors dressed as Rambo for a Halloween party. His motive for killing women is rather pathetic and weak and he's just not interesting. In part, because he's not kept a mystery, the character has little allure, and villains need to be just as interesting as the good guys. Keller and Agnew's screenplay offers a stew of psychological makeup from gialli past in the killer and Enzo's characters, paralleling them in many ways. The characters both have flashbacks regarding their childhood traumas, explaining their motives for their adult behavior: Enzo murdered his mother's killer as a child and "Yellow" was taunted and teased by children at the orphanage he grew up in, triggering his psychopathic behavior. The clunky pairing of these two characters along with Linda's outburst at the end of the film — where she yells at Enzo, "You're just like him!" — puts a little too fine a button on things.

With her exclamation echoing through his brain, Enzo walks off into an uncertain psychological future, realizing he has possibly cost Celine her life, leaving Linda to twist in the wind at the prospect of a life without her sister. Enzo's problem is that, of course, Linda is right: he is just like "Yellow." He has to do what he thinks is right, no matter the consequence for anyone else. If he had only played along with the killer's demands, they could have found Celine. The coda on the film removes the ending that would have echoed *Suspiria*, *Inferno*, and *The Card Player* in having the protagonists walk off toward the camera and into their future, wherever that leads. What we are left with, instead, is a strange ending where a security guard hears Celine in the back of a car while she is bleeding a puddle onto the ground. Yet we don't know if she is seen by the guard, but he acknowledges the sound she is making. Keller noted of the coda, "The movie, I think, would benefit from it ending with Linda yelling at Enzo, 'Where is she? Where is she?' and then cut to black. It would have been crushing. I think the coda let a little of the air out." Keller and Agnew's script makes an unexpected comment on the Italian government and justice system: "This is Italy; sometimes you need to grease the wheels of bureaucracy," Adrian Brody says to Linda as they go to bribe Sal for the records he is having pulled of a list of taxi cab drivers who have a criminal record. It's not only Avolfi taking jabs at Italian society and culture, but "Yellow" does as well by his decisions of where he dumps his victims. Keller describes the character's motivation for where he places his victims as "…a biography of his shame, in a way. And that he would leave the bodies in places where he had some kind of rejection or disappointment." But when he puts one of the bodies in the courtyard of a convent, it could be read as a jab at the ineffectiveness of the Catholic Church to prevent against the evils in the world — something all religions are in constant struggle with.

First-time Argento composer Marco Werba looks back into the past of the thriller and contributes a score influenced by the work of Pino Dinaggio and Bernard Herrmann. For a film that was written and intended to be a tribute of sorts to a particular style of film, the score doesn't fit into what it's attempting to do. The issue isn't with the score, however. Werba has talent, but the problem lies in the way it is used. The score is well written and arranged; it just belongs in a different movie. It seems to consist of three cues that are used repeatedly to little effect because you can almost predict what will be used where and when. Also, there's just too much of it. Silence is a key in creating suspense and horror; unfortunately, the film is wall-to-wall music, it seems.

Giallo unfortunately is the weakest film to date that Argento has made. The talent is there, but it seems nothing caught fire the way it should have. For a film to be called *Giallo* and have it not be a giallo is a risky move that ultimately doesn't pay off, since it sets up expectations that cannot possibly be met. The film's ugly, "torture porn" environment feels cheap and reductive, and the central villain isn't terribly interesting, which is a huge blow against it. Leaving the modern world behind, Dario would adapt Bram Stoker's immortal novel, *Dracula*, with Rutger Hauer and Thomas Kretschmann playing Van Helsing and Count Dracula respectively.

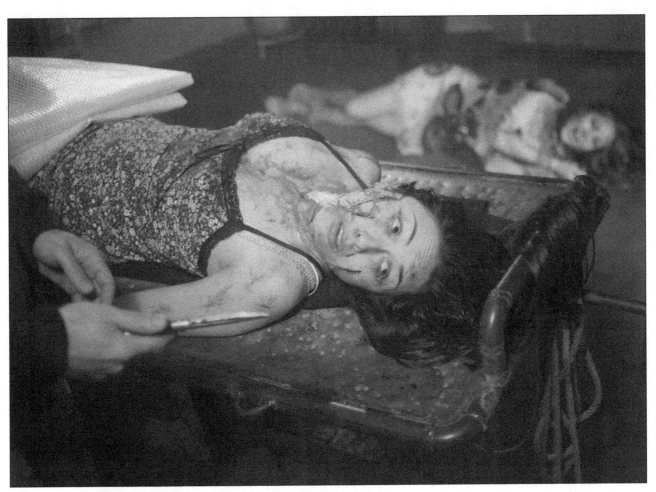

Is this Hostel? *Dario Argento gets ugly.* COURTESY HANNIBAL PICTURES.

INTERVIEW

SEAN KELLER

(Co-writer, *Giallo*)

With writing partner Jim Agnew, the two have created five produced screenplays to date, *Tokarev* (2014), with Nicholas Cage being the latest. Keller is also a musician and actor, having appeared in the first national touring production of the musical Rent as Roger. I'm still waiting for his cover of Weird Al Yankovic's "I Lost on Jeopardy."

DB: Can you tell me where you two got the idea for the script and when you first wrote it?

SK: I think it was 2004 when we wrote the first draft. And the idea, well, we're horror lovers and horror writers and we were just exhausted by J-Horror. Little girls with wet hair and extreme torture seemed to be all that was selling. Jim and I were thinking, well, what do we want to see? I don't mean this as a derogatory term, but Euro Sleaze. You know, sleazy, garish, brightly colored, obnoxious horror from Italy has been something we've loved and loved for years. As soon as he suggested it, we thought yea, we should write a giallo. And just trying to be clever, we thought, well, we'll make a film about a killer whose skin is yellow and we'll call it "Giallo." We never had any concept this would cross Dario Argento's desk. This was meant as homage to Argento, Bava, and Martino and all these other fantastic, stylized directors so we could do something scary and horrific and also kind of make a comment on that genre at the same time.

DB: Did you then go and look a bunch of gialli as reference to see what clichés you could play with?

SK: We were both big fans and we'd seen quite a few. And we dove into a few just to really get the most important conventions to hit. We wanted to make it a more encompassing homage. The initial draft had cats in it and we had jazz singing with the flashback of Enzo's mother having the party and signing. We had to have psychosexual motives for the killer because that seems to be the buzzword that went through all these films. We had to have people being impaled on glass and models, just all these tropes. We watched *Black Belly of the Tarantula*, *Who Saw Her Die?* It's not like we took a refresher course on Argento. We dove into the

other films that we weren't as familiar with. We decided to make it a slightly more Americanized version. We wanted to try and hopefully use the film as a gateway for people who'd never seen a giallo. "Oh there's this whole genre that exists." We got crucified for the fans for that, I think. We made it for the new audience and not for the hardcore fans. We decided to roll with that and take our lumps. Oddly enough, it seems to have succeeded on that level.

DB: Well, if you want to see an American giallo, look at DePalma's thrillers or maybe *Alice, Sweet Alice*. But, yeah, there hasn't been too many, it seems.

SK: Look at John Doe in *Seven*. How does he appear? When he shows up in the hallway, he's got the long coat, the fedora, and he's got gloves on. And his motives are bizarre and you know nothing about him, but he looks just like a giallo killer. That movie owes a lot to the giallo. Those do exist, but we were trying to push it; we were hoping it would be a super stylized version. As soon as we hooked up with Dario, which was just amazing, he sort of dropped the bomb that "I don't want to do that style anymore. I want it to be more realistic." So we thought, well, you're the master, you're the one who inspired us to write this, so of course, we'll listen to you and do it your way.

DB: You mentioned John Doe in *Seven*; would you say the scene when "Yellow" escapes Enzo is inspired by that appearance of Spacey on the stairs taking photos and then just walking away?

SK: Yes. That iconic scene was something we thought could be played back into the genre from which it clearly sprang. It was a fun bit of referential overlap.

DB: Back to what you mentioned about the movie's style or lack thereof, I think most people watching it assume that it looks and feels the way it does, is born out of pressure from the producers or what have you because it's light-years away from anything he's done.

SK: That's exactly it. Dario wanted to make it more modern and less stylized. He said he had done that and why repeat it? And I totally respect that.

DB: Well, maybe *Giallo* is the cousin to *The Card Player*. They're both police procedurals, they're fairly sterile…So what was the rewrite process like on this?

SK: It was really minimal, honestly. We sent the script to Dario and he read it on Halloween weekend, actually, which is really cool. He got back to us the Monday after we sent it to him. So we're like, "OK let's go!" We talked to him on the phone a few times. It was difficult; my Italian sucks and his English is a million times better than my Italian will ever be. One of the things he said right off was that he loved the title. Of course, we called the script "Yellow," but as you know, translated into Italian the word is "giallo." He wanted to keep that and we were a little hesitant because it would open up a whole can of worms, but we're absolutely willing to go on this ride with Dario because he knows better than us. But back to the rewrites, it was when Adrien [Brody] came on board that things became more specific. All Dario wanted to do was to tone down some things that he thought would be too difficult to shoot. He wanted to bring the level of violence down a bit. It was kind of over the top. It was gloriously over the top. The whole thing was to write this splattastic homage to gialli; it was ridiculous. So Dario wanted to take that down a bit. He had us take the cats out of one scene because he thought it was too much like the other films. Once Adrien came on, he had character notes. It's funny because Enzo didn't change at all. The killer he portrayed, he became a different character and it was an idiosyncratic thing that Adrien did because it was loony and weird and really kind of perfectly in keeping with the history of gialli, even if a lot of people said it's too much, it's so over the top. And it does stand out in this sober version of a giallo. I have to admit, I kinda love it. It's loony and delirious. It's the most "Italian" thing in it.

DB: Speaking of Brody, he's a big name and he had a lot of potential weight to push around. And I don't mean that in a negative way, but was he involved with the look of the character? I would think Dario and Stivaletti would have had that ironed out somewhat already.

SK: Absolutely, he had a very specific notion of how he should look, behave, and that's what good actors do. As an actor myself, I expect that from my lead. I want the person to come in and say, "I want to do it this way." The writers should be left out of it. That's something the director and actors deal with because we're turning the film over to them.

DB: It's nice you can be humble and not feel the need to hang onto everything you've done.

SK: Well, that's foolish. Film is the most collaborative of the arts by far. And it's the most commercial. So everyone does have to have a say in it. Sure, if you want to be an auteur, you better be a director and a writer. My job is to write. My job is to get everyone on board to go make a movie and once we're there, I just facilitate as much as I can without getting in the way. That's my job, to be egoless and just drive the project.

DB: So would you say you're drafting a blueprint that you then hand over to the builders and you walk away and trust they know what they're doing?

SK: Let's say the final draft is the first draft of the movie. So you have the script, so you act it, you shoot it. It's done sometimes as written, sometimes not. Then you edit it. There's no controlling what happens in between all these steps. You just try and give them the best script you can. We kept doing these little passes with Dario. And Jim [Agnew] did more of this than I did because he was in Turin to shoot second unit. So he not only shot a lot of the kills, he was also the hands of the killer when he's choking the kid. He got to be the gloved hands in an Argento film. How cool is that? So he did a lot of the day-to-day rewrites. He didn't consult me because we're in different time zones and I was here taking meetings and keeping our Hollywood presence down while he was off in Italy and we divide duties like that up regularly. Little rewrites were done all the way through, which is common. But yeah, give a blueprint and you hope you have a cool house when it's done.

DB: Did Jim shoot the entire butcher shop sequence then?

SK: Yeah and he also stabbed the dummy when the person doing it wasn't doing it hard enough. He put on the gloves and the jacket the kid was wearing and just slammed the knife into the dummy in a single take. Jim also directed the entire sequence, the fight, all of it. He shot most of the kills and the special effects shots and Stivaletti was always there to help with how the effects should be shot and lit. He did a lot of work. The schedule was tight. He also did a lot of the exterior shots. Poor guy was doing rewrites at night and doing exteriors during the day. He lost some weight working so much.

DB: Yeah, but you can eat all the pasta you want and you'll burn it off later not eating and running around like a maniac. So back to the killer's look. To me, I've always thought he looked like Jim Naybors dressed up as Rambo for Halloween. I can't help but think that the face was built up that way to cover Brody's really prominent features. Even his eyes give him away. The shape of his face, everything about him is very distinct.

SK: That's pretty good! It's a challenge to disguise his very distinct look. When we got him in the movie, he said he wanted to play both parts. Originally, it was Ray Liotta playing Enzo. Vincent Gallo playing the killer, that would have been interesting. Asia Argento playing the lead, but she got pregnant and dropped out. Then Ray and Vincent dropped out. So then we started to get worried. But then Adrien came in and said he wanted to do both roles. Then we realized we weren't making a traditional giallo, which is a whodunit, we're making a meta giallo at that point. It's not who is the killer, but who's playing the killer? That was a Herculean task for Stivaletti to try and pull off. In some scenes, it works great and others, maybe not so much.

DB: As to Adrien's character ideas, was it his idea to have the killer masturbating looking at pictures of his victims with a pacifier in his mouth?

SK: I believe that was all him. I don't recall ever writing that in the script. I remember seeing that and thinking it was an interesting choice. It was his call all the way. Some people really love that and others really hate it. Which means it's probably good because it's so divisive and I love that.

DB: So in the film, how is it possible that the killer is having a flashback about his life before he was born? We see his mother shooting up drugs, dropping him off at the convent.

SK: That was an odd bit of editing. There was a sequence where Enzo was going over the file for "Yellow" and this is all written in the report. There was some narration with visuals. So then this was all filmed and put in a flashback. It's either impossible to follow or amazingly weird depending on your perspective. That's one of the things that happens in editing. It was a choice that was made, but no, that was never intended. It was simply supposed to be his case history being looked over by the cops. And the idea behind the motive was that it was a biography of his shame, in a way. And that he would leave the bodies in places where he had some kind of rejection or disappointment.

DB: You said the film isn't a whodunit, but more of a "who's playing the killer." So we're with the killer and the heroes at different times.

SK: Yeah, it's more in line with, say, *Silence of the Lambs* structure-wise.

DB: Well, I was going to ask if there was ever more to the detective aspect of it because for Enzo and Linda, it's still a mystery, of course, but was there ever more to their detective work or was it always just the one big clue at the hospital and that's how they catch him.

SK: It was always very lean. The point of it wasn't the whodunit for us. We wanted to make an overt statement about the sort of inherent misogyny of the genre. And sort of fuck with the structure and the giallo as is and turn it into a comment on the price of hyper masculinity. In the end…why isn't it good enough in any Hollywood film for the good guy to catch the bad guy? They have to blow him away or nobody is happy. It's not good enough to just catch someone and lock them up, put them on trial, and have justice served. It's not accepted. There's this hyper masculine need to punish. And Enzo is the embodiment of this need to punish and as a result, he kills the girl. The two girls could have had a plan and could have made it through. Celine could have been saved. Linda and Celine could have gotten away and that would have meant letting the killer go. So what's the price? You let the killer go or do you kill him and as a result damn the victim? And that's why the movie ends as jarringly as it does. It was written slightly differently, there were some editing things, but the point still rings and so the whodunit aspect, the mystery, was there mostly to serve this statement. And that is one of the things Dario reacted strongly to. He enjoyed the fact that it was making a clear statement. This isn't the misogyny that you expect.

DB: With the motive of the killer as well, there is nothing sexual about it. He doesn't rape them. He's not interested in that, he gets off on it differently. There isn't the typical male, macho, sexual aggression.

SK: He gets off on the destruction. Which is why I think Adrien adding the bit with "Yellow" jerking off to the photos adds that sexual weirdness in a different way. It's interesting.

DB: You mentioned the ending and the film and how the killer dies, but to what cost to the victims? That ending with him hanging from that window frame cutting his hands on the glass, is that a conscious nod to the end of *Cat O' Nine Tails*?

SK: Yes, absolutely. *Cat O' Nine Tails* is one of the biggest tonal rips for *Giallo*. A lot of people don't hold it in that high of esteem as I do. But it's one of, I think, the better procedural gialli. And I love that ending and that's one of the reasons he wanted the cats out of the script because it was too many references. At one time, there were cats crawling around where the victims were and they were chewing on the girls. It was a little much. One of my favorite references, though, was from Aldo Lado's *Who Saw Her Die?*, which is an often overlooked giallo which started George Lazenby, the one off Bond. There is a sequence where there are kids playing ring around the rosie, singing a song. They all get called away and then all of a sudden it cuts to a butcher shop and a door slamming shut. And I'm thinking, "What the fuck is going on in the butcher shop?" So that's where we got the butcher who kills Enzo's mother. And that was sort of one of my favorite sneakier references. That butcher shop sequence is where Argento really did go stylized in the film and gave us sort of the thing we were really lusting for out of the film.

DB: Back to that butcher shop scene. Enzo has his vengeance as a child and it gives him some closure in a way, but when he's older, he doesn't get that same satisfaction because he fucks it all up. With that coda on the end, was it ever going end with him walking away from Linda? Or was it always there with Celine in the trunk of the car?

SK: That coda was always there, and Jim and I take full credit for that. But it didn't really work. The idea was that she's stuck in the trunk of the car, time is running out, and she's bleeding out. It seemed a clever way to end a script, but not the best way to end a film. There's two big differences. One will get the reader in love with it, the script, but that may not translate on screen. The movie, I think, would benefit from it ending with Linda yelling at Enzo, "Where is she? Where is she?" and then cut to black. It would have been crushing. I think the coda let a little of the air out.

DB: I think the coda could have worked OK if Dario had the security guard not hear her or if he wasn't there at all. It's just her stuck in that trunk and bleeding.

SK: In the script, I think it was a guard walking around who didn't hear her because his phone rings, he picks it up, and walks right by the car and doesn't hear it because he's distracted and he just walks away. In concept, that's fine, but in a film, I don't know if it works. That was us trying to be tricky and maybe not getting the best thing out there. It was also an out for the producers. They didn't want us to show a girl die or cutting it really ambiguously. That way, some will think she's OK and some will think she's doomed. We went back and forth on the end quite a bit, we shot it, and then just tested it out in editing. I wasn't even certain how it was going to end until I saw it the first time.

DB: So what was the first time you watched the film like?

SK: It was in a screening room with potential buyers. So it was a very quiet room. It was the worst possible way to watch it. I didn't get to watch it with friends or fans of Dario's stuff, horror people. It was strictly business. It was a cold, quiet room. But it was a thrill to see Dario's name and our name up. Fuck, we made a movie with Dario Argento, which is awesome. It wasn't until I saw it with some friends that it was really fun. And my friends made fun of me, of the movie, of some things in it they didn't like. But that's OK because it seems with Argento, it takes a few movies ahead for people to really like the ones a few back. And they'll go, "Oh, I really like that."

DB: It's interesting you say that. I was going to bring up something similar. It seems like his movies in retrospect only get some kind of love or respect. Yeah, *Suspiria* kind of blew everything out of the water because it's so unique in every way. Now you have people looking at *Phantom of the Opera* and liking it and praising it in ways they weren't when it was released. Where were they when it came out?

SK: *Tenebrae* is my favorite Argento film and it was savaged by many when it came out. What is this? The transference in that film is weird. It's straight up fucking weird. It's loony and brilliant and I love it to death. But everything was so bright white, the white outdoors, there's no place to hide, it's so brightly lit. That didn't go over well. Now people talk about and love it. You brought up *The Card Player* earlier and now there are people who dig it, but at the time it was released, most people seemed to hate it.

DB: The first time I watched the movie, I was expecting it to be revealed that the killer and Enzo are related or they are the same person or something.

SK: A lot of people think that; it was never intended. But that kind of misdirection I love. I love that there's a bit of ambiguity.

DB: I was just going to say that the movie does set it up, though, it's constantly drawing comparisons between the two of them. And maybe it's just the fact that you go in knowing they're played by the same actor, so you assume there's going to be some, "Oh, they're twins" or something like that. In fact, the first time I saw it, when the mother drops off the baby, I thought there's gotta be another baby.

SK: Jim had the horror of shooting the baby in the bag sequence. When you want to film a baby in a bag in Italy, you put a baby in a bag and film it. Jim said that scared the crap out of him. He asked them to double bag the baby. It actually really upset him and he had to rush that to get the baby out of the bag. But we knew while writing it that there was going to be this parallel between them for this to work. And then the fact that they're played by the same person brings an odd level of expectation that we refused to satisfy, which I appreciate. It sets up an expectation and then undercuts it at the end. Again, I don't know if it's just me being sadistic, but I enjoy subverting an audience's expectations; it pleases me. So Jim and I intentionally set that up, but we didn't realize that people were going to be so hung up on it. We hear it a lot that people thought they were the same guy.

DB: One last thing: even though the script was really close to what ended up on screen, was there anything you wanted that you didn't get?

SK: Well, the casting is very weird. It was written to be an Italian detective and two American girls and what we got was an American detective in Italy and a French woman and a Spaniard playing American sisters. And we changed them to Canadians, so they have a French Canadian accent or something. But that aspect makes it true to the original concept of the giallo. The multicultural cast that's all shot M.O.S. and dubbed later. That's one thing I would have really loved is if the whole thing were dubbed. I think it really would have brought it to that level where everyone would really get it and realize it was a throwback. I don't know if there was any one thing. Actually, there was one beat I would have loved. In creating this character "Yellow" and with his name being yellow like giallo, we had a beat in which he became the giallo killer where he shows up at Linda's apartment and he shows her the footage of Celine and says he has a plan. The way we wrote it, he was putting makeup on to cover up his yellow skin and donning a big black hat, a black coat, and the black gloves. And at that beat, it was supposed to be a supervillain origin. This is the proto-giallo killer emerging. And once again, Dario said, "I've done that to death." And so we respect Dario's wishes. So we did without it. It's a cheap beat that's not essential, but I love it. In screenwriting, there's a very common phrase that you have to kill your babies, kill your darlings. The things that you love the most are inherently the things you're going to have to cut out of the script because they're in there because of fetishistic love and not because they serve the story.

Argento and "Botelho" in Los Angeles, 2010. FROM THE AUTHOR'S COLLECTION.

MY DINNER WITH DARIO...

In 2010, Dario Argento was the guest of honor at the Weekend of Horrors in Los Angeles. It had been a decade since I saw him last, and seeing as he rarely comes to California for any reason, I had to see him again. I wasn't living in Los Angeles at the time, so I drove down with my friend Steven from Northern California for a weekend getaway to the Los Angeles airport! It was an awful location for anything; the surrounding restaurants and hotels were depressing. Even the "nicer" ones have the look of the communist bloc.

As Steven and I pulled into our hotel, his cell phone rang. With a look of pure shock and then horror, he said, "This isn't Derek. I'll get him." Very slowly, he handed the phone to me, his mouth slack, his eyes puzzled. "It's Dario on my phone! He wants to talk to you," he whispered. Maybe he was afraid Dario might jump out of the phone and attack him?

"Hello Derek, it is Dario Argento!" Dario exuberantly announced himself.

"Hi, how are you?" I said, pulling the car into a parking spot.

"Good. We should meet tonight, have dinner. The writers of *Giallo* will be with me, OK?"

"That sounds great. What time were you thinking and where?" What else could I say?

"At the Marriott. I will be there at five to see some people. Meet me and we will eat and talk, yes?"

"Of course, I'll see you then." "And bring your friend who answered the phone." Click.

After a short nap and washing the travel off of us, we walked over to the Marriott where the convention was to take place. If you've ever been to any of these things, you know just how slow the first day can be if it's a Friday through Sunday ordeal. A long and frustrating registration line later, Steven and I were on the floor of the convention. It was fun for a while, wandering around looking at the various booths with everything from no budget, self-produced films being hocked to women's lingerie, on the other side of the spectrum.

Right on schedule, we spotted Dario walking around the main hall. I approached, said hello, and he asked how we were. Honestly, I was surprised he even remembered me by sight. Steven could barely manage to mumble a "nice to meet you" under his breath and wouldn't get anywhere near him, not even to even shake his hand.

"I am trying to find this room where Bill Lustig is showing a film, do you know where it is?" Dario asked me.

I didn't, but a quick glance at my program told me, so together, we found the room. It was empty except for the chairs and a projector. Dario proceeded to sit in one of the seats and motioned us over to him. I sat next to him and instead of taking the seat opposite Dario, Steven chose to sit on my other side, explaining quietly, "I can't sit next to him, I'm nervous."

After a short conversation in which I told Dario that he looked good — the weight he had gained in the intervening time looked good on him — people started to trickle in. I will never forget the guy who was in charge of introducing the film, upon seeing Dario, asked, "Are you Dario Argento?"

Dario stood up and very matter-of-factly said, and I assume expecting something more to the question, "Yes."

"Wow, cool man."

Dario smiled somewhat awkwardly, laughed, and sat back down next to me. Bill Lustig came into the room and made a beeline for Dario, gave him a hug as if they were fellow soldiers of war and were reuniting victorious after some terrible incident. They were absolutely giddy and it was infectious. I didn't even know the guy and I was grinning at him from ear to ear. "This is Botelho. He is writing a book for me," Dario introduced me to Lustig. A book *for* me, I thought… well, that's even better than *about* me!

After a short talk to introduce one of his films, the four of us left the screening room and took a good deal of the audience with us once the crowd realized that: one, Dario Argento was there; and two, Dario Argento was leaving! There was a strange Pied Piper thing going on; Dario attracted little crowds of people everywhere we went and they would just hang back a bit and continue following. Usually, they wouldn't approach him — afraid of what, I don't know. He's one of the calmest, most approachable people I've ever met.

Inferno was scheduled to screen a bit later, and Dario was asked to answer a few questions and introduce the film. At his insistence, we all went back to the same screening room a bit early, and there was a small group of people watching old cartoons — with a horror bent, of course. Standing in the doorway, recapturing my childhood in a beam of candy-colored light next to someone I greatly admired, brought me back to watching this particular cartoon as a child around Halloween time. The Pink Panther meets Count Dracula in Transylvania at his castle, Dracula being a small, round man with an enormous head. He ran around making that stereotypical "bleh, bleh" sound and this really made Dario laugh. He turned to me and said, "My Dracula won't say, "bleh, bleh." At this moment, it all hit me. It had been a decade since I saw him last and would this be it? I couldn't help but get a little emotional, so I turned my head away from him so he wouldn't see me shed a few tears of gratitude at being able to know him. I began to remember the time in Italy I spent with him, and now he was in my homeland as I was in his. Once the cartoons were done, I stood right outside of the room with Steven and watched Dario give his short introduction and answer a few questions about the movie. At the end, he told the moderator, "Have I said enough? I think so," to great applause from the crowd.

After signing a few autographs, we all walked over to the steak house in the hotel to meet Sean Keller and Jim Agnew for dinner. After some small talk, we started to order food and drink. When the waitress came back to the table with a bottle of Pelligrino and put it on the table in front of Dario, he asked, "What is this? I asked for a bottle of Pino Grigio." The poor woman, tripped up by his accent, wouldn't do much better the rest of the night, so we had to "translate" his order back to the waitress.

After some talk of Dario's first trip to the Bay Area, where we met, and a little on Sean and Jim's new projects later, we all sat and watched as Dario ate the steak he ordered in a rather interesting way. I remember looking over to Sean and Jim, and then with a smirk to Steven, saying, "Only Dario Argento would eat his steak with a knife instead of a fork." As he continued to stab the pieces of meat with his knife and put them into his mouth, I must admit I was a little nervous, waiting for him to impale himself on this rather large implement. Someone at the table took a photograph of him with this huge knife, I don't recall who, but memories are like movies: you can "watch" them again and again and relive the moment…

DRACULA 3D

Before the film was in preproduction, I had a chance to speak with Dario over a break in the show at the last Weekend of Horrors in Los Angeles in 2010. We got on to the topic of *Dracula*, Dario mentioning that Carl Dreyer's film *Vampyr* is his favorite vampire film. I used the opportunity to inquire into what he planned to do with this newly announced film. Right off, I asked if he wanted Asia in the film, and he confirmed he did and wanted her to play Mina. Respectfully, I suggested, if anyone, Asia should play Lucy, as her persona would fit with the character's modern, sexually bold traits against the quiet and humble Mina. I broached Coppola's film of *Dracula* and how Winona Ryder's portrayal of Mina was a nice counter to Sadie Frost's Lucy. However, Stoker's novel paints Mina as a much stronger character than the films ever have, so my opinion, as many others, is probably based more on the numerous films, which mix and match these characters in various ways, bleeding one into the other into utter confusion where the source material is concerned.

Speaking of Coppola's film of *Dracula*, Argento once said, "I hate it. It was terrible. The reason why it wasn't any good was because director Francis Ford Coppola was sick, depressed, and hooked on the drug lithium when he made it. That's what the film was really about and why it was so awful. It was just his drug-addled fever dreams. Who's interested in that? I'm not." If only Argento had known years ago, when he made this statement, that he would be making his own version of the classic Stoker novel. With the near unanimous disdain for *Phantom of the Opera*, it seems surprising Argento would be willing to mine another period literary work of fiction, and the granddaddy of them all, Bram Stoker's *Dracula*. In the 1970s, a reportedly political take on *Frankenstein* never saw

the light of day; ironically, this *Dracula* is a patchwork of other films much like Victor's monster is cobbled together from various sources. Certain elements here are derived from *Horror of Dracula*, the first of the Hammer cycle centered on the Count, starring Christopher Lee. Setting the film in Germany being the most obvious choice, however, given Thomas Kretschmann's Germanic lineage, it's understandable. Jonathan Harker's entire character, and the resulting staking after being turned into a creature of the night, seems lifted from the film. A rather minor and surprising bit of homage is the maid's daughter, Tania; in the Hammer film, she is the maid's young daughter who alerts the police of Lucy's activity. Argento opens the film with a different Tania, this time out, a very voluptuous Miriam Giovanelli, having a literal roll in the hay with her married boyfriend. Beyond borrowing from Hammer's location and script, the sets at times resemble Jess Franco's *Count Dracula*, also starring Christopher Lee, with their threadbare, barely lived in look. Both films also share a disappointingly hurried and pathetic end to an allegedly great and powerful creature. Argento's overuse of CGI technology in the film is understandable given the budgetary constraints of building such creatures, but there is simply too much of it, and for the most part poorly rendered. Dracula's trasformation from wolf to human reminds one of the Gabriel Knight computer games of the 1990s from Sierra. Sergio Stivaletti, Argento's longtime creature and corpse designer has surprisingly little to do it seems with the bounty of computer graphics work being thrown about.

The film's poor special effects take a back seat to the biggest flaw of the film: the script. *Dracula* should be full of high drama, great conflict, and emotional turmoil for all involved. Given the high camp of *Phantom of the Opera*, *Dracula 3D* could have easily gone the same way, but seems to take itself much too seriously at times. This only seems to highlight the corniness of the proceedings bringing forth many unintentional laughs, not a new experience in an Argento film. Here however they seem more troubled than usual because the story isn't interesting or insane enough to keep it above water.

I realize characterization has never been a strong point for Argento in many cases, but this script lacks the core component of an interesting story — drama, whether it is cloaked in comedy, horror, or any other tonal guise. With a now near decade-long law of diminishing returns on his output, in part it seems due to handing over scripting duties to others, it's not hard to see the effect of this creative choice. Perhaps he has lost some faith in his own creative power or does not care to write solo any longer. Whichever the cause, his work has suffered for it.

With Dario Argento's name above the title, one would hope for a bit more, at least in terms of style, than what is offered. The entire film is doused with the feeling of community theater with none of the charm of seeing your friends put on a show. The decision to shoot the film in 3D, while admirable given Argento's love of technology, does nothing to enhance the film's story, mood, or characters who seem to rely on the stereoscopic process for their depth. One would be hard pressed to tell this film was co-written and directed by Dario Argento, photographed by Luciano Tovoli, and scored by Claudio Simonetti unless the credits informed as much. Tovoli's lighting looks nice in some scenes but overall has the feeling of an expensive Mexican soap opera. Perhaps due to the 3D process requiring so much light, the image feels a bit flat and dulled at the edges. Thomas Kretschmann as the Count seems game to go anywhere the character requires, but the script and Argento's directing leaves him with a wooden and lifeless performance, which is at least partially intentional, I would imagine. He seems to be restrained when not on the hunt or murdering someone. Human interaction and seduction are not this Count's strong points. Argento's vision of the character has no flamboyant touches like Gary Oldman in the Coppola film nor does he have any of that elusive hypnotic power that is attributed to

Asia and Dario Argento on the set of Dracula 3D. MULTIMEDIA FILM GROUP.

Jeremy Mincer's design for the Dracula 3D *poster.* COURTESY JEREMY MINCER.

nearly every version on screen or stage through the years. Although, he does mesmerize a police officer to shoot himself in the face with his own gun, complete with a CGI effect that recalls the bullet shot in *The Stendhal Syndrome.*

The rest of the cast, Marta Gastini withstanding, are equally as awkward in various ways. Gastini's slight frame, large expressive eyes, and small mouth give her a physicality to match her gentle nature as Mina. Unax Ugalde plays Jonathan with a dead-eyed boredom that makes Keanu Reeves's performance revelatory. Rutger Hauer's line readings as Van Helsing are especially embarrassing considering this was the man who gave such great performances in *The Hitcher* and *Blade Runner*, to name a few. He enters his first scene announcing himself to Mina, with a question "stating" his name. Asia Argento, displaying none of her usual fire, which would seem a natural mode for Lucy, seems merely there to wear the clothes and eventually bare her fangs at Van Helsing before he kills her.

I do have faith there are other cinematic statements to be made, but they cannot be written by anyone but Argento since he understands his creative internal workings and how it will translate to the screen better than anyone, naturally. Yet, on the other side of the coin, he cannot surround himself with crew and assistants who will say anything to appease his ego. If something doesn't work, it must be addressed. Sadly, with *Dracula 3D*, it seems there are nothing but "Yes" men all the way around. With a rumored giallo film in the works, perhaps Argento can catch some of his own fire again and show the world why he is so respected among genre-film fans the world over.

INTERVIEW

MARTA GASTINI

(Marta Harker, *Dracula 3-D)*

Currently part of the cast of the TV show *Borgia*, Gastini has also appeared in the 2011 film *The Rite* alongside Anthony Hopkins. She got her start on another TV show in Italy called *Good and Evil.* Gastini has also written and produced the short film, *Life on Loan,* which was released in 2013.

DB: When you went out for the film, were you intrigued by yet another film of *Dracula*? What drew you to the project?

MG: I was intrigued! *Dracula* is, in my opinion, a timeless classic that can still be discovered, revived and revisited. When Dario Argento, the horror master, offered me the role of Mina in his *Dracula* I could not resist.

DB: How familiar were you with Dario's reputation before taking this role?

MG: As a movie lover first and as an actress later on I've always come across Dario Argento's name and work and I've always admired it. Dario has been a great innovator and creator of masterpieces characterized by a very personal style that distinguished him in his entire career.

DB: Upon reading the script, what were your first thoughts?

MG: When I first read the script I found it very interesting. Dario had an extremely appealing vision of Dracula. Without losing the purely horror dimension of the character, with cruel, bloody scenes worthy of the most famous bloodsucker, Dario revealed the human side of the Count, almost creating a romantic hero, tormented by his eternal life and moved by his sempiternal love for Mina.

DB: Tell me a bit about being directed by Dario, how does he compare with others you have worked with?

MG: Dario is a legend and his presence on set was very strong. He has a very clear view of what he wants to the point he is able to shoot the scenes as if they were already edited. despite his long career he is still very passionate about his craft and it was great to see him get excited for some specific scenes. I enjoyed the fact he trusts his actors, giving them the chance to experiment. I felt very priviledged working with him.

DB: Was there much time to get to know everyone in the cast? Your relationship with Asia, you're life long friends in the movie, did you spend any time together outside of the shoot to bond?

MG: There was time to get to know many members of the cast. I especially created friendships with Thomas, Miriam Giovannelli, Unax Ugalde, Christian Burruano and Asia. Her and I spent time together, especially on set, talking during breaks. Asia is a very strong woman, extraordinary. Apart from her availability, I was struck by her humility: she suggested to never take anything for granted and told me that this is a profession where commitment pays off. I admire her courage: she moved to America and put herself in the game as a director.

DB: The scene with Asia in the bath tub, was it uncomfortable to shoot? What are your feelings about nudity in films? Especially when it's a father/daughter team.

MG: No, it wasn't uncomfortable to shoot. In the story Lucy and Mina are bonded by a life long friendship and this is the only way I could perceive the scene. I don't mind nudity in films, as long as it's dealt in a very artistic way and it has a meaning in the story. Dario and Asia are father and daughter but they are artists as well, and when they are on set together they are professionals creating art.

DB: Thomas Kretschmann can be a very intense actor, what was he like?

MG: Thomas *is* a very intense actor. I enjoyed working with him, it was fun. He is like a 8 year-old trapped in an adult body and I think that's his strenght in his work.

DB: Rutger Hauer is famously strange…tell me a bit about working with him.

MG: Rutger Hauer is a great artist. He is genius and intemperance. It was very inspiring working with him. He is a very hard worker, his script is covered in notes and suggestions. A quality I do admire.

DB: The 3D process, are you a fan? Is it any different than making a normal film?

MG: From the actor's point of view working with the 3D technology makes no real difference, apart from the fact that it requires a lot of preparation time therefore the actual shooting time needs to be shortened making it more challenging for everybody. Normally I'm not a big fun of the 3D, especially when it's used uniquelly as a visual effect, but I must say I enjoyed our 3D. I found it very high quality and used to support the story.

DB: After working on a bigger budget horror film, *The Rite*, how did *Dracula 3D* compare?

MG: I didn't find substancial differencies. As it often happens Hollywood productions have bigger budgets, even if *Dracula*, being a European production, had a very good one. But from a purely artistic point of view, by that meaning enthusiasm and joy in doing what you love to, I didn't see many differencies. In both cases I had the privilege to work with movie legends, Dario Argento in *Dracula* and Anthony Hopkins in *The Rite*; I had the chance to play beautiful, challenging and very different roles, Rosaria, a 16 year-old girl possessed by the devil, and Mina Murray, one of the most famous female literary characters.

INTERVIEW
MAITLAND McDONAGH

Lifelong New Yorker Maitland McDonagh is a writer and film critic whose work has appeared in publications as diverse as *Film Comment, Fangoria and The New York Times*. She co-founded and edited of *Columbia Film (Re)View* and has written four books: *Broken Mirrors, Broken Minds: The Dark Dreams of Dario Argento, Filmmaking on the Fringe: The Good, the Bad, and the Deviant Directors, The 50 Most Erotic Films of all Time: From Pandora's Box to Basic Instinct* and *Movie Lust: Recommended Viewing for Every Mood, Moment,* and *Reason.* She spent 15 years working for New York City Ballet, taught film history/theory criticism at CUNY and in 2013 founded 120 Days Books to republish two-in-one editions of vintage gay erotic novels of the 1970s and '80s.

DB: Maitland, thank you very much for your time, first off.

MM: You're welcome.

DB: So I was doing some prep for this interview and coincidentally, I was sent in the mail yesterday the issue of Video Watchdog with the *Mother of Tears* round-table discussion in it.

MM: Oh, I'm the negative voice there. Well, not the only one.

DB: Well, the reason I bring it up is that I was writing a bit more about the film and I watched it again. It's really violent and ugly in a way that none of his other films are. And as a woman, and the misogyny accusations that are always being flung at him, how do you as a woman react to that pike through the vagina scene?

MM: Well, the misogyny accusations were always there, in thrillers at first and then the straight-ahead horror like *Suspiria*. And that was very much part of a concern of the seventies when movies were becoming more graphically violent in general. Peckinpah got raked over the coals so many times, I'm sure he had an extra layer of skin burned off because people were troubled by seeing things that had previously only been suggested. And clearly violence and sex went hand in hand there. People were also seeing far more sexually explicit material than they had ever seen before and some people were really disturbed by it, especially because it started in the '60s and coincided with any number of seismic social shifts both in the United States and Europe. And it seemed, I think, all of a piece to a lot of commentators that generally the world was becoming cruder, more chaotic, more out of control. That's what bothered people so much about student activism. It wasn't so much that students were being politically aware and making their voices heard, but they were actually coming out on campus and making a big noise and resisting when the national guard was sent out to round them up, which of course backfired profoundly given the shooting of unarmed college students no matter what they're doing short of, I don't know, stabbing each other with their fingers is never going play well. It's not going to look good in the papers the next day. So Dario's movies were, I think, part of all of that. And Dario was part of all that. He is a product of a very political time in the '70s in Italy. God knows in Italy the students were not joking when they came out in the streets. In Europe, generally, a lot of that youthful protest movement was a great deal more violent than it was in the United States. So all of that is a long way of saying that's always been the rap on Dario. But I do think that he is not unaware, but he has lost a lot of ground in the last fifteen years. I personally do not think the problem isn't that he didn't get the idea for torture porn first, I think the problem is that he has kind of run out of ideas and is really hashing things that he did before and frankly did better the first time around. I don't know what you do about that. There is a problem, I think, of people generally and artists in particular as they get older. In some cases, you've said what you have to say. So what do you do now?

DB: Well, it really takes the polish off the first two movies.

MM: Exactly and that's why I have such a negative reaction to that movie because it is the conclusion to the trilogy. It did take me a while to come around to *Inferno*. I know I really didn't care for it much the first time I saw it.

DB: Part of what I think is the problem with a lot of his work lately is that he stopped writing the scripts himself or with a European collaborator. And I think having that American voice is dulling something. And something is literally lost in translation.

MM: Absolutely; it doesn't come naturally to him. His English is still terrible.

DB: I saw him last year in L.A. and we had dinner and his English is better than he thinks it is, maybe. You can at times see the hesitation in him to say something, but when he just kinda lets it go, I think, you know, he gets by OK.

MM: He gets by OK and I'm making a huge generalization. He's good at non-verbal communication as well. If you watch his hands and his body language and listen to the words, you can pretty much piece together what he says without problems. That's fine in person; it's not fine on the screen. Because clearly, he can't hear the difference between a line of dialogue that works and one that flops on the ground like a mackerel because he's not truly fluent.

DB: And thank you for saying that because when I saw *The Card Player* in a screening in Los Angeles as part of some film festival —

MM: It was painful…

DB: If you recall that scene with Stefania Rocca and Silvio Muccino where he's smoking a joint and there is that bit of nonsense about "the wind." What is this conversation? It's really silly.

MM: I think that was meant to be a reference to *Night of the Living Dead*. I think it's Judy's boyfriend who says, "This isn't like the wind passing through." It just doesn't play; it sounds like a terrible fart joke.

DB: You're right and I bring that up because one, I think that you definitely have a point in trying to argue that with some people over the years. But even in Italy, I heard one of my friends say that during that scene, people were howling with laughter at that scene. So it may just be a case of writing crap dialogue.

MM: Well, I don't think Dario cared about dialogue, even in the early days. He's not a verbal filmmaker, which sounds like a contradiction in terms anyway. But he is intensely visual and I think in his newer movies, there are always moments when the visuals are really holding up, but he never cared about language. I doubt he ever rehearsed a scene for dialogue the way he does for blocking. I've only ever seen him rehearse blocking and I haven't been on that many of his sets. The dialogue doesn't matter to him, people have to say things, and we don't make silent movies anymore. Although that's not true with something like *Amer*, which is virtually a silent movie and it's just stunning. And it's so Dario that you know clearly that's what it's meant to be. But it's not the thing Dario ever cared about and it hurts him more and more with each passing film.

DB: I'm hesitant to be one of those people to say "he's losing it" or dismiss him because there have been moments in the last decade where he has done some really good work. The "Pelts" episode of *Masters of Horror*, for example, is quite strong.

MM: I think you're right. I think what's caught up with him are things that were always problems for him. It's not that he's lost anything in particular. It's the things that were always problems have just become more so. Part of that is money. He can't command the kind of money he used to be able to and that hurts the visuals. And when you hurt that, you're really stabbing at the heart of what he's good at. And it makes the things that he was never that great at look even worse. Now you don't have something like *Suspiria*, one of the high points of his visual tapestry. You don't have the visuals to distract you from those ridiculous pieces of dialogue. Women with names that begin with S are the names of snakes. It makes me laugh in an affectionate way because the rest of the movie is so beautiful. But that completely dead-eared dialogue is not so painful. But in *Mother of Tears*, every bit of it grates on the ear horribly.

DB: One thing that I commented on about *Mother of Tears*, I hate to keep going back to it, but I sat in a screening of it at USC with Jace Anderson and Adam Gierasch in attendance. Throughout the movie, people were laughing at stuff that I'm thinking wasn't supposed to be funny as is the case; these things happen. But this, you would think it was some kind of slapstick comedy up there. At one point, I think it was right after the murder of Marta with the pike through the vagina, a few people got up and walked out, which I was a little surprised at. If you can make someone react that strongly, you've made some kind of impression, which I know Dario has said in the past —

MM: All Dario wants is a strong reaction. He doesn't care if you like it or not.

DB: Yeah, he's very John Waters in that regard. *Mother of Tears* could have been so much more and should have been so much more. Back to the budget thing…it was made for around four million dollars, which is nothing for something of that scope. And the film was trying to reconcile itself with what it should have been and had to be because of that.

MM: Well, I don't think he could reconcile that. And I think that it is difficult to get to the age Dario is at now and to have made as many films as he has made and have to completely rescale your thinking. Romero has managed it, though. I think *Diary of the Dead* is actually a really good little movie and clearly he didn't have anywhere near the kind of money that he was able to put together even for *Land of the Dead*. Clearly, he is pragmatic in a way that Dario's not. Which is why I think it's a wonder the two of them got along so well in so many ways. Maybe it's just because he's Italian.

DB: I wanted to ask you about this gay pulp novel project you're working on. The blog is 120 days of Sodom(y).

MM: To which my husband said, "Christ, Maitland, you are not calling it that."

DB: I've always been intrigued by Dario's use of gay characters in his films. I can't think of another film director, and a straight one at that, who makes horror movies who so consistently has gay characters in his movies. And who comes from a very macho, Catholic culture to boot.

MM: I'm glad that's something you've noticed. Again, there is a real rap on Dario that his gay characters are stereotypes and that they are offensive and that they pander. For example, the detective in *Four Flies*, he's treated like a mincing pansy. Although he's also the guy who says, "What do you think, I'm going to jump on a chair when I see a mouse?" In fact, he dies very bravely and you feel bad for him. Dario clearly is very accepting and doesn't have an issue with it. I've always thought it was a nice thing about him. The characters aren't written to forward a pro-gay agenda or anything. They're just there. And again, maybe it's because he's Italian.

DB: It's interesting with Silvio Berlusconi basically owning Italian media and running literally everything. He's a very, I don't want to say he's a misogynist, because I don't want to be accusatory, but Berlusconi is —

MM: He's a world class man whore; that's all there is to it!

DB: Thank you! I just can't help but think in that kind of environment if maybe Dario hasn't been kind of throwing stuff back at the politicians and the culture and saying, "Look, it doesn't have to be like this." A rebellion in a way…

MM: I think if it is a rebellion it's an unconscious one. Dario has said himself…I don't think he thinks that deeply about these things and he works on a very instinctive level. And I think this issue and in many others, it's just his instinctive reaction. What's the problem here?

DB: Back to the detective in *Four Flies*. It's interesting that you brought up that he takes back the accusation that just because I'm a gay guy, I'm just going to fall apart and jump up on a chair when I see a mouse. In fact, he's the only character that figures out what's going on. And he has to pay for it. So he literally is the hero, but before anyone else, really.

MM: Absolutely and he's also very self-aware. He has no compunction about invoking those very stereotypes. It's a very forward thinking kind of piece of character writing. It's always puzzled me why so many people don't see that at all. I just don't get it. And I've certainly run into plenty of people who say, "You're joking, right? That's a very elegant sense of Dario, but you don't really think he thinks that way?" But I absolutely do!

DB: In fact, it's one of the things that has struck me about the horror community in general. Being a gay guy and liking horror movies, some people look at me like my head's on backwards. Going to the conventions there is kind of, and I'm sure women experience it, too, it's such a straight boys' club that —

MM: Indeed it is. I've had a long conversation with David DeCoteau, who didn't come out until he made that movie *Leather Jacket Love Story* and he said he spent years going to conventions with movies like *Sorority Babes in the Slimeball Bowl-O-Rama* and having these guys trail after him and say things like, "Oh man, you have such a great job! Was she really naked in that scene?" He told me, "I have Beavis and Butthead's dream job." These guys don't have a clue. And he presents quite gay and did even before he came

out. If your eyes and ears are open, I don't get how you could miss it. But apparently people did for years and years. He said he would go home and laugh at it. It's not only a boys' club, but a young boys' club.

DB: Can you tell me why the new material in the newest version of *Broken Mirrors, Broken Minds* is so short?

MM: The gist of it is that I wasn't given a whole lot of room to write more. University of Minnesota didn't want to do five or six new chapters. And I wasn't sorry because I don't think it's possible, without being intensely negative, to write at length about the newer work the way I did with his earlier work.

DB: I don't know if you have children or not.

MM: No, I don't. I don't like children.

DB: Well, I can't say I disagree. I have two nephews and an hour with them is enough.

MM: I married a man with two children from a previous marriage, so there you are.

DB: I bring it up because I wanted to ask you about Argento's theme of maternal problems. Since you aren't a mother, I don't know if it carries more weight, but you are a woman.

MM: I notice that he rarely mentions his mother.

DB: It's true. People bring her up and all he says is that she was a photographer of some note.

MM: And that she was Brazilian.

DB: Well, the women or mother specifically problem goes back to *Suspiria*, in a way. The trilogy tells the story of the three women who are evil and then *Deep Red* has the murderous mother. What's going on? There is that Freudian thing with all the trouble in life being traced back to mom.

MM: He doesn't say much about her at all. I have no idea how long his parents were married. It's all a great big mystery. That said, though, he does have a volatile family. He's gone through years without speaking to his brother and then they made up and work together. He and Asia certainly have gone through periods of keeping quite a distance from each other. I don't know about Fiore and how volatile that is. You generally recreate the family environment you grew up in for better or for worse.

DB: The interview you conducted with Asia on the U.S. DVD of *Scarlet Diva*, you seem to be a fan of the film. A lot of critics seemed to hate it and said it was a vanity project and how dare she pat herself on the back for an hour and a half. It couldn't be praised without also being kicked in the face. It was very oddly received. Anyhow, you said you were a fan of the punk rock sensibility of it. What were your thoughts on the film upon first watching it?

MM: I recall watching it and feeling a sense of relief. I thought it was a good movie. I was afraid it was going to be bad. I was also relieved that it didn't do what so many first movies do, especially ones made by people who grew up in the film industry. There are a set of things that they do that first time filmmakers who didn't grow up in the business do. They include being very in on technical aspects of filmmaking. And this comes up on *Scarlet Diva*. I think the storytelling is quite strong. It's very harsh and disconnected in places. But I think it's a function of the character and milieu, not an inability to harness the language of filmmaking. It's pretty clear to me that every set she was on as an actress, she was watching. Not just her father's films, but everyone else's as well. And looking at how you get the raw material that you can put together into a coherent film. And how you can play with that coherence to suit your story, character, and whatever is of primary concern to you. I thought it was remarkably accomplished. It's very clear how much of it is about Abel Ferrara. You can completely see how much of it is about her relationship with him. He lives in New York. He used to work on a block I worked on. He's a character. There is a lot of his style of storytelling in the movie. And frankly, you could model on far worse people than him. So that, in a somewhat less than elegant form, is what my basic first thoughts were.

DB: What were your thoughts on *The Heart is Deceitful Above All Things*?

MM: I have a lot of reservations about the source material. But I can see what appealed to her. It's also about a child who is hauled into an adult world and has to figure out a way of surviving in a very chaotic environment. And I think casting herself as the mother was something that shows she may have a vanity about what she is willing to do. But she has no vanity about what she *will* do, if you see what I'm saying. She's willing to play a horrible character and look like shit. A lot of people find the glamour in the drug culture. It's like the Saint Augustine thing, just wallow in all of the destructive glamour in it and then clean up from it at the end. You never get that sense of that from her. There is no underlying moralizing to the way that she treats that character. Which is very much, I think, what that material needs.

DB: I would agree and I have to say that I read the book when it first came out and I had friends in San Francisco who said, "Oh, I know J.T. Leroy," but it's funny, I read that book and *Sarah*, the second book, and I went to one of my friends and said, "Look at the photos on the back of the books and look at photographs online. Something isn't right." I was suspicious pretty early on.

MM: I remember being struck by how unauthentic that literary voice seemed, but I couldn't put my finger on it. It picked at something from the beginning. And you can say to yourself that you don't want to believe that this was written by someone who was shaped by these experiences. There was something so polished about the voice itself, not the prose. And I guess I realized what I was trying to get at is that it feels constructed. And clearly, everybody's persona is constructed to one degree or another. There was such a consciousness there that felt artificial that it kind of bothered me.

DB: My reaction to first reading that it was all based on real life, it seemed too much. It's so piled on. There is so much bad happening that it can't be real.

MM: It's a J.G. Ballard novel.

DB: I said to one of my friends, here read this novel, which I dubbed "Bad shit happens." And then the hoax was being revealed and I had an "I told you so" moment with some people. It was all a very strange, unnecessary play to mount. Why not just write the novel and publish it as fiction?

MM: Well, there are many ways to fake your way to fame. But I think there is something very damaged with this case. I would love to know what it is. I am fascinated by people's damage. So there is much more I want to know. But the other thing that I found myself wondering is really, what was Asia's role in this? There was that time where she was supposedly dating J.T. Leroy and there are photographs of her and one of the many J.T. impersonators. She's not dumb. I have to believe she was perfectly aware of what he was or wasn't. But I'm still very curious.

DB: Speaking of Asia and her films with her father, for my money, I think *The Stendhal Syndrome* is the best film they've made together. I think people don't want to deal with what it is. It's got this weird two-act structure, almost two stories shoved together. It has a lot of psychological things he doesn't really put into his movies and deals solely with this one character. There are no subplots to speak of, really, and it's very uncomfortable and confrontational in a very singular way in his canon. It seems to have unraveled something in him that he hasn't dared to look at again.

MM: I think that's absolutely true. I think being called the "Italian Hitchcock" from the very beginning, it's the most Hitchcockian of all his films and in the *Vertigo* realm. His own interest in shifting identity suddenly becomes very like Hitchcock. And I have to believe the way it turned out the way it did is because of Asia. She is clearly a more disciplined thinker than he is. I think she has inherited a certain impetuous boldness from him, but I think she is more analytical by nature. And I think she did a great deal of thinking about her roles and brought a lot of the intensity to that that is there. Although the one time I asked her about it in an interview, she was very evasive. It clearly made her uncomfortable. And in shooting the rapes scenes with her father, she told me, "Oh yeah, the raping. He wouldn't watch it on the set. He would go watch it on a monitor." And clearly, she wasn't going to say another word about it. Again, I'd like to know a little bit more there.

DB: The first time I watched it, no joke, was with my grandmother. What does that say about me?

MM: That must have been interesting.

DB: She is a fan of thrillers and murder mystery movies. She told me after seeing several of Argento's films that she liked them, but wished they weren't so violent. She didn't have a major problem with the content —

MM: Just the way it's presented? Well, good for your gran! It's a very disturbing movie.

DB: The whole Italian Hitchcock label, I think, is rather cheap now that you bring that up.

MM: I would agree. And it's rooted in not even a misunderstanding or a lack of interest, but more a cheap way to pigeonhole him as a filmmaker. It was never a serious comparison and clearly, he's felt it his whole life. Clearly, he wouldn't have made *Do You Like Hitchcock?*

DB: And for him to make the film and deconstruct the comparison almost to say, "Here it is, now shut up." Speaking of *Do You Like Hitchcock?*, and I may get slapped for saying this, but I think that of the three latest films, alongside *Giallo* and *Mother of Tears*, I think in a way, it's the most successful and interesting of the three.

MM: I'm not going to slap you because I completely agree. When I finally saw it and it landed with such a bad reputation, I needed to see it because I've devoted a major chunk of my life to Dario's work. And I'm sitting there watching this and thinking it didn't seem so terrible at all. And I thought it was actually kind of good and smart. So yeah, I would say I do like the movie. There are things in it that are very funny in a deliberate way that isn't usual for him because he's basically not a funny guy. He is so much sweeter than people think. I love how much he loves his kitty cats. But he's not a "funny" guy. It's not nature. I mean, he's funny, but he's not someone who is a joker. But to see his humor in his movies work was nice. They are the mark of a guy who just isn't funny. It's kind of squirm-inducing to watch.

DB: Sometimes it's hard to tell if things are supposed to be funny or not in his movies. And I've grappled with that. In *The Card Player*, for example, you have the singing and dancing morgue attendant. OK, well, if you look at a lot of older Italian comedies, they are very broad and buffoonish and in a way, I can see that character as the "buffoon." But you stick that character in the middle of what is basically a police procedural and the set just falls down around him.

MM: I think that's something important to remember. Going back to making broad cultural stereotypes here, but by in large, the Italians are not the French. It is not subtle humor in most cases. They like buffoonery in a very serious way and that doesn't make a good fit with genre films. I think a lot of Claude Chabrol films are funny, but it's in that very dry French way, the big boffo laugh that does not work. All I have to hear is comedy-horror and I've checked out.

DB: Thank you for agreeing with me! On a tangent here, but I don't see the appeal of these movies. I think they're lazy and just fan boy-induced nonsense. I don't get the mentality. *Shawn of the Dead* works, but for the most part, I can't stand them.

MM: Well, *Shawn of the Dead* works as a comedy and it's touching and actually scary at times!

DB: Sorry for the detour, but back to Dario. Have you been following the Dracula project?

MM: Yes and I don't have good feelings about it. It doesn't seem like it's something that suits him well; he's clearly a product of the 20th century. And while he has great respect for the classics of literature and film, it's not what suits him or his style. I love *Opera*, but I think it works less when it's dealing with the *Phantom of the Opera* allusion. That fascist Frankenstein project he was always talking about, that never happened. I'm glad it never happened. But with Dracula, vampires are so incredibly malleable that maybe he can find a way to bend the material to make it work.

DB: Speaking of that "Fascist" Frankenstein that never happened, what do you know about it?

MM: Not much; I'm pretty sure I read about it in *Variety*. It would have been a little mention "Italian thesp Argento." That's all I know. I can see, although he is not an overtly political filmmaker, I can see how it was a take that would appeal to him, that it would have been something that came out of a conversation with someone else, perhaps. And this is my interpretation, mind you. But I could see this idea of building the perfect human being. Having it go pear-shaped really fast. Allegory is not his strongest mode, so...

DB: I've heard that Dracula, the character, will be bisexual. And he alluded to as much when I talked to him last.

MM: Of course he is! It's interesting in Dario that once again, he's going back to that if it is true.

DB: Well, it's more of his sexual subversion, let's call it. In *Deep Red*, you have the effeminate gay man played by a woman and in *Tenebrae*, the woman on the beach who is a transsexual.

MM: I think that is one of the most finely tuned things he has ever done, that scene on the beach.

DB: *Tenebrae* is one of my favorites of his; it never ceases to fascinate me.

MM: I would say it's my favorite of his movies.

DB: It's definitely up there for me. In fact, I cut a trailer for it in film school. None of the other students had seen it and my teacher loved the trailer and asked me how she could watch this movie. I ended it with Daria Nicolodi's scream from the end of the film over Franciosa with the shoe in his mouth.

I wanted to get back to the sexuality we were briefly discussing with Dracula and bring up Argento's use of human sexuality in general, not just homosexuality. In *Four Flies on Grey Velvet*, you have Michael Brandon's character having sex with his wife's cousin, but never with his wife. And Argento rarely shoots sex scenes and this one, you don't want to be OK with it because it's his wife's cousin, but you're on board because it seems they genuinely care for each other.

MM: It's probably the healthiest sexual relationship I can think of in terms of sex scenes in any of his movies. Perhaps not healthy in a social sense, but it feels like a love scene and not a fucked up sex scene. And another thing along those lines is the sexual androgyny. Look at the two of them in *Four Flies*. From the back in some of the scenes, you can't tell the husband and wife apart. And clearly, I think Dario modeled a lot of his male characters in the early movies on what he looked like at the time. It's basically what he looked like. It's the same build, physical presence. But the consistency in the women is really striking and very suggestive.

DB: You bring up the androgyny and doubling and *Tenebrae* is full of that, too. A lot of the characters look alike, dress alike.

MM: And it's not an accident. The confusion is very much intentional.

DB: And sexuality is a weird thing in his movies. Even the more normal characters like Sam and Julia in *Bird* can't have sex without something interrupting them.

MM: It's coitus interruptus for an hour and a half.

DB: And I know this is an interview, but I keep doing all this talking because I have never talked to anyone about his films who sees what I see in them.

MM: Well, I think it goes back to the Beavis and Butthead mentality. This kind of fluid sexuality makes a lot of people uncomfortable. And it makes a lot of people who like horror movies uncomfortable. I think they truly choose not to see it as a consistent factor in his films. I think women who are horror fans see it faster than most men do. Maybe it's not as threatening to men as to women and it's not as troublesome.

DB: It's interesting you use the word threatening. The sexuality in horror movies, it's often about sexualizing lesbians in a way that men aren't. There's that threat of male homosexuality that female homosexuality doesn't bring.

MM: Oh absolutely, come on! How many straight men have huge collections of lesbian porn? They like that stuff; it's fun to watch. But they don't want to see two men because it forces them to identify with someone there and it makes them uncomfortable. They can just watch two women.

DB: Well, *Tenebrae* has the lesbian couple and *Hitchcock* has some lesbianism in it. But he goes back to gay men much more often. The scene at the kitchen table between Stefano Dionisi and Roberto Zibetti in *Non Ho Sonno* almost has echoes of *Chuck and Buck* to me. They're both sitting there, one with his shirt off and one with his shirt unbuttoned and open. And they both have "girlfriends." What was just happening?

MM: We all know the "I have a girlfriend" excuse.

DB: Then every time we see these two guys with their girlfriends, they can barely stand to touch each other.

MM: And that is culturally very anti-Italian, that lack of physical affection, that you have to believe it's coming from somewhere deliberate. I think it's following a pattern of thinking in Dario's movies. It's not culturally what you would expect.

DB: Totally off topic, I was wondering about the *Eye for Horror* documentary. I'm still waiting for a really good retrospective doc on Dario. Can you tell me anything about this? Why it's so short and glosses over a lot of his career. It's frustrating.

MM: Well, funny story about that. I did that interview a year and a half before that came out. There was a crew in New York, so they asked me to do it. And honestly, I had kinda forgotten about it. I was still working at *TV Guide* then. We got a copy of it and I was asked to write about it. I throw it into the DVD player and the first thing I hear is my voice and seeing those billowing curtains. Well, I guess I'm not reviewing this! It was meant to be a DVD extra, the documentary.

AFTERWORD

With *Dracula* completed, Argento turned back to television, this time in Italy, to host a new film series titled *100 Pallattole D'Argento/100 Silver Bullets* for RAI. The series ran almost an entire year from August 2012 into July 2013, with a bi-weekly slate of films shown at night. Luigi Cozzi, who created Dario's introductions for the films, also had the task of selecting all 180 (not the 100 alluded to in the show's title) films to be shown. He explains, "The show was born from discussions between RAI Movie's chairman (and film critic) Enzo Sallustro, Dario, and TV producer Guglielmo Ariè. When the project was set, Dario asked me to join him in writing the introductions and to assist in shooting."

The process of picking the films that would be aired seemed quite the chore according to Cozzi.

In the show, there are no Hammer or Universal horror classics and it's a shame as Dario and I wanted to air many of them. The Italian state network didn't have any of them under contract, so we couldn't put any of them on the program. The same applies for Dario's movies. I could select the few that RAI already owned: The Bird with the Crystal Plumage, Cat O' Nine Tails, Suspiria, Tenebrae, Phenomena, Two Evil Eyes, Door into Darkness, and both of Lamberto Bava's Demons films.

There proved to be another challenge with showing older horror films, as RAI wasn't keen on anything in black and white. Cozzi goes on:

RAI refuses to air any black and white movie before one a.m.; they insist people hate to watch anything black and white. I insisted and selected many of them, but I had to schedule them as the second or third film of the evening, very late at night and into the morning. Usually the show starts at 11p.m. and Dario introduces one film, but often does introductions for two, three, up to four a night.

As of this writing, with *Bullets* wrapping up, Argento has plans to direct a production of Verdi's *MacBeth* sometime in 2014. It seems Argento has also been working on a miniseries for Italian television called *The Fourth Dimension*, which has been trapped in endless rewrites. As for feature film work, there are rumors of a few giallo scripts being worked on; sadly, *Occhiali Neri* seems to be dead in the water for fans who are hoping it will one day see the sun. Whatever comes next for Argento, it promises to be divisive among his fans. In the last decade, many fans have rung the death knell for his career, while Argento soldiers on. Dario told me once when I asked what he thought of the fans' reception to his American work, "I can't worry about that or else I won't get anything done. I know the audience won't like everything I do, but I have no choice. I tell stories that I find interesting and I hope they do, too."

Derek Botelho
April 17, 2013
Los Angeles, California

INDEX

CPSIA information can be obtained
at www.ICGtesting.com
Printed in the USA
LVHW061403061019
633322LV00011B/270/P